THE KEY TO HAPPINESS AND SUCCESS IS IN YOUR HANDS WHEN YOU DISCOVER THESE COMMON DENOMINATORS OF SUCCESS:

- Dream big and never stop dreaming of more.
- Have faith in yourself. Hang in there when all hope fails and believe there are unlimited opportunities.
- Learn how to define success for yourself and don't let others define it for you.
- Create goals with one-, five-, and ten-year plans, and don't leave anything to chance.
- Be ambitious and driven, and make success happen.
- Have networks of people who support what you're doing.
- Constantly affirm your ability to be successful, and believe in a higher power.
- Be a "prosperity thinker," and develop a mental attitude that guides you to success.
- View obstacles as challenges.
- Work through fear and take bold, calculated risks.

BEATRYCE NIVENS is a consultant and motivational speaker who has addressed hundreds of professional and educational organizations, including Citicorp, TWA, the National Association of Female Executives, NASA, Essence Communications, Chevrolet's Strategies for Success, the National Association of Black MBA's, the National Association of Urban Bankers, and the Coalition of Black Career Women. Beatryce Nivens is a former career columnist for *Essence* magazine, and her articles have also appeared in *Family Circle*, *New Woman*, *Black Enterprise*, *Glamour*, and numerous other publications. She is the author of five previous books.

D0831382

By the Same Author

The Black Woman's Career Guide
Careers for Women Without College
How to Change Careers
How to Choose a Career
How to Reenter the Work Force

SUCCESS STRATEGIES FOR AFRICAN-AMERICANS

A Guide to Creating Personal and Professional Achievement

BEATRYCE NIVENS

A PLUME BOOK

PLUME
Published by the Penguin Group
Penguin Putnam Inc., 375 Hudson Street,
New York, New York 10014, U.S.A.
Penguin Books Ltd, 27 Wrights Lane,
London W8 5TZ, England
Penguin Books Australia Ltd, Ringwood,
Victoria, Australia
Penguin Books Canada Ltd, 10 Alcorn Avenue,
Toronto, Ontario, Canada M4V 3B2
Penguin Books (N.Z.) Ltd, 182–190 Wairau Road,
Auckland 10, New Zealand

Penguin Books Ltd, Registered Offices:
Harmondsworth, Middlesex, England

First published by Plume, an imprint of Dutton NAL,
a member of Penguin Putnam Inc.

First Printing, July, 1998
10 9 8 7 6 5 4 3 2 1

 REGISTERED TRADEMARK—MARCA REGISTRADA

LIBRARY OF CONGRESS CATALOGING-IN-PUBLICATION DATA:

Nivens, Beatryce.
  Success strategies for African Americans : a guide to creating
personal and professional achievement / Beatryce Nivens
      p. cm.
  "A Plume book."
  ISBN 0-452-27524-5 (alk. paper)
  1. Afro-Americans—Life skills guides.   2. Success—United States.
I. Title.
E185.625.N58   1998
640'.89'96073—dc21
                                                            97-49893
                                                            CIP

Printed in the United States of America
Set in New Baskerville
Designed by Leonard Telesca

To all of our children,
who can and will dream again—

Contents

Acknowledgments

First, I would like to thank God for giving me the strength to compile and complete this book. He saw me though a great number of challenges to the end. To Leslie Farquharson, my fiancé who has been my Rock of Gibraltar, steadily supporting and reading every word that I've ever written. To my deceased parents Thomas and Surluta Nivens, who gave me every opportunity in the world to soar.

A book of this magnitude can't be written without the sharing, cooperation, and help of many people. My sincere thanks to Kym A. Whitley, my dear cousin who opened her home, extended wonderful hospitality, and took me to the Ira Aldridge Acting Competition where I met a number of the individuals profiled in this book. To my friend Sheryl Lee Ralph and her children, Ivy Victoria and Etienne, who made my stay in Los Angeles wonderful.

Many successful African-Americans gave generously of their time for interviews; their wonderful stories have added so much to this book: Joe Dudley, Bessie Nickens, Ruby Bridges, August Wilson, Sheryl Lee Ralph, Bobbi Humphrey, Ruby Dee, Nikki Giovanni, Angela Bassett, Senait Ashenafi, Carl Gordon, Susan Taylor, Pamela Warner, Jasmine Guy, Dr. Craig Polite, Kim E. Whitley, Terrie Williams, Lawrence Otis Graham, Marie Brown, Dr. Donna Mendes, Elza Dinwiddie Boyd, Vondie

Curtis Hall, Marcia Gillespie, Franklin Thomas, Carolyn Baldwin, Audrey Smaltz, Pierre Sutton, Robert Johnson, Carole Riley, H. Jerome Russell, Ted Lange, Leonard Dunston.

To the people who wanted to be a part of this book and couldn't be accommodated, I thank you for your time, consideration, and openness: Woody King, Herb Boyd, Ortheia Barnes, Oyanfunmike, Janine Coveney McAdams, Dr. Coyness Ennix, Jr., Tony Lee, George Subira, Michael Ralph, Calvin Brown, Rob Williams, Roy Roberts, John Wesley, Linda Griffin, Adilah Barnes, Richard Lawson, Queen Afua, Art Evans and Jeffrey Anderson-Gunter.

Behind all the book's successful African-Americans are support people who offer important help. Without their assistance, my job would have been a lot tougher. Many thanks to the following publicists, attorneys, and assistants for their tireless efforts in sending materials, arranging interviews, and/or other good deeds: Suzy Berkowitz and Emily Bear for Jasmine Guy; Lisa Kasteler and Stephanie Casat for Angela Bassett; attorney Safronia Johnson for Ruby Bridges; David Lust for Vondie Curtis Hall; Tom Estey for Sheryl Lee Ralph; Sharon Arthur and Deborah McGee for Ruby Dee; Lillian Smith for Carol Riley; Gary Krasny for Carl Gordon; Robert Baskin, director of corporate media relations of the Coca-Cola Company for Carolyn Baldwin; Dena Levitin for August Wilson.

Many sisters went out of their way to make this book a success. They cajoled, prepared, and made sure the interviews went as scheduled. And I made some good friends in the process. Many thanks to Karen Malone for Pierre Sutton; Valerie Carter for Carolyn Baldwin; Michelle Curtis for Robert Johnson; Dionne P. Boissiere for H. Jerome Russell; Marge Thomas Ennis for Franklin Thomas; Debra Parker for Susan Taylor; Karen Stevens for Marcia Gillespie; Andrea Heyward for Lawrence Otis Graham; June Williams for Joe Dudley; Norma Sanchez for Dr. Donna Mendes. I take my hat off to all of you!

Dear friends are priceless! Dr. Arthur Rouse generously shared all of his contacts, made calls, and just arranged things. I'll never forget his help with the interviews of Franklin Thomas and Carl Gordon. Thanks to my friend Randy Sher, who spent nights thinking of people for me to interview. To Elza Boyd who thought of all ways of helping me. To Herb Boyd, her husband, who lent his expertise in trying to reach people. To my students at the College of New Rochelle who provided some of the Bible quotes.

To my agent Carol Mann, who kindly offered assistance. Deirdre Mullane, my editor, was very understanding about missed deadlines, illnesses and deaths in my family, and other crises. I will always remember her thoughtfulness.

To all of the African-Americans who have struggled so that we could have our own successes: Your work wasn't in vain.

Introduction: We Have Come This Far by Faith

Knowledge is gold!

—Swahili proverb

Because we've had such steady shoulders to stand upon, African-Americans are successful in so many ways. Our success lies in the solid foundation that our ancestors have laid for us. It can be traced back to our African forebears who made it to these shores and survived. It's the Black woman who worked to educate her children and give them what she never had. It's the African-American father who held three jobs so that his daughters and sons could have better lives. It's our families who sacrificed to make it possible for us to even desire success. And it's our teachers, preachers, and community leaders who beat the odds themselves to now serve as our shining examples of success.

At a memorial service for Secretary of Commerce Ron Brown, Alexis Herman, our secretary of labor, described her and Brown's phenomenal climb up the ladder of success into the highest echelons of the Democratic Party and eventually to their cabinet positions. She made note of how they had stood on the shoulders of Fannie Lou Hamer. For it was this African-American sharecropper who, along with other delegates of the Mississippi Freedom Democrat Party, fought to take her place as a recognized state delegate at the Democratic National Convention in 1964, and forged a new day in politics.

In another example of noteworthy praise to our pioneers,

Oprah Winfrey devoted an entire show to those who integrated schools, including some members of the Little Rock Nine and Ruby Bridges, one of the four Black children in the New Orleans public school system's struggle. In her closing remarks, the popular talk show host thanked them for being "the bridges" on which so many of us have walked. For without their courage and bravery, a great number of us wouldn't be privy to the vast opportunities that we know today.

Both Herman's poignant example and Winfrey's salute to those who had once battled segregation confirmed my own thoughts regarding the important role of our ancestors and trailblazers. Their cumulative efforts gave us the strength or determination to aspire to the highest rungs of our own success. And with this in mind, it's my deepest feeling that no book on success that speaks to an African-American audience should be written without paying tribute to them. So when we begin our journey toward finding more successful lives, let us not forget to pay homage to their valiant struggles.

As it was for many of those who came before us, our own walk down the road to more successful lives won't be easy. Success isn't some magical carpet that descends from the heavens, sweeps us on board, and sprinkles luck upon our paths. Nor is it a quick fix or some lottery win. But just what does it take?

Is this elusive thing called success strictly material? Does it mean having large sums of money, fine homes and cars, going on long, luxurious vacations, and never having to work again? Or is it spiritual and emotional, a kind of peace of mind, happiness, and harmony with God? Are you born with it? Or can you develop it along the way?

During my many years of doing counseling and consulting work, I used to counsel many African-Americans who wanted to improve their lives and become successful. They wanted more money, better-paying jobs, productive children, bigger homes, larger cars, a winning lottery ticket—the list goes on. Yet many of them weren't sure about how to get what they wanted. Some just hoped for the best. Others prayed for a miracle. And some gave lip service to wanting success but never really believed that they could achieve it.

Many had low self-esteem, self-confidence, and self-worth. A good number thought negatively about themselves, which chased away any thought of success. A few felt that life had dealt them a bad hand; others were trapped into inertia by fear. As I closely observed these people, common themes began to emerge:

1. They didn't believe in themselves or the enormous possibilities in their lives.
2. They had stopped dreaming a long time ago.
3. They had no real, solid goals or road maps to make their success happen.
4. They had extinguished their ambition, drive, discipline, and passion.
5. They lacked the support needed for success from their family, friends, associates, or networks.
6. When they encountered obstacles along their paths, they viewed them as large, insurmountable stumbling blocks that couldn't be overcome.
7. They were consumed with fear.
8. They were afraid to take risks.
9. They wanted to become rising stars but were frozen into apathy.
10. They didn't see any hope of really becoming successful.

It was painful to see. Here were some very bright and honest people who had only wanted the best out of life but had fallen victim to their own mind-sets. If only they could have developed the right attitude, dreamed big, put into action an organized set of strategies, followed through and persevered, they could have found the success that was so badly desired. As I later assisted many of them in seeing this possibility and worked with them toward helping them actualize it, the seeds for this book were planted.

When I started on my writing journey, I decided to interview successful African-Americans in search of some common threads or a philosophy. I talked to more than fifty people, including Ruby Dee; Joe Dudley of Dudley Products; Susan Taylor of *Essence* magazine; Marcia Gillespie of *Ms.* magazine; playwright

August Wilson; actors Vondie Curtis Hall of *Chicago Hope*, Jasmine Guy, Sheryl Lee Ralph, and Senait Ashenafi of *General Hospital*; Franklin Thomas, the former head of the Ford Foundation; Robert Johnson of Black Entertainment Television; Carolyn Baldwin of Coca-Cola; public relations advisor Terrie Williams; flutist Bobbi Humphrey; Pierre Sutton of Inner City Broadcasting; and Marie Brown, literary agent.

As I conducted my interviews to discover whether they also had a similar attitude, a striking commonality became clear. Not surprisingly, most of them looked at the world quite differently from those whom I had once counseled. Their views and actions were entirely positive:

1. They had big dreams and never stopped dreaming of more.
2. They had enormous belief and faith in themselves. They hung in there even through failure, and believed there were unlimited opportunities for themselves.
3. They knew exactly how to define success for themselves and didn't let others define it for them.
4. They had goals with one-, five-, and ten-year plans and didn't leave things to chance.
5. They were ambitious and driven, and made their own success happen.
6. They had excellent networks of people who supported what they were doing.
7. They constantly affirmed their ability to be successful and believed in a higher power.
8. They were "prosperity thinkers," developing a mental attitude that guided them to success.
9. They saw obstacles as challenges and sometimes welcomed them.
10. They walked through fear and took calculated or sometimes bold risks.

Rather than focusing on the rewards that success could bring, those profiled were more concerned with improving their lives and being happy in what they did. As a result, they were more apt to become successful. Their attitudes and concerns were simple. They were most interested in:

1. Finding something that they loved to do in life and becoming passionate about it.
2. Finding happiness and peace of mind, as well as having fun at what they did.
3. Having the ability to learn more about life and expanding their horizons.
4. Finding something outside of themselves with which to connect—family, a support network of friends, God.
5. Helping others in their communities by giving back.

I think that this concept of success is universally correct. By changing yourself in certain ways, success will beat a path to your door!

But can you learn how to change your outlook in order to become successful? I think so! And *Success Strategies for African-Americans* can help. Like a road map, it will steer you toward the strategies used by generations of successful people, and highlight every aspect of mind, body, work and livelihood, and soul that you need for success. In each chapter you'll find basic, universal success strategies as well as profiles of and advice from more than thirty successful African-Americans. Their stories are meant to inspire and challenge you, and may even remind you of your own plans for success.

"Uplift Yourself: Boost Your Self-esteem" will help you develop the correct attitude for success and raise your self-esteem and self-confidence. It will help you filter out negative thoughts and replace them with more positive ones. Included are the uplifting profiles of Joe Dudley, the president and CEO of Dudley Products; Bessie Nickens, who changed careers and wrote her first book after age eighty; and Ruby Bridges, who integrated the New Orleans public school system.

"Think Big, Dream Large" gives you a unique opportunity to resurface your dormant or lost dreams and begin dreaming big again. You'll learn why having big, bold dreams can often lead to success. You'll travel with and hear the stories of playwright August Wilson, actor Sheryl Lee Ralph (*Moesha*), internationally renowned flutist Bobbi Humphrey, and our treasured Ruby Dee.

Although dreaming big is crucial to success, you must also set goals. "Wade in the Water: Set Your Goals" helps you turn your dreams into realities. By clarifying your goals, you'll learn how to make success happen! Within this chapter, you'll read the success stories of poet Nikki Giovanni and actor Angela Bassett.

"Peace Be Still: Affirm Your Success" begins to help you incorporate some of the more spiritual or metaphysical aspects of success into your daily life. By exploring the power of affirmations, visualizations, faith, and prayer, you'll soon tap into the vast powers and spiritual wonders that the Universe unfolds. In addition, you'll read about the triumphs of actor Senait Ashenafi (*General Hospital*), actor Carl Gordon from the beloved television show *Roc*, and Pamela Warner (mother of actor Malcolm-Jamal Warner and owner of Warner Management).

"The Power of Prosperity Thinking" explores how thinking positively can propel you to success. Without the proper attitude, you'll never find success. *Essence* magazine editor-in-chief Susan Taylor explains how correct thinking has impacted her life and brought success.

"Standing on the Banks of Jordan: Release the Fear" gives you specific ways to combat fear, move on to a more successful life, and stop being held back from achieving. Actor Kym Whitley tells how she took matters into her own hands and created a career. "Blast out of Your Comfort Zone: Taking the Risk" tackles the courage you will need to make calculated risks and blast out of your apathy. Looking at the advantages and disadvantages of risk taking will free you to soar. Actor Jasmine Guy, literary agent Marie Brown, public relations advisor Terrie Williams, and author Lawrence Otis Graham will show you how they did it.

"Put Your Principles Into Action: Work Your Way to Prosperity" helps you develop ways to uncover the divinity or happiness in your work, and guides you to finding more fulfilling work that can enhance your soul as well as your pocketbook. The following people will explain their strategies for finding satisfying work: actor Vondie Curtis Hall of *Chicago Hope*; *Ms.* magazine editor-in-chief Marcia Gillespie; former Ford Foundation President Franklin Thomas, who was the first African-American to head a major U.S. foundation; and top-ranking Coca-Cola executive Carolyn Baldwin.

"Empower Yourself: Success Strategies for the Entrepreneur" gives you the keys to successful business ownership and the principles that can lead to financial independence. The entrepreneurs profiled include Audrey Smaltz, owner of the Ground Crew (a fashion backstage management company); Pierre Sutton, head of Inner City Broadcasting; Robert Johnson, president and CEO of Black Entertainment Television; H. Jerome Russell, president and chief operating officer of H. J. Russell & Company (the fifth-largest African-American business in the nation); and Carole H. Riley, former proprietor of four McDonald's restaurants in Harlem USA, who now owns forty-five Pizza Huts.

"Honor Your Temple: Take Care of Yourself" puts the emphasis on you. Being successful means eating right. "Manage Your Stress" helps you learn to reduce stress in a variety of ways. "Manage Your Time" explores many ways to gain control over your time and life.

I've also emphasized the need to "Give Back." Many of the people I interviewed for this book spoke about the importance of giving back to their communities as a major component of success. In an echo of the sixties sentiment "Each one, teach one," there was a real spirit of "Each one, give back to one!" Learn about the philanthropic works of many successful African-Americans. For example, actor Ted Lange, who played Isaac Washington on the television series *The Love Boat*, sponsors an annual competition through which many young actors have found success in Hollywood. And Leonard Dunston of the National Association of Black Social Workers discusses Black adoption as a way of giving back.

Finally, I urge you: "Go for It!" I recap the strategies that you need to become successful. This motivational and inspirational chapter will prompt you to live out the dream that the Creator has chosen for you!

Success Strategies for African-Americans will empower you and change your life by giving you the tools for success. Remember that it's not too late to follow your dreams, have a more successful life, and take your rightful place in the Universe. If you're willing to try, you're about to begin one of the most exciting chapters of your life. So, what are you waiting for? Just turn the page, and go for it!

‹I›

Taking Care of
Your Mind

‹ 1 ›

Uplift Yourself:
Boost Your Self-esteem

For as he thinketh in his heart, so is he.

—Proverbs 23:7

We all want success and all the positive things it brings. For many of us, we try and try to become successful but it never seems to happen. What do we have to do? How do we begin on the journey of obtaining our own personal success?

The first step is to take a hard look within and begin feeling good about yourself and your achievements. By doing so, you'll begin building up your self-esteem, self-worth, and self-confidence, which are vital components. Dr. Nathaniel Branden, the author of *The Power of Self-Esteem*, explains that we must have "confidence in our right to be happy, the feeling of being worthy, deserving, entitled to assert our needs and wants and to enjoy the fruits of our efforts." For without this sense of healthy self-esteem, we'll constantly be standing in the way of our own success.

Beam a Little Love Your Own Way

If you look at successful people, most of them possess a strong sense of self-esteem and self-confidence. They feel good about themselves and their accomplishments and have a positive attitude toward life.

Think about your own thoughts and what you feel about

yourself, your life, and your accomplishments. Are they positive or negative? Do you truly believe that you can achieve your goals? Or are you constantly putting yourself down?

If you are negating your abilities and let more negative than positive thoughts surface, you must now begin to change that perspective and clear away all that is eroding and damaging your self-esteem and self-confidence. Start by replacing your thinking with more positive messages:

Filter Out	*Filter In*
I'm a failure. I can never do anything right.	*I have beaten many odds in my life and am proud of these successes. I can be successful in everything that I do.*
I have no joy in my life.	*Joy is seeking me out.*
I'm not good enough.	*I am very good at doing _____. My strengths are in _____ and my prior successes have been in _____ and _____ and _____.*
I'll never be pretty or handsome enough.	*I'm beautiful both inside and out. Because I'm strong and have high self-esteem, I know that my inner beauty is far more important than my outer beauty.*
My life is so unhappy. Nothing ever works out for me.	*I am reversing my negative thinking by taking charge of my life. By doing so, I am not leaving my destiny to anyone but myself.*

I'm so miserable and feel like giving up.	*Life is a miracle. There are hundreds of miracles just waiting out there for me. All I have to do is look and really see my own miracles unfolding.*
People don't like me.	*I'm becoming a person who is liked and respected. I am making it happen. It's a matter of attitude!*
My self-esteem and self-confidence are at an all-time low.	*I'm picking myself up, dusting myself off, and learning to love myself. I'm no longer willing to put myself down or let others do it. I'll fight for my right to be here and cherish all that is good about me.*
No matter how hard I try, I can't become successful.	*Success is finding me because I'm earnestly seeking it out, want it badly, and am doing all the work necessary to achieve it.*
I fear the unknown.	*I look fear in the face, knowing that I'll cross paths with my purpose and destiny. So I have no reason to fear all that is mine by birthright!*

Though only the first step, thinking positively can influence how you believe, feel, and act. As you replace your negative thoughts with more positive ones, your self-esteem will begin to improve. And when you filter out the old and filter in these new messages, your attitude about yourself will begin to change for the better.

See Success in What You Have Already Achieved

Another way to start feeling good about yourself and building stronger self-esteem and self-worth is your past successes. In each of our lives, we've had times when we were successful. Regardless of who you are or what you do in life, you've done something, no matter how small or what you might consider insignificant, that can be considered a success. Perhaps you have raised money for your church group, made a room of people laugh or feel good about themselves with your talk, created an idea that made your organization function better, or received an award for a job well done.

Ask yourself the following questions:

- What have I done in my life that I consider to be successful?
- What kind of attitude did I have to make it a success?
- What did it take to make it a success (planning, natural abilities, the help of others)?
- What challenges did I have to overcome to make it successful?
- How did I overcome them?
- How did I feel when I was successful?
- What were the rewards of my success?

Moving Beyond Feeling You Can't Be Successful

The next step in building up your self-esteem and self-confidence is to stop feeling that you can't succeed. Many people damage their self-esteem by thinking negatively about themselves, their circumstances, and their abilities. Consequently, they never get to the point where they can let go of those thoughts enough to attract success.

Compare Your Problems to Other People's

It's easy to point to your particular circumstances in life and feel unhappy. I used to hear my former college students grumble and complain about their hard lives. They were convinced that if they had been born free from poverty or hardship or had better educations their grades would improve. They would say things like "But my family is poor!" or "I had a lousy education in high school," or "I've had some tough breaks." While listening to them complain and moan, I would often shake my head in amazement. Before me sat some neatly dressed students with good minds. They had the benefits of eating three meals a day and weren't afflicted by any catastrophic illnesses. I attempted to challenge the way that they felt about themselves and tried to keep them from feeling sorry about their circumstances. I would ask them, "Are you blind, crippled, crazy, deaf, dumb, or physically disabled in any way?"

After they told me no, I'd tell them a story. It was about the young men and women with disabilities who were at Hofstra University on Long Island, where I once worked and did graduate study back in the early seventies. As an inspiration to all who came in contact with them, these young people would roll around campus in wheelchairs or zip everywhere in scooters. Not feeling even a bit sorry for themselves, they surmounted their obstacles, graduated from college, entered a variety of professional fields, and became productive citizens.

After telling that story, I would ask my students, who were by then ashamed of feeling so badly about their own circumstances, one more question: "Do you have two legs that walk, two eyes that see, two arms that move, two ears that hear, and a body that works?" When they nodded yes, I'd say, "Then there's not one reason on this earth why you can't come to school and achieve!" And right before my eyes, their attitudes shifted and changed. In time, many of them would buckle down, do their schoolwork, and improve their grades.

Do you feel sorry for yourself? Were you born into poverty? Has life dealt you some horrific blows? Well, take a look at the life of one person who was told that he could never achieve anything in life.

●<>●

He Would Never Amount to Anything

I first learned about him when my plane landed in Greensboro, North Carolina. As I walked through the airport, I saw a picture of a Black businessman towering over me. "That's Joe Dudley of Dudley Products," my late mother proudly explained. And right at that moment, I decided to find out more about this man.

Joe Dudley grew up in a three-room farmhouse in Aurora, North Carolina, with thirteen other people: his parents, ten sisters and brothers, and his grandfather. He was held back in the first grade, labeled "mentally retarded," and had a speech impediment. "Now, here's a kid who'll never amount to anything in life," people thought. But his mother, Clara, had high expectations for her son and encouraged him to "prove them wrong!"

He did more than that. Today, Joe Dudley Sr. is the CEO and president of Dudley Products, a line of more than 120 high-quality hair care products that are sold throughout the United States, Europe, Zimbabwe, South Africa and Brazil. Reigning over a fifty-four-acre empire in Kernersville, North Carolina, as well as more than seventy-five thousand square feet of manufacturing/office plant, a $3 million hotel, a cafeteria, the fully accredited, four-site Dudley Cosmetology University (DCU), and a travel agency, he has proven to be a potent example of willpower.

His climb to this successful plateau wouldn't be an easy one or hard to forget. Readily, he remembers the journey that would take him from that old farmhouse of his youth to the twenty-room mansion where he now lives with his family.

His trek to becoming a successful entrepreneur began

early. Joe Dudley remembers that his father, a farmer, never wanted any of his children to be beholden to other people for their livelihoods. "We believed in working for ourselves. My daddy worked for himself. My granddaddy worked for himself. And of the eight boys in our family, we are all self-employed in some form or fashion," he proudly states and points to the fact that all eleven Dudley children graduated from college.

Because he was determined to fulfill his parents' dream that all of their children become educated, Dudley enrolled in North Carolina A&T State University as a poultry science major with an eye on owning a farm in the future. Working his way through school, he used the skills learned from his family's farm to collect eggs and feed chickens on the college's grounds for fifty cents an hour.

While pursuing his studies, fate intervened one summer, and changed his life forever. It was around that time he learned about Fuller Products, a prosperous company run by the late S. B. Fuller, who was one of the richest African-Americans at the time. Seeking out an opportunity with the renowned entrepreneur by journeying to New York, Dudley became inspired by Fuller's philosophy. He paid the initial sum of ten dollars to join the organization and began working as a door-to-door salesperson. "I started working for them in 1957. They talked about being self-sufficient and that meant a great deal to me," he remembers. "On my first day, I made about one dollar and ten cents. My first week, I made twenty-seven dollars." However, his sales and confidence soon skyrocketed and he began making $100 a week, which helped him comfortably pay for his tuition. Realizing his success and newfound love of selling, he readily switched his major to business administration.

During the summer of 1960 while still working for Fuller Products, he met Eunice Mosley, the daughter of a Selma, Alabama, Baptist preacher and schoolteacher, who was also selling for the organization to earn money for school. This meeting would ultimately become a marriage and a lifetime business partnership. But before agreeing to dating him, Mosley, a business major, expected Dudley to honor his commitment of meeting his daily sales quotas. After he did so, the couple were married the next summer.

Once college was completed, Joe Dudley returned to New York to join Fuller Products on a full-time basis and rapidly rose up the company's ladder to success. Along the way, he became a team member and gained the respect of S. B. Fuller, who was a mentor and a guiding light to the young sales leader.

Five years later, Dudley returned to North Carolina and started a Fuller distributorship. However, there were difficulties during this time with getting Fuller products for his sales force. Not to be discouraged, he bought a small cosmetics company and set his sights on owning a much larger business. "I was already selling products and knew what customers wanted. So that wasn't a big problem. And Mr. Fuller gave his blessings."

And with that important support, he was on his way to starting Dudley Products. "The problem was that I had to learn how to manufacture and formulate products. But Mr. Fuller had shared some of his technology with me. And I just remembered how he did it. I went to the library to do research and also bought some formulations from other companies."

Determined to make it despite the overwhelming odds, the struggling entrepreneur began an inspirational journey to making Dudley Products a reality. And the kind of story of which successes are made. He explains those modest company beginnings: "I started making the products on my kitchen stove. I didn't have the money so I went to beauty salons and they gave me their old containers. Then I would take old milk jugs and make shampoo. We just took what we had. My wife would type the labels. My kids would put the tops on the containers. I would make the products by night and sell them during the day."

With that kind of drive and determination, his company mushroomed to one with almost five hundred employees, a chain of beauty salons, and a cosmetology college. But just when he was having his most successful year, Joe Dudley put his life on hold and rushed to the side of S. B. Fuller, whose company was experiencing financial difficulties. In 1976, sales at Fuller Products had sharply plummeted. Answering his mentor's call for help, the enterprising Dudley packed up everything and relocated to Chicago. Using his expertise and business savvy, he boosted Fuller Products' sales to $2 million, and was glad to do what was necessary to help his old friend and inspirational leader. "Everything I know came from that man. There's no question that he changed my life. He is gone now, but I still follow his program," he says while sitting behind an important memento of his friend and teacher—the very desk from which S. B. Fuller built his fortune.

After doing what he could to resurrect the failing Fuller Products, Dudley returned home to continue building his own company. And that success is due in part to a unique philosophy of marketing and selling his products directly to the cosmetologists and eliminating the middleman. "We had several beauty salons and I decided to make some great products for my own shops. And the people liked them and they kind of caught on." He explains his attempt to strengthen the revenues of African-American beauty salons: "I decided that we would do a lot with the cosmetologist. The manufacturers would use them to introduce the products. Then after the items caught on, they would take the products and put them in the retail stores. So, I wanted to help the cosmetologists to become more successful, create a line exclusively for them, and make a better-quality product. In this way, they wouldn't have to compete with the drugstores." And thousands of cosmetologists are thankful to him for doing this.

An astute businessman who strives to help others, he always seeks out ways to motivate people in his own company. Like a true leader, he gives his sales managers the latitude to operate as if they were running their own organizations. He also inspires his employees with an incredible team spirit and slogans like "We Are Job Makers, Not Job Takers!"

And he still employs the family who helped him in the early, unpredictable days. Eunice Dudley is business partner and chief financial officer of the company. Son Joe Jr., who has a master's degree from Northwestern University, is a vice president. Eldest daughter Ursula, a graduate of Harvard Law School, is both general counsel as well as head of the Customer Service Department and Makeup Division. Daughter Genea, the youngest child, is a graduate of Wharton. She is currently a marketing executive in her father's company and pursuing her MBA at Duke University.

Besides being a family man and business entrepreneur, Joe Dudley is a humanitarian who generously spends his time and money. "We send about forty students to college at North Carolina A&T and Bennett College," he remarks with pride about his community involvement, which includes sitting on the boards of several companies. His Dudley Fellows Program, a mentoring program for high school students, is renowned for helping teenagers learn leadership and life skills. And he has launched a new program, ComPass, which helps college-bound students prepare for careers in accounting and at the same time seeks to increase the number of African-American professionals in the field. He has spearheaded a fund-raising drive that collected $50,000 for cosmetologists whose shops were damaged or destroyed during the disturbances after the Rodney King verdict in Los Angeles. With an additional commitment to education, he donates eight acres of his complex's land to Forsyth Technical College. His company sponsors the National Miss and Mr. Black Teenage World Scholarship Program, and he has made commitments to the Adopt-a-School programs for local schools. DCU alumni, company employees, and others have given about five thousand speeches to schools and community groups. In the future, he plans to make 250 millionaires, which was the dream of S. B. Fuller.

His awards could fill an entire wall. In 1991, President George Bush honored him with the 467th "Point of Light" for his Dudley Fellows Program. He is the recipient of the prestigious Horatio Alger Award; an honorary doctorate from Edward Waters College in Florida; the North Carolina Master Entrepreneur of the Year Award presented by *Inc.*

magazine, Ernst and Young, and Merrill Lynch; The Maya Angelou Tribute to Achievement Award; The National Beta Gamma Sigma Medallion Award and Award for Excellence from Minorities and Women in Business; the Direct Sales Association's Vision for Tomorrow Award; a Non-Merchandise Supplier Grant Award from JCPenney, and many other honors, including an induction into the National Black College Award Hall of Fame.

Dudley's first book, *Walking by Faith: I Am, I Can, I Will,* is representative of his life. A phenomenal book, it should be read by every African-American and anyone who seeks inspiration.

"I took a little bag of ten dollars," Dudley says of his initial investment in Fuller Products. "I didn't have to borrow money and it kept on growing." And I know that if S. B. Fuller as well as Dudley's parents and grandparents are looking down from heaven, they have to be proud of Joe Dudley, the man who people thought would never make it.

❀<>❀

Has Age Stopped You in Your Tracks?

I remember seeing and counseling many people who used to cry the blues about their age and how the rapidly passing years were holding them back in life. Many felt that they were just too old to follow their dreams or make new starts in life. Startled, I looked at some of them who were just in their thirties and forties, and couldn't believe my ears. Even though life should have just been starting for them, they still considered themselves "over the hill." Perhaps a look at Bessie Nickens can help us reconsider the limitations of age.

◉<>◉

The Date of Her Birth Is in Her Daddy's Bible

"I don't feel like I'm ninety-two!" exclaims Bessie Nickens who says that she has only her father's Bible to determine the exact date of her birth. Back then, marriages, births, and deaths were recorded in Bibles because many states didn't gather vital statistics. "And my daddy's Bible didn't lie!"

Although eight years shy of being one hundred years old, Nickens is a remarkable and accomplished woman who didn't get going good until age eighty. After her retirement, she started a brand-new life and broke with a tradition where many her age would be saddled into rocking chairs or wallowing away in nursing homes. Changing careers from silk finisher to artist in her eighties, she authored a children's book titled *Walking the Log, Memories of a Southern Childhood*. And she proves that if you live long enough, you can do everything that your heart desires.

I first met her at the Grace Congregational Church in Harlem at a celebration of her life for Black History Month about two years ago. Although I had interviewed her over the phone, I really didn't know what she looked like. Expecting a frail, white-haired, ninety-year-old who was possibly in a wheelchair, I looked around the church's audience at every little old lady in sight. My eyes settled on an old, bent-over lady with white hair. I figured that it must be Nickens and my eyes became misty. Wasn't it wonderful that she could even lift her fragile fingers to paint and write? Wasn't life great?

Boy was I surprised when they introduced Bessie Nickens. Dressed to the nines in a black designer suit and black coiffed hair without a single strand of gray, she strutted up to the stage and began speaking in a strong voice that belied her age: "I can't believe I'm ninety!" And the congregation roared back, "And you don't look it, either!"

Born just after the turn of the century in the segregated

South, she had the kind of life struggles that many African-Americans experienced back then. There were no public schools for Black children in her little Louisiana town, so she had to wait a year until her parents moved before she could attend school. Undaunted, Nickens saw the benefit of a high school diploma and resolved to get as much education as possible.

Through no fault of her own, it would be many years before she would get that cherished piece of paper. "I didn't finish high school until I was twenty-one years old. We had to pick cotton when I was a child and so we would miss classes. But I was determined to get ahead in life." She recalls her burning desire for an education. "For four years, I went to high school and worked every evening after school. And in my last year of high school, I had to get up and go fix a woman's breakfast. I had to get to school by nine and sometimes I had to run to get there on time. But I didn't get discouraged. I finished school because I realized that you had to have at least a high school education before you could do anything in life."

She climbed over every obstacle to get that coveted diploma, including the numerous moves that her family needed to make to find work. In those days, it was quite common for African-Americans to journey from town to town seeking employment. Her parents relocated several times, from Louisiana, to Arkansas, to Texas, to find jobs in the sawmills, oil fields, and cotton fields of the South. Nickens and her siblings had to pull their share by doing something that she grew to dislike immensely. "I found no joy in picking cotton and only made thirty-five cents a day," she recalls. But despite having to do the arduous labor, she soon discovered something special that could occupy a child's active mind.

When she wasn't working or going to school, she used her vivid imagination to color and paint. There were no televisions or other distractions and children had to be more creative. "When I was seven, I started tracing from an old Sears Roebuck catalog. That old catalog used to go throughout the United States and my mother ordered all of our shoes and clothes from it," she remembers. "I used to get tissue paper and press it out with a warm iron and then I'd trace pictures and paint them with crayons. I did that for a long time and learned how to draw freehand by teaching myself. Then I learned how to paint with oil and pastels, but oil is my medium!"

However, art was an unlikely field for an African-American woman of Nickens's era to pursue. So, like many others, she worked as a domestic after completing high school. In the following years, there would be employment in the dry cleaning and silk finishing business.

After retirement, at an age when many people would pack it in, she decided to re-create the memories of her childhood through art. Those paintings found their way into the Paul Robeson Cultural Center at Penn State, Lock Haven University in Lock Haven, Pennsylvania, and the homes of many avid collectors. "Sometimes you don't see a future but you just have to stick to it. If you continue doing what you're doing, something will open up for you," she says with the optimism that has carried her this far.

"I had no idea when my paintings were seen that I would write a book." She smiles while thinking of one of the most gratifying accomplishments of her life. Because her artistic work showed great style and wisdom and offered a historical look at the days that many of us have only heard or read about, the publishing company Rizzoli, which specializes in art books, commissioned her to write the children's book that includes seventeen of her artistic works.

The title *Walking the Log* refers to a favorite log on which she and her siblings played. "In Fullerton, Louisiana, there was a creek nearby where we lived. My sister, brother, and little dog loved walking that log," she recalls of the inspiration for the painting that adorns the book's front cover. Then there is the painting that depicts a church scene of a time many of us can't imagine. "I painted about the old church where we went. During those days, I had never seen a car. People came to church on horseback, in buggies and wagons. We lived nearby. So we walked." Other pictures recapture her childhood remembrances of playing Hide-and-Seek or the game Snap the Whip, getting a Saturday-night bath, or having her hair pressed with a straightening comb.

Having made this impressive transition from one field to another, Nickens is still looking forward to all that life has to offer. She continues exhibiting, and her works have been shown at Baruch College and Cinque Gallery in New York. And in the future, she will publish another book and hopes to go to college.

As this amazing woman spoke in Grace Congregational Church, she concluded her talk by presenting vividly colored, hand-painted butterflies on white pieces of paper to each child who had gathered around to hear her stories from *Walking the Log*. Explaining why she had attached pencils to each piece of paper, she told them, "Use them to write yourself out of high school and into college!"

Bessie Nickens shows all of us that at thirty, fifty, sixty, seventy, or ninety life is still worth living. If you want to succeed, age shouldn't stop you. After all, it's only a number in your mind!

Is the Weight of the World on Your Shoulders?

Many of you may feel dragged down by life. However, if you look at those who have tackled the world for the betterment of the African-American race, your burden may seem a little lighter. Witness the case of Ruby Bridges Hall.

She Took Her Place Among Them

The year was 1960. It was six years after Thurgood Marshall of the NAACP Legal Defense Fund and others took the landmark case that was instrumental in bringing about school desegregation to the Supreme Court—and won. But although *Brown v. Board of Education of Topeka* was applauded as a new era for African-Americans' educational opportunities, many whites in Southern cities bitterly fought this attempt for change. The white residents of New Orleans were hostile and braced to do battle by preventing their children from integrating with Blacks.

On November fourteenth of that year, Ruby Bridges became one of four Black children who were selected to integrate the New Orleans public school system. Accompanied by federal marshals sent by President Dwight D. Eisenhower, she bravely walked through the color lines up the steps of William Frantz Elementary School and wrote herself into history. It was a triumphant moment forever captured in the Norman Rockwell painting *The Problem We All Live With,* and in John Steinbeck's book *Travels with Charley.* This January, *Ruby Bridges,* the acclaimed Disney motion picture, appeared on ABC television, and had a special opening statement by President Bill Clinton. In addition, there are two books about her life: *The Story of Ruby Bridges* by Dr. Robert Coles and Bridges' own *My Story.*

On that winter 1960 day in an era rife with sit-ins and marches for freedom, Ruby's mother rode along with the marshals with her to the school. When they arrived, a crowd of hostile whites awaited them. And little Ruby Bridges, who was told to look straight ahead, thought all the excitement was about New Orleans's festive celebration known as Mardi Gras. Besides, she was too busy focusing on what her mother had told her. "She said, 'You're going to a new school today and you'd better behave!' "

What many people didn't realize until recently is that Bridges sat alone in an empty classroom for the entire first grade with only a white teacher, a newcomer to New Orleans. Because none of the white parents would allow their children to go to school with a little Black girl! It's a sad commentary on racism.

This painful time held dire consequences for Bridges' entire family. Their street had to be blocked off to keep away the potentially dangerous mobs of whites who might harm them. But they found comfort and humanity in an African-American community that kept them away from danger. "My parents would not have been able to successfully do what they did without the whole community. People on my street actually protected us. Some stood guard outside my house. Others helped dress me for school. Everyone came together to take care of me and my family." She remembers the community feeling that she hopes can be resurrected one day. "We as African-Americans don't do that anymore. And it's very important . . . not simply when a child is doing something like what I did but every child needs this same type of support!"

Those were trying times. And even though white New Orleans eventually had to accept school integration, life would never be the same for the Bridges family. "My father was a gas attendant. One night, his boss said, 'I have to let you go because my customers know that it's your daughter in that white school.' And so, he let him go, fired him solely because of my integrating the school." She thinks back on the event that would begin a cycle of hurt and pain. The retaliation even spread across state lines to her grandparents, who had been sharecroppers on the same farm in Mississippi for twenty-five years. "People there soon found out that they were my grandparents. They threatened them and they had to move on to Louisiana, where they live now."

Still, Bridges' role in integrating the school system would bring about some personal benefits for her. Despite the hardships that she had been through, she found a lifelong friendship with Dr. Robert Coles, the Harvard psychiatrist who, as a young man, happened by the angry mob scene in front of the William Frantz Elementary School. Struck by this lone little girl marching to take her place in history, he would later arrange a meeting with her, write about her in his prizewinning books *Children of Crisis* and *The Moral Life of Children*. He would also pen a children's book about her life titled *The Story of Ruby Bridges*, and proceeds of its sale go to the Ruby Bridges Educational Foundation, which she now heads.

Decades later, Coles is still Bridges' friend, and there have been many rich rewards. On August 18, 1995, both were reunited more than three decades after her historic walk when they received honorary doctorates from Connecticut College.

Today, a youthful-looking Ruby Bridges is in her forties, married, and the mother of four sons. She began working as a parent-liaison in the same William Frantz Elementary School, which is now all Black, and is the president of her education foundation. Through it, she is trying to increase diversity within public schools with cultural arts programs. "We need to come together and have a sense of community again. I think that all of us— I *know* we African-Americans were raised that way, and somewhere, we forgot that."

Ruby Bridges has shown us that despite overwhelming circumstances, we can still be strong and succeed. Today, she is a symbol of the strength of those who have sacrificed so much for us all.

Dudley, Nickens, and Bridges are a few examples of those who have overcome and beat the odds, and should be an inspiration for all of us. They had a strong sense of themselves and met their challenges. By uplifting themselves, they overcame the obstacles in their paths. And through their examples, we can use their lives as models of how to lift our ourselves high above our own present adversities.

Strategies to Uplift Yourself

Positive Things to Do

1. Feel good about yourself!
2. Improve your self-esteem and self-confidence.
3. Improve yourself.
4. No longer feel sorry for yourself.

5. Change your lot in life.
6. Resolve to be happier.

Negative Things to Avoid

1. Continue to put yourself down and be negative.
2. Remain in the same emotional place.
3. Stay the way you are.
4. Continue thinking life has dealt you a bad hand.
5. Think it's only happening to me!
6. Don't believe you have the ability to change, and stay stuck in the same place.
7. Continue being miserable.

< 2 >

Think Big, Dream Large

Ask, and it shall be given you; seek and ye shall find; knock and it shall be opened unto you!

—Matthew 7:7

Do you want to become successful and take advantage of all the riches that the Universe can bestow? If so, you must begin to think big and dream large. By doing so, you can overcome your present circumstances and become all that you're supposed to be.

Just think about some of the greatest feats ever performed, inventions designed, cures discovered. The seeds for many ideas, from launching an airplane into the sky to inventing the automobile and computer to discovering cures that have prolonged our lives, came as a result of dreams and were born right in the minds of big dreamers. And those people who dared to dream the impossible were no different from you and me. In fact, many had much more to overcome in life.

Look at some of the greatest people in our race who had little more than their dreams and went on to propel their visions into subsequent successes:

- Frederick Douglass was a slave but that didn't stop him from dreaming of freedom. Once freed, he went on to fight for others who were caught in slavery's throes through his abolitionist work. Becoming one of our greatest orators, he tried his hand at many things, including being a newspaper editor and lecturer. And, of course, he was certainly one of our greatest authors and thinkers.

- Madame C. J. Walker had big dreams for a laundrywoman who could only eke out a meager living. Taking no more than a couple of dollars and some imagination, she refashioned the straightening comb for Black women, developed a hair pomade to use along with it, shaped a company to sell and promote her products, and became a millionaire in the process.

- Marcus Moziah Garvey, the Jamaican-born leader with big dreams, knew that people of African descent could unite. After founding and organizing the Universal Negro Improvement Association, he set his sights on instilling racial pride in his people and connecting them with Africa, our Motherland. A man of many dreams, he also envisioned providing our people with trading opportunities by establishing the Black Star Liner. And today, we know that his wisdom and Black cultural thinking lay the groundwork for much of the sixties' nationalistic philosophy, including the "Black is Beautiful" theme.

- With limited means, a dream, a few pennies and fortitude, Dr. Mary McLeod Bethune saw a day when she could help educate young African-Americans. Using her creative thinking and sheer willpower, she began building the institution now known as Bethune-Cookman College. A woman of incredible talent, stature, and foresight, she became an adviser to several presidents, including Franklin D. Roosevelt, and actualized the dream of founding the National Council of Negro Women, which is now headed by Dr. Dorothy Height, who is carrying on her dreams.

- The great and powerful A. Philip Randolph of the Brotherhood of Sleeping Car Porters dreamed of a 1941 "March on Washington" to protest segregation and discrimination in defense industries and the federal government. Through his efforts, President Roosevelt capitulated and signed Executive Order 8802. He also was instrumental in influencing President Truman to sign Executive Order 9981, which ended discrimination in the armed forces.

Steadily moving ahead in his fight against racial injustices, Randolph helped organize and carry out the 1963 March on Washington. More than 200,000 people from all over the country came by bus and car to Washington, D.C., for this historic moment. And on that day, Dr. Martin Luther King Jr., another dreamer of enormous magnitude, took center stage with the now-famous "I Have a Dream" speech.

- Sitting on a porch in Henning, Tennessee, Alex Haley reveled in the talk of his female relatives who told him about his African heritage and an ancestor named Kunte Kinte. Never forgetting those stories, he dreamed of tracing his roots back to Africa. Despite many years of financial hardships and extreme sacrifice, he was able to translate his hopes and aspirations into *Roots*, the best-selling book and television miniseries.

- A modern-day hero, Ron Brown always had big dreams. When he was a young boy traipsing around the Hotel Teresa, which his father, Bill Brown, managed, he prepared himself by shoring up the confidence to take those dreams clear up to the inner circle of the President of the United States. And by doing so, he became the first African-American commerce secretary. Desiring to leave a legacy for young people, he opened the doors for opportunity and provided the mechanism for many other African-Americans and women to dream their dreams, until his unfortunate, early death.

What are your dreams? Can you dream as big as Douglass, Walker, Garvey, Bethune, Randolph, King, Haley, and Brown? With their visions, talent, and a little imagination, they have turned their hopes and desires into realities and taken their places among the successful big dreamers of our world. Perhaps your dreams can take you as far. Did you ever wonder where you could land if you pursued them?

<> •

His Dreams Landed Him on Broadway

August Wilson learned life's lessons through firsthand experience. Without letting anything stand in his way, the two-time Pulitzer Prize winner dreamed big and succeeded. Today, he is the writer of some of the African-American community's best-loved plays, including *Ma Rainey's Black Bottom, Fences, The Piano Lesson, Two Trains Running, Joe Turner's Come and Gone*, and *Seven Guitars*.

Raised along with five other siblings in Pittsburgh, Pennsylvania, by his mother, Wilson set his sights high by considering a future writing career. A big and ambitious dream for a poor teenager who grew up when there were very few visible African-American literary role models in American classrooms. He found his inspiration in the works of great African-American writers like Richard Wright, Langston Hughes, and Ralph Ellison. And the seed for his own writing was planted.

Dreaming of following in their footsteps, his destiny was almost sidetracked. When he turned in a brilliant paper, a ninth-grade teacher dismissed it, thought it was not his own, and failed him. Disgusted, Wilson walked out of school and never went back. Despite disappointing his mother, who had big dreams for him, he just couldn't be in a place where his potential was so misunderstood.

Entering the real world, he moved himself closer to fulfilling his dream. Amid the Black Arts Movement of the late 1960s, he helped to found a Black theater and worked in an assortment of jobs to pay his way. By age twenty-eight, he had purchased his first typewriter, and his genius began taking form. A lover of poetry and the blues, he created works using their lyrical cadences and soon expanded into other genres.

After moving to St. Paul, Minnesota, he would try his hand at scriptwriting and gradually move into playwriting. However, it wasn't until he began incorporating the images, dialogue, and characters of his hometown that his plays received a literary jump start. With his work ringing with true brilliance and African-American authenticity, Wilson began down the slow road to bringing his work to the stage.

Without much luck at first, he would submit his early plays to playwriting competitions. "I was rejected five times," he recalls of sending his work to the Eugene O'Neill Playwriting Conference. But he persevered. Eventually he came to the attention of Lloyd Richards of the Yale School of Drama, the artistic director of the Yale Repertory Theatre and director of the stage version of *A Raisin in the Sun*. After seeing Wilson's formidable talent, the highly regarded director joined forces with the playwright to bring his plays to theatergoers' attention.

When August Wilson's first play, *Ma Rainey's Black Bottom,* opened on Broadway in 1984, it captured the hearts of the theater world and thrust him into the limelight. The warm man with the gentle soul continued writing and has dedicated himself to a ten-part cycle of plays about African-American life in the twentieth century.

Despite his fame, which could lead to a sort of celebrity-like exile, Wilson readily mingles among his audience. With a warm smile and genuine appreciation of their admiration, he takes the time to inscribe a different phrase on each person's book of his plays at a signing and lovingly autographs their old pictures of him, theater posters of his plays, and mementos of his hometown of Pittsburgh. And in a concerted effort to encourage African-Americans to go to the theater more often, he often journeys out into the community to give readings.

Wilson's dreams and persistence have taken him a long way from his beginnings in Pittsburgh. His acclaim has been rewarded with some of the theater's most prestigious awards, including two Pulitzer Prizes for *Fences* and *The Piano Lesson*, five New York Drama Critics Circle Best Play Awards, two Drama Desk Awards, and a Tony Award. He has dreamed big and those dreams have taken him straight to Broadway and into the hearts of many theater critics and devoted fans.

Never giving up on himself for one moment, he has continued building upon each success one step at a time. But to what does he attribute his phenomenal success? "Talent and determination," he readily admits. And it's this stamina and belief in his dreams that has given us one of America's most beloved playwrights.

August Wilson never let a lack of education interfere with his goals or hold him back. Instead, he became knowledgeable with the wisdom of life and kept sight of his vision, which has become a wonderful reality for all of us to enjoy.

If you dared to dream, can your dreams take you as high as Wilson's? When was the last time that you dreamed? A year ago? Five? Ten? Twenty-five years? If so, it's time to get back in touch with your lost dreams.

Deferred Dreams, Broken Lives

Once upon a time, we all were full of big, glorious dreams. However, many of us gave our power to dream over to those disguised as do-gooders or others who came along and trampled all over them. Perhaps they told you, "You can't do this!" or "You can't do that!" Or maybe you were made to feel guilty: "But everyone in our family has been a teacher. You can't break the pattern." Or some of you may have been tempted by the gold at the end of a rainbow: "If you do this, you'll get a great retirement package and gold watch at age sixty-five." Pity! Some of you bought into this so-called wisdom, which prevented you from dreaming your own brand of dreams. But think of what could have happened if you had given yourself permission to do so? And it's not too late. You can still resurrect those dreams and make them realities.

When I think of the consequences of losing one's dreams, I often recall the story of Malcolm X in *The Autobiography of Malcolm X*. A smart, bright boy, the young Malcolm dreamed of growing up and becoming a lawyer. However, a teacher ridiculed his ambition and told him to become a carpenter, a more acceptable occupation for Blacks at the time. Reeling from the disappointment that must have played incredible havoc with his self-esteem, he ultimately turned to a life of crime. Fortunately, he fashioned another vision for himself, rose above his adversity, and went on to become one of our nation's most profound and powerful leaders.

While everyone's life may not take such a downward turn from lost dreams, many of you are consciously or subconsciously suffering from the consequences of your unrealized or thwarted dreams. You may be depressed but don't know why. You may be craving something deep down inside but can't quite put your finger on it. And it just may be those lost dreams. Isn't it time to bring back the joy and passion into your life by rediscovering those desires? Without making excuses like "I'm too old" or "There are no jobs in that field" or "I can't do that because of my family responsibilities," you can resurrect them or develop new ones.

Rekindle That Fire

I remember once doing some workshops with a group of college students. When I asked them to tell me what their majors were, I saw a lot of frowns and heard a lot of moans. Finding this interesting, I went from one to the other and asked how each one had decided on his or her major. When I stopped at one young woman's desk, I questioned her about her future plans and she solemnly replied, "Nursing." But I could see from the sadness on her face that she wanted to do something else with her life. I asked her point-blank, "Now, tell me, why did you pick nursing?" Suddenly, her eyes lowered and she began stuttering. "Because they said that it is a good field!"

Who were "they"? I wanted to know. And it turned out that she had read about nursing being a good field in some newspaper. Concerned that this wasn't a particularly good way to select a major, I asked, "But what is it that you really want to do?" And she replied, "I want to sing."

I know of many cases where people have put aside their dreams or took on others and smothered their real desires. For instance, I had no idea that a friend of mine who is a successful salesperson really wanted to go into acting. Or another friend who is a business executive actually wanted to become a meteorologist. Or someone I know who is an educator really wanted to become a dancer. Somehow, these people and many others in our society have the idea that pursuing their dreams and passions is a fruitless, ridiculous, or ill-timed thing to do. As a result, many have ceased even paying attention to that which is calling out to them.

If you have stopped dreaming, it's now time to rekindle your dreams. Go to a quiet place where you can be still. Remember back to the days when you had big, bold, beautiful dreams. You were probably a child and wanted to soar to the moon or become the first doctor to develop a cure for cancer or nurse the sick or dance your heart out on the Broadway stage. Really try and connect to your dream. Get a firm picture of it in your mind. Experience it! And as you do, notice what's happening. Are you smiling? Is there a well of emotion making a lump in your throat? If so, good! You're beginning to feel your passion once more.

Now, stay with the feeling and start focusing on more recent dreams. Perhaps you want to start your own business or open a school for children or make a mint on Wall Street or invent the most needed product in America. Visualize your dream in your mind and ask yourself the following questions:

- What thoughts did I bring up?
- Is it a dream that keeps recurring at various times in my life, even when I try suppressing it?
- Do I still want to pursue this dream?
- What is holding me back from achieving it?
- What will it take to make this dream happen?
- How long will it take?

Now, let's disarm your reasons for thinking that this dream is unobtainable. Using the following chart as an example, let's say that you have dreamed of becoming a screenwriter. Look at five possible reasons why it can't be accomplished. Afterward, ask yourself whether these reasons are really insurmountable, or could they possibly became a reality. Next, study the five reasons why this dream can be accomplished. Now, think about your own dreams and complete the exercise.

Remember: You can still dream your dreams and accomplish them!

Obstacles to Dream Accomplishment

Why Can't I Acheive My Dream?	*How Can It Be Accomplished?*
1. I'm too busy doing _____ .	1. I can decide that I really need to do this. Nothing will stop me!
2. My job is too demanding.	2. I can stop blaming my job! I can better schedule my after-work activities to include _____ .
3. I have other responsibilities, like my family.	3. I will explain to my family the benefits of my pursuing my dreams. I will be a happier person. And if I am successful, there will be many rewards including financial ones for them.
4. I'm too lazy.	4. I will stop procrastinating and do what I have to to realize my dreams.
5. Doing _____ seems awfully hard.	5. I will focus on pursuing what makes me happy and refrain from looking at all the obstacles. I will write my screenplay!

In addition, let's work on what you are saying about ful-fulling your dreams:

Are You Saying . . .	*Instead of This?*
"Dreaming is for kids."	*"Without dreams, I'm a lost soul. I'll dream for the rest of my life."*
"I'm too old to realize my dreams."	*"Age is just a number. Many people wait until retirement to do what they really want to do. I'll have the courage to make my dreams come true now."*
"I might fail."	*"I'll never know unless I try. I'll consider my attempts as a learning experience. Win or fail, I've still learned and gained a great deal."*
"People might laugh at me!"	*"The worst criticism is from someone who knows the same or less than me. I am forgetting about what people think or say and concentrating on me."*
"If I pursue my dream, I might lose my job, my friends, my home."	*"People who are pursuing something that they love always seem to manage. Look at all the struggling actors and musicians out there. They may not be rich in the pocketbook but have plenty of peace of mind and contentment. I'll find a way to make my dreams survive!"*

Put Some Courage Behind Your Dreams

There are a million reasons not to dream. Will you be think-ing that you can't achieve your dreams and go for it? Will you have the courage to try?

She Had the Courage to Dream Big and Made It Happen

Sheryl Lee Ralph, one of our best-loved dream girls, portrays Dee on UPN's hit television show *Moesha*. Now also a film producer, she has always had the courage to pursue her dreams.

Although we know her best from *Dreamgirls*, the Broadway musical extravaganza that gave her name recognition, Ralph has made many of her dreams come true. She has appeared in a variety of films, including *Sister Act 2* with Whoopi Goldberg; *The Flintstones*; *The Distinguished Gentleman* with Eddie Murphy; *Mistress* with Robert De Niro; *To Sleep with Anger* with Danny Glover, which won her the 1991 Independent Spirit Award for Best Supporting Actress; *The Mighty Quinn* with Denzel Washington; and HBO's *Witchhunt* with Dennis Hopper. In addition, she has been in the television shows *Designing Women*, *George* with George Foreman, and *Codename: Foxfire*.

Considering herself a "Jamerican," or one of mixed African-American and Jamaican parentage, Ralph was born in Waterbury, Connecticut. Getting the creative bug early from two artistic parents—Dr. Stanley Ralph, a musician and former school administrator, and Ivy Ralph, a fashion designer—she made her stage debut at an early age.

After high school graduation, the perky coed would go to Rutgers University with the hope of becoming a doctor. However, she soon changed her mind and majored in English Literature with a minor in Theater Arts. With the courage to go into a field that was crowded with aspiring performers, she let her talent soar. After winning the Irene Ryan Scholarship, being selected as one of *Glamour*'s Top Ten College Women in America, which brought her under the tutelage of veteran actor Virginia Capers, and being named the first runner-up in the Miss Black Teenage

America Pageant, which attracted an agent, she was more determined.

Her first professional roles were as an understudy for the Negro Ensemble Company's production of Steve Carter's *Eden*, and a Broadway debut in *Reggae*. Inspired, she relocated to California and did *A Piece of the Action* in which her acting talents would become admired by, among others, Sidney Poitier and Bill Cosby, two of the industry's best.

However, it was *Dreamgirls* that would put her on the map. "*Dreamgirls* was all by accident. I was in California and doing films and guest television appearances. I had it in my mind that the real action was on stage," she recalls. "So, I came back to New York and had an audition with Tom Eyen, who was working on 'Workshop Number Nine,'" a musical workshop which eventually became the highly acclaimed *Dreamgirls*. Landing one of the lead roles as Deena Jones, Ralph received a Tony Award nomination and a Drama Desk Award.

With that kind of success, she thought that a return to Hollywood might open more doors, but it didn't happen so easily. "When I would perform, people would always make note of my talent and abilities. But there was always a 'but' . . . but you're Black. But Black isn't a hurdle for me. I know that I'm Black. It was finding out that it was a hurdle for someone else," says Ralph, who is an outspoken critic regarding the lack of roles and vehicles for African-American actors in Hollywood.

With a desire to tackle this problem, she began producing her own films through Island Girl Production Company. Taking all of the expertise learned from her own work in films, the film *Secrets*, starring Alfre Woodard and Robin Givens, was her first project. A second one is *Card* with Kathy Lee Crosby and Alex Trebec in leading roles. "I'd like to get much more into producing. I want to do films about Black women because we don't get a chance to work." She talks about future plans. "I realized that you really can't depend on other people for your success. And as long as you're waiting for someone else to come along and tell you that you're the best thing since Tom and Denzel, then you're in a different position. You're holding your hand out and waiting for someone else to make your dreams come true."

Despite having a busy professional life, Sheryl Lee Ralph is married to import-export businessman Eric Maurice, and the couple have two beautiful children, Etienne and Ivy Victoria. They own a mail-order business that sells African-inspired products, cloth, and furniture, and Ralph began a children's clothing line called Le Petit Etienne, which received extensive coverage in many publications, including *TV Guide*, *Essence*, *Working Mother*, and *Vibe*.

Ralph also spends a considerable amount of time and energy on coordinating fund-raising events. For the past five years, she has been the producer of "Divas Simply Singing," a musical show benefit for AIDS. With proceeds going to such organizations as the Minority AIDS Project, Baby Buddies (a program for AIDS-affected children), Project Angel (a meals program for people with AIDS), and Rue's House (a shelter for HIV-infected women), the event has been tremendously visible and successful. And she has been able to get some of Hollywood's most talented to perform in the show, including Mary Wilson, Liz Torres, Tisha Campbell, Linda Hopkins, Stephanie Mills, CeCe Peniston, For Real, Jenifer Lewis, Marsha Warfield, Marilyn McCoo, and Tichina Arnold.

Talented in so many areas, the lovely and vivacious Sheryl Lee Ralph believes that success is quite individual. "It is so many things. Success is what you consider it to be. What I consider success may not be what someone else considers it. And you have to make those definitions for yourself and not let anyone else define it for you."

An advocate of having a five-year plan for both her professional and personal life, she says, "I've always been a reader of success and self-help books. In one of them, it said that it was necessary to plan. And while making those plans, it was necessary to visualize those plans coming true." And dream girl Sheryl Lee Ralph took that information, supplied a little courage, and made her dreams happen. With so many more dreams to accomplish, she has just begun. And we believe in her possibilities!

❖<>❖

Put Incredible Passion Behind Your Dreams

Like Sheryl Lee Ralph, most successful people tend to be passionate about their dreams and believe that they can achieve them. And by having this type of passion, they become single-minded like Wilson and Ralph in the pursuit of accomplishing their goals.

❖<>❖

She Blew Her Passion Flute into the Heart of the Music World

They call her the "First Lady of the Flute," and she has stacked up a list of musical achievements over the past twenty years. Like the title of her latest release, *Passion Flute*, Bobbi Humphrey's passion to become one of the world's foremost jazz flutists has propelled her into the jazz world and fans' hearts.

Born in Marlin, Texas, she recalls her first experience with the instrument that would change her life. "I first heard the flute when I went to a *Peter and the Wolf* symphony in the second grade. After the chase scene, I asked my teacher what was that instrument they were playing and she said it was the flute. And I knew that I was going to play it one day."

However, it wasn't until later in high school that Humphrey had the chance to fulfill that desire. While participating in the ninth-grade band, she also joined the school's stage band, which afforded her the opportunity to play and fall in love with jazz. After school, she spent every second of her spare time listening to a local jazz radio station. Playing the songs over and over on her flute, she tried her hand at soloing, which helped develop her ear for music. When the band director heard her solo playing, he exclaimed that she had a real talent for improvisation, which boosted Humphrey's belief in her talents and her desire to follow her dream of professionally playing the flute one day.

After high school graduation, she won a full music scholarship to Texas Southern University, but became homesick and switched to Southern Methodist University. It was there that she came to the attention of the great Dizzy Gillespie. When she entered and lost a collegiate musical competition, Gillespie came to her and offered some words of advice. "Dizzy told me, 'I voted for you in the soloist category and thought you should have won. And I guarantee if you go to New York, the world will know your name. And the guy who won, I doubt that they'll ever know him.' " Humphrey fondly recalls the conversation with the legend who gave her the extra push to take her dream to the next step. "I was already thinking of going to New York. But I thought if Dizzy says I can make it, maybe I can!"

What happened next can only be explained by the Universe's showering of multiple miracles upon her. In 1971, she called the Apollo Theatre's amateur program, and was promptly sent a telegram which said that a spot had been reserved for her on the world-famous stage and to come to New York. With her family's blessings, she headed there and had no idea what big things were in store.

"My mother had told me to call a cousin who was in New York. When he came over to the hotel where I was staying, he asked whether I would like to go see Duke Ellington's band, and to bring my flute." She recalls taking the instrument along and encountering one of the many opportunities that helped propel her to fame. It was her third day in New York when more than the unexpected happened. "I met 'The Duke' backstage and he was larger than life. He asked me what was that in my hand and wanted to know, 'Do you play that?' I was really nervous and going 'Well ... I ... !' Then he said, 'Either you do or you don't! Speak up!' " She spoke up, sat in with him on that set and eventually performed with the master musician for the entire weekend.

Quite by accident, her second miracle came when two friends who worked on the television show *Positively Black* invited her down to the NBC studios. With flute in hand, she found herself in the studios where *The Tonight Show* was being taped. "Joey Bishop was hosting and they had this contest called 'Stump the Band' where you could sing and see if the band could pick up your song. So I said that I could play Herbie Mann's 'Coming Home Baby' on my flute. I started playing and Doc Severinsen said, 'Stop. This is no joke. This girl can really play!' And so they invited me onstage and I played with the band for the whole show and Joey Bishop said, 'Let's interview this girl!' " She remembers the havoc created by her impromptu appearance, which backed up scheduled guests' performances and interviews.

In the midst of all this commotion, there was still the Apollo to consider. After all, it was the reason for Humphrey's coming to New York. "I was tying for first place with another petite person named Stephanie Mills." She explains how her career would get yet another push. "One Wednesday, I didn't show up at the Apollo because I had heard that Herbie Mann was going to be in concert in the park. I went there and asked him if I could sit in with him. He said, 'What do you mean ... can you sit in with me?' And I told him, 'Well, Duke Ellington let me sit in with him.' " She smiles when she remembers how Mann finally gave in to her request. "He said, 'If you played with The Duke, you must be pretty good.' I went on to play the concert before ten to fifteen thousand people and the audience went into an uproar. I think besides *The Tonight Show*, more people remember me from that one affair when I played with him. That night, Herbie offered me a gig right onstage and I went on to do two records with him."

In the coming weeks, Humphrey would continue her

winning streak by making jazz recording history and becoming the first female artist to sign with Blue Note Records in
its thirty-nine-year history. Her LP album *Blues and Blacks*
became a huge commercial success along with the hit "Satin
Doll," both of which established her as a crossover artist.

While all of this may seem like some wondrous coinci-
dence or good luck, Bobbi Humphrey had long prepared for
those moments in New York. For years, she had practiced
and believed in positive thinking. "My father used to do gar-
dening for some rich people and they would give him
books, which he brought home. So when I was very young, I
read *Think and Grow Rich* by Napoleon Hill. I read its
premise, which said that whatever you believe and put some
action to, you can actually achieve. And that really framed
my way of thinking. When I went to New York, I said, 'Why
shouldn't I?' I believed that I was going to be a success!"

Because of that belief, she took an ordinary childhood
dream of playing the flute and turned it into a reality. Instead of forgetting about her musical talent, like so many
children who play in elementary or high school bands do,
she took her training and carved a future from it.

In a career that has had many milestones, she was *Billboard* magazine and *Record World*'s Best Female Instrumen-
talist, *Cashbox*'s Best Female Vocalist, and *Ebony* magazine's
readers poll's Best Flutist. She has performed with the gi-
ants, including Stevie Wonder who included her on his triumphant album *Songs in the Key of Life*. Today, Humphrey
still performs but also devotes time to her publishing and production companies, and Paradise Sounds Records, her own
record label. She also lectures at colleges and universities.

Bobbi Humphrey is a woman of passion who, like so
many African-Americans before her, received a powerful
legacy from her family. "My mom and dad encouraged all of
us kids to always go for it. My late father was very proud of
me. When he put me on the plane for New York, he said, 'I
don't want to see you back here until you've made a name
for yourself. Hold it up for the Humphrey name!' " And it
was his might and fortitude that encouraged her to reach for

the highest rungs of success. "I saw a lot of strength in my father. He worked two jobs to support us six kids. And I said that if he could survive and make a good living through working two jobs, I really don't have anything to complain about. And it's this legacy of strength and greatness that all of us, particularly Black people, have!"

A little child listened to the melodic sounds of a beautiful instrument, became fascinated, and decided to fly with it. Over and over, she had written in her high school notebook: "Bobbi Humphrey, Jazz Flutist!" and believed that her dreams could come true. When she added some passion and began cooking on that flute, there was no stopping her.

Give Your Dreams Another Dimension: Expand Them

Throughout history, there have been many examples of African-Americans who stretched their initial dreams, gave them another dimension, and took them to the next level. Think about the following African-Americans who did just that:

- Dr. Charles Drew dreamed of becoming a surgeon but took his dreams to another level and wrote himself into the history books. Although he did outstanding work as a physician, it was his research with blood plasma that made him famous. Pursuing a dream within a dream, he expanded his work, which led to the establishment of the first blood bank and the subsequent saving of millions of lives.
- Dr. George Washington Carver was an agricultural chemist who fueled his dreams by seeing beyond the possibility of ordinary uses for peanuts and other products. By doing so, he developed ways to produce more than 250 products from peanuts, sweet potatoes, and pecans. He could have remained a college professor but widened his vision.
- Adam Clayton Powell Jr. could have enjoyed a happy, pros-

perous life as the pastor of the Abyssinian Baptist Church, but he had bigger dreams. A champion against racial injustice, he fought for our rights. In 1943, he was elected to Congress and ultimately became the powerful chair of the Education and Labor Committee. Through his vision of helping his own, he became known to the world as our special warrior.

- Reginald Lewis could have been content with being a savvy lawyer but set his sights higher. With an eye for corporate entrepreneurship, he bought Beatrice International and created the largest-owned Black business, which still consistently ranks number one on *Black Enterprise* magazine's Top 100 List.

- Oprah Winfrey dreamed of making a name in television and could have been satisfied being a reporter or anchor or host of some local television show. However, she had a larger vision. Today, she ranks among the wealthiest people in the United States; *Forbes* magazine reports that her fortune is more than $400 million. With the ownership of a studio, she is a powerful producer and actress.

How can you expand upon your dreams and take them to the next level? By doing this, you may leave a great legacy like that of Drew, Carver, Powell, Lewis, and Winfrey.

Connect to Your Life's Purpose

While dreaming big and expanding those dreams are good, you must take this one step further and connect to your life's purpose. Why were you put here? What special qualities do you have? Did you come here for a specific purpose?

◉‹›◉

She Was Born to Perform

Early on, Ruby Dee knew that she had been given certain talents. "I think that I came with the equipment ever since I can remember. I had been reciting, painting, and doing creative things as a child. I was lucky enough to have parents who recognized that, gave me piano and dancing lessons, and encouraged me in the arts," she recalls. "I think that we are lucky as children to have adults in our lives who recognize what the particular bend of the twig is and seek to reinforce it. I should wish that for everyone."

And what wonderful parents she must have had to let her pursue her destiny. For in the decades prior to her seeking an acting career, there had been only a handful of Blacks on stage and in the movies. Josephine Baker had made her mark during the Roaring Twenties; Florence Mills had dazzled in Noble Sissle and Eubie Blake's spectacular *Shuffle Along*; the great Paul Robeson had found acclaim in Eugene O'Neill's *The Emperor Jones* and *All God's Chillun Got Wings*; Ethel Waters became known in *Africana*; Bill "Bojangles" Robinson, the fabulous dancer, had wowed the world with his tap dancing; Oscar Micheaux's films, such as *Hearts of Dixie*, had shot into prominence. In the thirties, Hattie McDaniel would win an Oscar; Lena Horne and Eddie "Rochester" Anderson would grace the silver screen. But by and large, there were slim pickings for African-American actors when Ruby Dee came along. Still, she would take her place on the stage.

Soon steered to a place where she could develop and perfect her craft, she began studying with theater greats such as Lloyd Richards, Paul Mann, and Morris Carnovsky, who were inspiring and teaching many rising performers of her era. "Through a young man whom I knew when I was fifteen or so, I joined the American Negro Theatre in Harlem on 135th Street where the Schomburg is now housed. A number of us got our start there . . . Sidney Poitier, Ossie

Davis, Harry Belafonte, Hilda Sims, Clarise Taylor, and Fred O'Neal."

Because of that experience, she is committed to bringing about a national theatrical training ground where African-American actors can study as many did at the American Negro Theatre. It would be a place that could provide crucial support for our actors. "All my life, I have been interested in encouraging and supporting those kinds of groups," she states. Perhaps the future will bring that type of creative forum.

And, as Ruby Dee knows, rigorous training forms the foundation for any actor's long-term survival. Because she had been blessed to find great acting training to augment her natural abilities, she has been able to keep landing choice parts. Her first role was that of an ingenue in the play *Strivers Row*. From there, she has gone on to portray many memorable roles. Among her favorites she includes Lutibelle in *Purlie Victorius*; Lena in Athol Fugard's *Boseman and Lena* for which she received an Obie; Julia in Alice Childress's *Wedding Band* for which she received a Drama Desk Award; Mary Tyrone in the television version of Eugene O'Neill's *Long Day's Journey Into Night* for which she received an Ace Award; Ruth in Lorraine Hansberry's *A Raisin in the Sun*; Cordelia in *King Lear* as well as Kate in *The Taming of the Shrew* for the American Shakespeare Festival in Connecticut. She has also been featured in television miniseries, including Alex Haley's *Roots—The Next Generation* and Stephen King's *The Stand*, and in major films, such as Spike Lee's *Do the Right Thing* and *Jungle Fever*. "As an actor," she says. "I want to explore life rhythms and the sounds in the silences."

Although Ruby Dee has had staying power in her field, she is still concerned that there is a lack of vehicles for African-Americans. "As actors, we are still on the periphery of the main event. Of course, it is a little better today." She refers to the problems that have plagued our actors for so long. "I suppose as a Black actor, I've had some longevity. I'm still looking for the 'success' that to me is the realization of roles I've envisioned doing all my life. They are the ones based on the work of the authors whom I admire. Because you can count on one hand those authors whose works get on film. So as actors, we still need to explore our writers and thinkers and put them on film. I have a strong desire to do that."

While enjoying the acclaim that she has had in both acting and producing, Ruby Dee has given the world yet another talent. Describing herself as a "word worker," the Hunter College graduate is also an accomplished author of several books, plays, and children's books. "I love the language and authors and music and how it can all interact," she says. Her works include *My One Good Nerve*, a collection of short stories, humor, and poetry. *Glow Child*, a poetry collection by and about children, will soon enjoy a new printing, and her children's books, *Two Ways to Count to Ten*, which received the Literary Award for Children's Literature, and *Tower to Heaven*, were adapted from African folktales.

She has also had a passion to extend beyond her performing and has achieved many milestones with her husband, Ossie Davis. Together, they co-host *The African-American Heritage Movie Network* series, and produce audiotapes, including the King James version of the New Testament, with their company Emmalyn Enterprises.

While many actors might be completely satisfied with performing, producing, and writing for the theater, Dee and Davis have tirelessly given back to the African-American community by participating in numerous activities that have endeared them to us. She explains why this facet of their work is so important: "We believe in group identity . . . not group exclusivity, mind you. We think that we can be good neighbors but first we must be good family members. We come from this Black family of Americans and it's a steadying thing. It gives you a place culturally in all kinds of ways. Then from that position, you can reach out to other groups. I think you have to love home first and you have to love yourself before you can really truly love anyone else."

And she is particularly proud of her own family. Considering her children as among her and her husband's greatest achievements, Dee proudly speaks about her three offspring. "If we can call one thing a success, we feel that it is our children, who have a sense of value, are caring and involved, and that's important." Son Guy is a musician, guitarist, composer, and author. With his mother and father, he collaborated on "Two Hah Hahs and a Homeboy," a musical theatrical piece. Daughter Nora is an academic support coordinator in the Office of Multicultural Programs at Emory University in Atlanta, and daughter Hasna is an assistant principal at the Monroe Woodbury School in New York and is working on her doctorate. In much the same way that Dee's parents gave her wings to pursue her love and dreams, she and Davis have done the same with their own children.

It has been years since Ruby Dee first entered our lives and gave us so many stellar performances. Riveted by her incredible acting, we have watched her perform in many cherished plays, television movies, and films. A visionary with a destiny, our beloved Ruby Dee came here to take her place on stage, in our community, and among our accomplished writers. And we are thankful for the opportunity to share in so many of her gifts.

◉<>◉

Dream Big and Claim All That Is Yours

Whether you're shoring up your destiny or dreaming about taking your place, know that your dreams can survive! Don't think you can do it? You can! The only thing that is holding you back is belief. So take away the limitations in your mind and believe in yourself! Dream big, dream strong, and dream long! It's up to you!

Dreams → Desire → Belief = REALIZATION

Strategies for Dreaming Big

1. Take a look at the big dreamers in our race!
2. Remember that broken dreams mean broken lives.
3. Rekindle the fire under your dreams.
4. Put some courage behind your dreams.
5. Put incredible passion behind them.
6. Take your dreams to another level and stretch them for added greatness.
7. Connect to your life's purpose.
8. Dream big and claim all that is yours!

‹ 3 ›

Wade in the Water: Set Your Goals

To make preparations does not spoil the trip.

—Guinean proverb

If you want to achieve success, you must anchor your dreams and that requires setting some goals. Like little guideposts, they'll help steer you in the right direction. Because without crucial goal setting, you may just maneuver off target and land anywhere.

In much the same way that a road map works, goals help keep you from getting lost in life's unpredictable waters. Just think about traveling by car to a completely new place but only having a vague idea of where you are going. More than likely, you'll need a map or directions on how to get there. Without this valuable help, you'll probably lose your way and never reach your final destination. And the same is true in life: you need some direction in getting to that destination called success.

Make the Plan or Plan to Fail

You have all heard the expression "Make a plan or plan to fail." If you haven't been getting anywhere in life, you may need to map out a good plan or a revise an old one. So take a few moments, use the Goal-Setting Chart on page 53, and determine the following:

- What goals do you have for your professional and personal life? What do you hope to accomplish?
- How can you achieve this?
- What is the target date?
- What are the obstacles or hurdles you must overcome?

Professional/Personal Goal Statement

Goal One

Short-Term: _____
Target Date: _____
Action Plan
  to Achieve: _____
Hurdles to
  Overcome: _____

Medium-Term: _____
Target Date: _____
Action Plan
  to Achieve: _____
Hurdles to
  Overcome: _____

Long-Term: _____
Target Date: _____
Action Plan
  to Achieve: _____
Hurdles to
  Overcome: _____

Goal Two

Short-Term: _____
Target Date: _____
Action Plan
  to Achieve: _____
Hurdles to
  Overcome: _____

Medium-Term: _____
Target Date: _____
Action Plan
  to Achieve: _____
Hurdles to
  Overcome: _____

Long-Term: _____
Target Date: _____
Action Plan
  to Achieve: _____
Hurdles to
  Overcome: _____

As you can see, the Goal-Setting Chart is broken into three parts (short-term, medium-term, and long-term goals).

This breakdown is done for a very good reason. Often when looking at a goal in its entirety, you may become overwhelmed by its largeness and never get around to achieving it. Therefore, it's better to chop it into smaller parts. For example, if you want to go back to school and get a graduate degree, you know that this will probably take some time to accomplish. If, however, you think of it in small chunks, such as taking one or two courses a year, it can seem more achievable or manageable.

Develop the Strategies for Implementing Your Goal Plan

By using the Goal-Setting Chart, you can begin thinking about how you'll implement your goals through planning. Basically, there are nine strategies that can provide you with this valuable direction:

1. Give some thought to your goals by working out the details.
2. Prioritize your goals.
3. Give them a time frame or target date.
4. Be prepared to overcome the hurdles.
5. Put some energy and drive behind your plan.
6. Be disciplined and weed out procrastination.
7. Persevere.
8. Pursue your goals with dignity.
9. Go for it!

With these nine strategies, you can begin to develop an excellent road map to guide you toward accomplishing your goals. If used properly, you'll find that they can make success a great deal easier to achieve.

Strategy #1: Give Some Thought to Your Goals by Working Out the Details

Think about how you'll implement your goal plan. Ask yourself, Exactly what will I do to achieve these goals? Let's say that your professional goal as a salesperson is to increase your sales threefold. What are you going to do to make this happen? Will you double or triple your cold calls? Will you attend a sales seminar where you can bone up on your selling techniques? Will you go out and network to get more customers?

Or let's assume that you want to start a business. Will you research all the possible ways to begin? Will you pound the pavement to test market your product? Or will you attend workshops and gather information to make it happen?

Suppose your personal goal is to send your children to college. Are you going to just hope for the best? Or will you start investing and saving some of your earnings to make this possible? Are you going to the library with your children and leafing through scholarship books?

Consider the story of Marianne Ragins, a Black high school student who had a goal of raising money for her college tuition. By going to the library and doing the research, she was eventually able to unearth $400,000 in scholarship money and wrote about the process in her book *Winning Scholarships for College.* What will you do to implement your personal goals?

Strategy #2: Prioritize Your Goals

Next, prioritize your goals. Which ones do you want to accomplish first, second, and so forth? For example, your personal goal of purchasing a house may take six months or less, but your professional goal of getting a promotion may take two to three years to accomplish. You need to decide which one you want to tackle first. Perhaps you'll want to work on the goal that can be accomplished in the shortest amount of time, Priority Goal A. In your Goal-Setting Chart write down your Goal One, Two, Three, and so on.

Strategy #3: Give Your Goals a Time Frame or Target Date

When do you want to accomplish your goals? Next week? Next year? Five years from now? Don't fall into the trap of being vague or ambiguous, saying things like "I want a lot of money!" or "I want to be free from all this debt" or "I want a new house." Be more specific by giving your goal a date and time when you want to accomplish it.

When I wanted to write my first book, *The Black Woman's Career Guide*, I read in books like Napoleon Hill's *Think and Grow Rich* that success would come by making goals, putting down a definite time to achieve them, repeating a goal statement day and night, and believing your dreams would come true on that date.

I decided on September 1, 1978, as the date for getting my book accepted, I wrote it down, and I repeated my goals every morning and evening. Almost immediately, I met an agent who showed me how to write a book proposal. Afterward, I worked on reaching my goal by spending a little time each day focusing on and dreaming about achieving it. And on the evening of August 31 of that year, my agent called to say that a major publisher had accepted my book proposal.

No one knows why, but giving your goals a specific time period to occur makes them happen. It has to do with firming up a time frame in your mind that helps you focus. So make sure that you know exactly when you want to achieve your goals, write down that date, and believe that it'll happen!

Strategy #4: Overcome the Obstacles

What hurdles must you overcome to achieve your goals? For example, if you want to buy a new house, will you have to clear up your credit? Or will you have to save enough money for the down payment? Determine what obstacles may get in the way of achieving your goals and decide how to get around them.

Suppose you want to buy a new house and have bad credit. What can you do to overcome this? Perhaps you could go to one of those credit-counseling programs that assist people in clearing up bad debts, or make payment arrangements with your creditors. Or if you need a down payment, you or your mate may get a part-time job and save the money from it. Be imaginative and come up with innovative ways to surmount your hurdles.

Remember that there will be many obstacles to success. Many successful people had to overcome daunting challenges:

- James Earl Jones, the brilliant actor, overcame stuttering that would have crippled the average person. Yet, his distinctive melodious voice is now known the world over.
- Wilma Rudolph, Olympic track and field champion, was afflicted with many childhood illnesses, including polio. Instead of giving in to those circumstances, she went on to become one of the world's fastest women.
- Athlete Jackie Joyner-Kersee has asthma but that didn't stop her from winning gold medals in the Olympics. She learned to control her disease and runs like the wind.
- Gail Devers overcame the debilitating effects of Graves' disease and the threatened amputation of both feet to become an Olympic gold medalist.
- Two little blind boys used their musical genius and talent and grew up to become Ray Charles and Stevie Wonder.

There are and will always be obstacles to your goals. You decide whether to surmount them!

Strategy #5: Jump Behind Your Goals and Push

It's good to dream about achieving your goals. In order to accomplish them, however, you have to put some drive behind them. As all successful people know, they must put plenty of energy behind what they hope to achieve. On the other hand, those who are not successful lie back, skid along life's road and hope for the best.

Why are some people achievers and others simply spectators? Psychologist Dr. Craig Polite, coauthor of *Children of the Dream* and a former talk show host on New York's WLIB-AM, uses a scene at a public swimming pool to try to explain the difference. He says that the majority of people are swimming by the sides of the pool, a small number are in the middle, and very few are in the deep water. He believes that by swimming out in the deepest waters, a person must work hard to maintain his or her performance level or risk drowning. In the shallow water or out in the middle, however, that kind of rigorous performance is optional. "In the same way, people have difficulty swimming or operating in life when they have to exert the effort, do it every day, and really put it out there. So most people swim by the sides of the pool. Most of them operate at that lesser level, which is actually beneath what they really could do if they stretched out," Polite explains. "And the difference between some of your very high performers and your average ones is really the extent to which they are willing to operate at those other levels."

However, until you can swim in that deep water and do it consistently, you may be letting success pass you by. Do you have the drive that is required to make it happen? Are you willing to put some hard work behind your goals? Or are you a person who is all talk and can't get past that talking stage? "Set goals and work quietly and systematically toward them," Marian Wright Edelman, president of the Children's Defense Fund and author of the best-selling *The Measure of Our Success* and *Guide My Feet: Prayers and Meditations of Loving and Working for Children*, told a 1990 Howard University graduating class. "Too many of us talk big and act small!"

What are you willing to do to make your goals happen? Are you a hard worker or just a talker as Edelman says? Are you willing to spend long hours learning a new skill? Are you prepared to go back to school and learn a new field? Are you willing to spend hours networking with others to assure the success of your business? Many people think that there are short cuts to success, but they're wrong. Without putting ambition and drive behind your goals, you'll never get what you want out of life or become successful.

Take the case of best-selling author Terry McMillan who dug in and made her success happen for her, long before there was a *Waiting to Exhale*. While many authors would be stumped as to how to supplement the promotion of their books, she did her own mailing for her previous books to thousands of people, including bookstores. And this ingenuity paid off. By the time *Waiting to Exhale* appeared, McMillan already had a built-in market. And there are other examples of this fortitude.

She Did More Than Talk About Her Goal—
She Rolled Up Her Sleeves to Make It Happen

In the late sixties, a rebirth of the Black cultural movement was gradually exploding and renowned poet Nikki
Giovanni found herself taking center stage. Because of her
ingenuity, hard work, and determination, she helped guarantee her success.

Yolande Cornelia Giovanni Jr. grew up in Cincinnati,
Ohio, and Knoxville, Tennessee. Like most promising African-
American high school students, she set her sights on going
to college, and eventually attended Fisk University in Nashville, Tennessee.

Like many historically Black colleges of its day, Fisk had
strict rules for its female coeds. Going to men's apartments,
riding in cars without permission and leaving campus on
weekend jaunts without written consent were strictly forbid-
den. When Giovanni ventured off campus to visit her grandparents in Knoxville, word drifted back to the Dean of
Women, who promptly expelled her.

During this hiatus from the school, she worked as well as
studied on and off at the University of Cincinnati before returning to Fisk. By then, the petite student with an Afro
would find a campus in the throes of student activism. The
civil rights movement had gained tremendous steam. In the
midst of it all, Fisk University became a stopping-over point
for many movement people who were making their way
through the South.

It was also a time when the Black Arts Movement was
gaining recognition. Giovanni explored her own writing talent. Coming under the influence of the novelist John Oliver
Killens, who was the writer-in-residence at the school, she
joined his Creative Writers Workshop. More than just a
teacher and workshop leader, he brought influential writers
to the campus, including Don L. Lee (now known as Haki

Madhubuti), LeRoi Jones (Amiri Baraka), and Pulitzer Prize winner Gwendolyn Brooks.

Giovanni relished this important, creative time. No longer was there an emphasis on the stilted, lyrical, Euro-centric-bent cadences, but a new bebop form of Black-oriented poetry was emerging that spoke more to our culture. Influenced by those times, she wanted to become a part of the growing cultural tide and to show her gift for writing. She recalls the desire to join the scores of new-generation African-American poets: "I've always enjoyed writing and thought that I should at least give myself a chance. How do you know unless you try?"

Upon graduating from Fisk, she wrote and self-published *Black Feeling, Black Talk*, which was distributed by Dudley Randall's Broadside Press in 1968. Immediately, her poems struck a responsive chord within many African-American readers and her reputation began spreading. Becoming a speaker in high demand on college and university campuses, Giovanni was setting the stage for what was to come.

By 1969, she was on the brink of enormous success. A teacher, she decided to promote her books through poetry readings. This was a move that caught the attention of a *New York Times* reporter who wrote an article about her. After the article appeared, her book sales increased dramatically.

Soon after, *Black Judgment,* her second book, was published, as well as *Night Come Softly*, an anthology of Black women poets. She then came to the attention of William Morrow Publishers, and the association with the main-stream publisher helped bring her books to a wider audience. Over the years, she has published twelve books of poetry, two essay collections, and two colloquies, including her recent *Selected Poems of Nikki Giovanni*.

In the early seventies, Giovanni reached another plateau. Her record "The Truth Is on the Way," which included her poetry and gospel/spiritual music by the New York Community Choir, helped push her over the top, opened up new markets, including older, churchgoing African-Americans, and made her a household name. She further expanded her fame by teaming up with such literary greats as James Baldwin and Margaret Walker for dialogues and books. Her poetry readings sold out much like a musical performer's concert.

Giovanni had a plan to write, publish, and bring her work to us. Much through her own efforts, she accomplished this end and rose to the top. In the process, she has stacked up many awards, including thirteen honorary doctorate degrees from, among others, Wilberforce University, her alma mater Fisk University, Indiana University, and Smith College. In 1979, she was named honorary commissioner to the President's Commission in the International Year of the Child and has received *Mademoiselle*'s Highest Achievement Award.

Today, she is a professor at Virginia Polytechnic Institute and State University. Having a chance to give back some of the knowledge that she has obtained throughout the years, she is now content with the slow-paced, academic life and enjoys teaching a great deal.

She is also the proud mother of twenty-six-year-old Thomas, who graduated with top honors from Morehouse College, and recently, Giovanni waged a successful battle against cancer.

For nearly three decades, Nikki Giovanni has been in our lives, enjoying enormous achievement as one of our most honored poets. She looks thoughtfully at what it takes to become successful. "You have to define success in a narrow term. You are successful in that you have tried to do it. Now, whether you get a financial gain, that is something else. But you will have the reward of completing the project. Otherwise, you can sometimes find yourself having done a wonderful job yet you're dissatisfied."

Giovanni also believes that attitude has a great deal to do with success. "The main thing is to remain cheerful. People say that but it's so easy to get down on yourself."

Always cheerful and optimistic, she is a model for our own success. She had a dream, put action behind it, and achieved a great deal by making it happen. Taking her talent and imagination, she launched her career by publishing her book on her own. Nikki Giovanni has captivated the world and shown others what dreams, energy, and drive can truly accomplish.

◈<>◈

Strategy #6: Be Disciplined and Weed Out Procrastination

The twin strategy to putting energy behind your dreams is developing some discipline. When I think of the kind of discipline that goes into writing my books—the research, the interviews, the outlining, and the writing—it's sometimes hard to believe. But without this kind of structured discipline, it would have been impossible to successfully complete one.

Unfortunately, many people make goals and vow to achieve them but something happens along the way. They promise to do the required things but never quite get around to them. Time goes by and they start making excuses for not accomplishing what they have set out to do. Some of them just wait idly for a miracle to drop from the sky but realize that isn't going to happen. Without discipline, goals just don't work.

To develop the kind of discipline needed to achieve success and your dreams, try setting aside a few minutes, an hour, or a couple of hours each day and work on what you hope to accomplish. If you can only stare at your written goals in the beginning, do that every day at an appointed time. Then build up to taking action.

When I'm writing a book, I usually make a goal of writing five to ten pages a day and nothing gets in the way. I'll write those five or ten pages on the bus, in a waiting room, even in a restaurant. Everywhere I go, waitresses joke with me: "Bringing your work along to lunch again?" But that's what it takes!

In addition to discipline, you must also begin to weed out procrastination, which can be the most insidious and destructive obstacle on your path to success, and one of the biggest enemies of discipline. How many times have you said that you were going to do something but never did it? As time went on, you just procrastinated more and more until nothing was accomplished. In the end, you were mad at yourself and no closer to your goals! So decide now to stop this damaging pattern. Left unchecked, it'll keep you from achieving maximum success.

After I wrote *The Black Woman's Career Guide*, a few women came up to me and said, "That's exactly the book that I wanted to write!" I'm sure that they could have done a great job, but when given the opportunity, I actually wrote the book! I didn't procrastinate but jumped right in and waded through the waters toward success. Instead of just giving lip service to my desires, I worked like a beaver until it was completed. To paraphrase Marian Wright Edelman, I did not talk big and act small. I decided also to stop procrastinating and achieve what I wanted to do!

Think about all the successful people in the world who put procrastination behind them and moved ahead with their dreams.

Do you have the discipline to make your dreams come true? Take control of your dreams, be disciplined, and do it now!

Strategy #7: Persevere

Winners always stay in the game while others stop at the first little problems put on their paths. If you want to win at your goals, you must have stick-to-itiveness until success comes your way.

There are many people in our race who have stuck it out and become successful in the process. Think about Rosa Parks, Dr. Martin Luther King Jr., and the many extraordinary African-Americans in Montgomery, Alabama, who persevered until breaking down the wall of segregated resistance that prevented them from sitting in the front of buses. Or look at the Freedom Riders whose spirits and sacrifices eventually tore down the walls of discriminatory interstate travel. In their own specific ways, they and others kept at it until achieving.

If you want to succeed and win, never give up on your

dreams. Although all types of problems may come your way, you can't and must never give in to them. And if you persevere long and hard enough, you'll find success!

Strategy #8: Do It with Dignity

There are two ways to become successful: the right way and the wrong way. Today, there is a big void in which good, solid values have taken a backseat. Unfortunately, many people are willing to do anything and everything to succeed. But these aren't the values that our parents, grandparents, and ancestors taught us. So as you journey toward success, reclaim those values and achieve it in a way that will make you proud of your achievements. With a little dignity and integrity in everything that you do, your rewards will be much more satisfying.

She Does It with Dignity and Reserve and Makes All of Us Proud

Angela Bassett is beautiful, talented, and one of our most highly respected actors. She is a symbol of having the kind of dignity and principle that warrants our admiration. With it, she has shown us that success can be accomplished without compromising or sacrificing honor.

Born in New York City, this incredible actor has all the charm and stateliness we associate with a well-raised African-American woman. These qualities have been translated into her powerful screen roles, making her one of Hollywood's hottest properties and top-paid Black performers.

Bassett learned early to excel from a loving mother who raised her and her sister and expected nothing but the best from them. The future actor would work hard and gain admittance to Yale University, where she pursued business. Switching to acting somewhere along the way, she completed her studies and ultimately received a master of fine arts from the university's school of drama. With degree in hand, the superbly trained actor headed for New York and graced its stages both on and off Broadway.

While some might have been satisfied with pursuing a stage career, Bassett wanted to explore the many facets of her talent and set her sights on doing films in Hollywood. It was the late eighties and a particularly good time because the industry was more open to new and innovative African-American filmmakers like Spike Lee, John Singleton, and Matty Rich. Believing that "success takes talent, timing, and tenacity," Bassett headed for the land where dreams can come true. Soon John Singleton would begin filming *Boyz N the Hood*, and she would be cast in the role of an ambitious single mother who sends her son to live with his father. Although this was a small role, she showed the depth and scope of her acting talent.

By 1992, Spike Lee began tackling the awesome project of portraying Malcolm X's life on film. It was an unsettling time for the seasoned filmmaker, the director of *She's Gotta Have It*, *Do the Right Thing*, and *Jungle Fever*, among other films. Though many critics had different opinions about how Malcolm X should be portrayed, Lee tackled the project head on. Angela Bassett and Denzel Washington would land the leading roles as Betty Shabazz and Malcolm X.

But playing Malcolm X's dutiful wife had to be done in a special, dignified way. After all, the late Dr. Shabazz was our former leader's widow and the mother of his children. The role had to be portrayed with sensitivity and respect. With the thoughtful approach she uses for all of her performances, Bassett took this unique opportunity to demonstrate her considerable acting skills and imbued the role with a quiet reserve and presence that earned her wide acclaim in our community.

She would go on to portray Katherine Jackson in the well-received ABC miniseries *The Jacksons: An American Dream* and received critical raves for her touching and sensitive performance as the woman who nurtured the Jackson family into fame and success. Again, Bassett would show the world her acting strengths by playing the Jackson matriarch over a thirty-year span.

When she was given the lead in *What's Love Got to Do With It*, based on the life story of Tina Turner, Bassett would give a riveting and memorable performance. The talented actress was finally beginning to gain the worldwide acclaim that many actors wait their entire careers to experience. She received an Academy Award nomination and a Golden Globe Award for Best Actress.

Once again displaying a remarkable screen presence, she played the vulnerable and abused Turner. Clearly comfortable with costar Laurence Fishburne, who had acted with her in *Boyz N the Hood*, she gave a startling reenactment of Turner's delicate dance between love and torment, making it hard to know where Bassett began and Turner ended. When Bassett as a bloodied Tina stumbled across a highway into a hotel and asked for refuge from Ike, we all sighed in relief as the character finally extricated herself from a devastating and often abusive relationship.

After her Academy Award–nominated performance, we would again be astonished by her wide acting range in the movie based on Terry McMillan's best-selling book *Waiting to Exhale*. This Touchstone movie has broken all box-office records for an African-American film.

Bassett plays Bernadine, the wronged wife of a highly successful African-American man who leaves her for a white woman. Bassett's quiet determination and dignified composure is startling, even as her character whirls through his closet taking all of his clothes off hangers, hauling them in a child's wagon to his beloved car, and turning it all into an inferno. She received an NAACP Image Award for Outstanding Lead Actress in a Motion Picture for this role.

Bassett has also played opposite Eddie Murphy in *Vampire in Brooklyn*, appeared in the Kathryn Bigelow–directed *Strange Days*, and had roles in *F/X*, *Kindergarten Cop*, *City of Hope*, and *Innocent Blood*. In addition, she will star in the upcoming *How Stella Got Her Groove Back*, based on another McMillan book.

Despite the fame that she has come to enjoy, this reserved and soft-spoken actor has remained centered and grounded. Part of this is due to the enormous amount of love and support that she receives from her supportive network of family and friends.

Offscreen Bassett is a warm, serene, and cordial person with a special quality about her that is both striking and sensitive. Unlike many who seek fame and all of its trappings above all else, she is not smitten by all that Hollywood has to offer. Rather, she is focused on becoming a better person and actor. "It's wasteful for me to pursue celebrity. I desire instead to be more gracious," she says.

It's this wonderful, gracious quality that has helped make her one of our most loved actors. With integrity and style, Angela Bassett has proved that one can pursue a dream and still maintain a sense of dignity. There's something so endearing about her that we'll forever keep going in droves to see her light shine on-screen.

Can you, like Bassett, pursue success but still maintain dignity and integrity? Remember that people who'll do almost anything for success often ultimately reap the exact opposite of what they want. You decide whether to choose the right or wrong way to success!

Strategy #9: Go for It!

Go out into the water, stick your toes in, and wade toward success. Make a plan or plan to fail, work out the details of your goals, prioritize them and give them a time frame, battle the hurdles or obstacles in your way, jump behind your plan and push, be disciplined and weed out procrastination, and persevere. Then, whatever you do in life, commit yourself to putting a little dignity and integrity into it. Give it your all and succeed!

Strategies for Wading in the Water

1. Make the plan or plan to fail.
2. Design your goal-setting plan.
3. Give some thought and work out the details of implementing your plan.
4. Prioritize your goals.
5. Work to overcome the hurdles.
6. Jump behind your plans and push.
7. Be disciplined and weed out procrastination.
8. Persevere.
9. Go for it!

‹ 4 ›

Peace Be Still: Affirm Your Success

I am that I am, a shining being and a dweller in light who has been created from the limbs of the divine.

—Ancient Egyptian incantation

If you want some real change in your life and desire success, affirmations can offer tremendous help. By saying these short, upbeat, and positive messages out loud on a regular basis, you'll begin affirming your potential good and tap into the wonders of your subconscious mind, which can help manifest whatever you desire.

Although we often hear the term *subconscious mind*, it's something that's very misunderstood. There are three basic parts of the mind: the superconscious, the conscious, and the subconscious. The superconscious mind connects us to a higher being and our higher selves. The conscious is our everyday, logical, reasoning mind, the one of which we're most aware. The subconscious mind is "beneath" the conscious one and is the master depositor of our thoughts. As Florence Scovel Shinn, the author of *The Game of Life and How to Play It!*, describes, "The subconscious mind is simply power, without direction. It is like steam or electricity, and it does what it is directed to do; it has no power of induction. Whatever a man feels deeply or images clearly is impressed upon the subconscious mind, and carried out in the minutest detail."

If you tap into the subconscious mind and deposit positive messages there, it can help you become more successful. Since it will accept either good or bad thoughts, the saying of affirmations can directly fill it with more positive ones.

Below are some affirmations that you might find helpful. Select one or two that appeal to you and can foster your belief in the reality of your success. Say them aloud on a regular basis until you begin to believe.

"I have received my power from God and the Universe. No one can take it away from me!"

"All things are possible with God!"

"I am the wealthy, abundant child of my heavenly Father."

"Today is the most joyous day of my life! I go forth and do all that I can do!"

"I am in charge of myself! No man can stop my good!"

"I am exceeding all my expectations for myself."

"I feel confident, alive, and happy! Nothing can stand in my way!"

"I have accepted God's plan for me and am awaiting its fulfillment."

"I have overcome my obstacles and broken through to success."

"I am prosperous in all my ventures!"

"I have harnessed all my good that overflows from the Universe."

"Today is the first day of my new life! I will affirm my greatness and rise above my circumstances!"

"I beam out love. All my relationships are prospering and growing."

"I have no more trouble from _____. I beam her/him with love."

"I dream big and accomplish all my goals."

"I have centered myself and taken my rightful place in the Universe."

"God made only one me and I celebrate my uniqueness!"

"God's creativity flows through my veins. I create the best that I can!"

"I stop and celebrate all the beauty in the Universe!"

"I am thankful for all that God has given me!"

"I can have anything that I believe is mine in the Universe!"

"Doing it tomorrow are words used by other people. I do mine now, get the job done, and receive my just rewards!"

"Every day, I am evolving into a more beautiful human being that is at peace with myself, my success, and the Universe!"

"Like a tree, I am rooted in all the wonders of the Universe."

"I can overcome my obstacles because I am built on the very rock of my African and African-American ancestors."

"I have the blood of my ancestors running through my veins. I can do no wrong!"

"I walk in the glory of all my ancestors."

"I respect myself, my elders, my children, and my community. I will be a success in a way that uplifts them."

"I love myself unconditionally!"

"I love my family and friends unconditionally! Through my example, they will prosper!"

"I have my divine and perfect mate who supports my success and all that I can be."

"I am accepting success as my master plan in the Universe!"

"I love my people and community unconditionally! Through my example, they will prosper!"

"I give God praise for my being, existence, and abundance that he gives me!"

"I think about the wonders of my body and know that I have been blessed a hundredfold!"

"I have all the blessings that are overflowing from the Universe."

"I am not selfish with my abundant blessings but give to others."

"I give back to my community knowing that I am giving back to myself."

"I give back to my family and friends knowing that my blessings will be tenfold."

"My heart is good. I claim my success."

"I celebrate my success!"

"I feel happy, content, and successful!"

"I believe in myself. My success is based on my own sense of myself!"

"Today, I shut out all negative forces and concentrate on positive and successful images!"

"I choose to be positive instead of negative."

"Today, I beam love to all those who would stand in my way to my higher good!"

"I am doing God's work and receiving his blessings!"

"Today is the first day of my redemption. With God's love and help, there is nothing that I can't achieve."

"I feel good about myself because I am me!"

"I choose to change me, my environment, and make a difference in the world!"

Affirmations offer a way of bringing the subconscious mind to a place of belief. If spoken often, they can work miracles through daily repetition.

To understand how they work, think of the way that cheerleaders help their teams win. Through the repetition of cheers, the team members' subconscious minds are filled with the desire to achieve. For example, in my high school, our basketball team had just been marginally performing until a friend made up a fiery cheer that was chanted in a gospel-like, foot-stomping manner. When she stood up in the bleachers and let out this cheer with her booming voice, we cheerleaders and all the spectators for our team began joining in, rocking our bodies and clapping our hands. In a matter of moments, the entire place became electrified. And every time this happened, our team was pushed to victory through our rousing belief and support for them. After constantly being bombarded with all that positive reinforcement from that powerful affirmation or chant, we couldn't help but become winners.

In much the same way, Muhammad Ali used the power of affirmations by saying, "I am the greatest!" and "I'm so beautiful!" By saying them over and over, his strong belief was imprinted upon his subconscious. And there is no doubt that these very strong affirmations helped push him into becoming heavyweight champion. When Reverend Jesse Jackson says, "I am somebody!" we see another example of the power of positive affirmations. When he calls upon us to repeat them, we're literally inspired to be all we can be!

If you learn to incorporate affirmations into your daily life, you will see the positive results. Say, sing, or chant them, and say them morning and night. And pretty soon, your subconscious will begin delivering.

Visualize Your Success

Along with affirmations, visualizations can help make success happen for you. Can you see yourself as a success? Can you imagine everything happening for your best good? If not, start visualizing and you'll soon be able to see, believe, and make it so.

Start the visualization process by bringing the image of what you want to achieve into view. At first, you might find this difficult, but keep trying. To begin, set aside some "quiet time" a few minutes every day and go into a "quiet space" where you won't be disturbed. Sit or lie down and close your eyes. In this silence, try concentrating on seeing yourself as a success. Let's walk through a visualization exercise for happiness in your career or business that you can try:

> *You're in a beautiful room. It's the most beautiful room that you've ever seen. There are many people in this room. You see yourself standing at the head of a large table in the middle of the room. You're in the center of all of the attention. You're happy and smiling. You've never felt like this before. For the first time in your life, you're doing exactly what you want to do. There's a peace within you. What are you doing? Are you a master salesperson? Or the owner of your own business? Or a top executive? A speaker? A performer? Visualize what is making you so ecstatic! Is it something that you would like to do for the rest of your life?*

Now, you can also use visualization to help see what is blocking you from success. This exercise might also be helpful.

> *Imagine that you're in a warm, safe place. It's the most beautiful place that you have ever seen. Suddenly, something wonderful appears in front of your eyes. You start walking toward it. In the distance, there's a beautiful stretch of green grass and the most beautiful, comforting place that you've ever seen. You begin moving toward this little piece of paradise and gently sit down. This is now your little piece of heaven. Bring images of your possible good into*

view. In almost a movielike frame sequence, flash the pictures of your wonderful dreams before you one by one. Focus on each one until you see what is standing in the way of your receiving this good. What do you see? Is it your attitude? Are you putting in enough work to accomplish what you want? Do you really believe in yourself? Next, stop at each frame and see yourself correcting the problem. See your attitude changing to a better one. See yourself working very hard to accomplish your goals. See your work paying off. You've achieved it and see the benefits. Close this visualization with a positive outcome to each scenario and hold on to these beautiful impressions for as long as you can.

You'll be better able to achieve success if your visualizations are strong and true. So do your visualizations each and every day. And within even one month's time or sooner, you'll be surprised at the results.

Now, ask yourself the following questions about your visualization:

- Do I really want what I am visualizing?
- How badly do I desire it?
- Am I open to receiving that which I am visualizing?
- Do I accept the energy that flows from God and the Universe?
- Do I believe in the power of the Universe?
- Am I flexible in the visualization process, allowing the Universe to gently tilt me down another path?

Believe in the power of visualization and it'll work wonders for you!

The Power of Faith

Along with affirmations and visualizations, you must anchor your dreams for success in faith. As Hebrews 11:1 says, "faith is the substance of things hoped for, the evidence of things not seen." Put another way: Faith is the belief that there is a force greater than ourselves that is operating on our behalf, making all things possible.

If you are seeking success, you must develop the kind of abiding faith that the old folks used to talk about. You must have faith in yourself, never falter in that belief, or give up turning to God for help. If you continue in faith, you'll always be on the right road to success.

Begin today by renewing your belief and faith. And know that even in your darkest hour, God will hear you and provide. As the Bible so beautifully notes, "According to your faith, be it unto you!" (Matthew 9:29). Or as Romans 10:17 describes: "So, faith cometh by hearing and hearing the word of God."

Let Go and Let God

When you were a little child, how many times did you hear the preacher say, "Ask, and it shall be given you; seek and ye shall find; knock and it shall be opened unto you" (Matthew 7:7)? I know that I heard that phrase often but never fully understood its true meaning. In time, those words slowly became crystal clear and made an impact.

That beautiful Bible verse is so simple, profound, and within its meaning provides one of the most significant keys to success. At its basis, you must believe in God as the most powerful provider of the Universe and the source for all accomplishment. When you let go and let God, miraculous things begin happening.

◉<>◉

When She Let Go and Let God,
It All Came Together

"My life literally turned around when I made God my priority," says Senait Ashenafi, the Ethiopian-born actor whose first name means "peaceful one." Many of us have seen her as Keesha Ward in the Emmy Award–winning ABC soap opera *General Hospital*. Although always in tune with her spirituality, it would take time to ultimately let God intervene and "manage" her career.

Prior to that, there had been many obstacles to a successful acting career. As a student, she had become dismayed with the lack of acting roles for Blacks in collegiate productions. "I became very frustrated at Florida State University and thought 'Why am I sitting here when I'm not doing what I really want to do?' " She dropped out after a semester, packing her bags and driving cross-country to Los Angeles.

Once there, she had no contacts in Hollywood: the land where dreams can be fulfilled is also a difficult place for newcomers. The pretty actor did commercials and waitressing jobs to make ends meet until landing her first television role on *Generations*, the first African-American soap opera. Although it was only an "under five" (a role with fewer than five lines), she was ecstatic and appreciative of the opportunity.

She came to the attention of choreographer, director, and actor Debbie Allen, director of the enormously popular series *A Different World*, who took a chance on the relative unknown. After two auditions, Ashenafi was cast in a recurring role as the sister of the Ron Johnson character and began making some significant inroads into the highly competitive arena of television acting. All along, without letting anyone know, she still kept her part-time waitressing job— her secret security blanket.

In 1990, there was a major casting for a role in *General Hospital*, and many female actors in Los Angeles, Chicago, and New York were scrambling to get auditions and take subsequent screen tests for the part. It would mean steady work on a weekly show and security in an industry where few such roles exist for African-Americans. In the end, Ashenafi made it into the group of finalists. "It was narrowed down to five African-American women," she recalls.

"I didn't get the role, but the casting director really liked me. He told me that I was so close and to just stay with it."

Waiting for another opportunity, Senait Ashenafi felt frustrated when her career stalled. After all, she had come to Los Angeles to act. It was her lifeblood and dream. Perhaps something was wrong. "For years, I really thought that I was in control. And even though I have always been a really spiritual person, it was only when I worked on the spiritual side of myself that it really opened up." She speaks softly about having a little talk with God. "I said, 'You know, if this is not what I'm supposed to do, then I'm willing to give it up. Show me what I'm supposed to do.' And it was only then that I was able to get what I wanted."

Almost immediately, her circumstances began changing and her good manifesting. Four long years had passed from that first audition on *General Hospital*. But soon she would learn of another opportunity to work on that show. And this time, she landed the role of Keesha. And recently, she was nominated for a NAACP Image Award for it.

Today, Senait Ashenafi is still very spiritual and believes that it keeps her focused and on the correct path. When obstacles come her way now, she can surmount them. "I am able to deal with them on a higher level. And there is no obstacle that can't be overcome with God in your life," she says.

"There are some people who put God first in their lives and then don't want to do the work. They want to be successful, have a lot of money, and drive fancy cars, but it takes more," she says of the hard work that goes into becoming a success and maintaining it. "A person has to put in that work on every level—physical, spiritual, and mental. And you have to have all three. If you have only one, the other two are going to suffer."

Now successfully working steadily at her profession, Ashenafi strongly feels that "to conceive and to believe is the starter button to achievement." And she is constantly exploring new ways of accomplishing other goals. Once a singer with the jazz band Silk while still in college, she has continued to expand upon that talent by writing songs and recording. Her first single, "Rock Me," was listed in *Billboard* magazine as a "recommended hit." And venturing into the beauty industry, she has recently launched her own skin- and hair-care line called Egyptian Goddess, which is available both nationally and internationally.

And she attributes all this success to her belief in a higher being. "I made God my priority and one positive thing after another happened for me," Ashenafi remarks. "Even when negative things happen now, I look at it differently and let it go. I say this is OK as long as my heart is in the right place. I'm a good person and things will work out the way they are supposed to!"

She let go and let God, and the Universe began shifting positive things her way. And in a land where strong spirituality helps to override rejections, frustrations, and numerous obstacles, she has found a way to survive through a new-found spirituality.

⊚<>⊚

Speak to Him Through Prayer

When you let go and let God, call out to him through prayer and ask for the success you want. As the Bible says, "Delight also in the Lord, and he shall give thee the desires of thine heart" (Psalms 37:4).

Remember that there was a very good reason your parents took you to church each and every Sunday morning. Wanting to expose you to the spiritual power of God and the positive effect of prayer, they gave you this exposure. You were told to pray before meals and at bedtime because prayer helps bring forth your desires through God's good graces. And when you correctly call out to him in prayer to ask for what you want, he'll answer your request.

Although many of you may have forgotten this powerful way to actualize things in your life, reacquaint yourself with the power of prayer. And know that if you believe, you'll receive because God is hearing you!

Can you pray and let God become the master of your ship? Can you bring spirituality into your life? By doing so, he may sprinkle a little success on your path.

He Prayed to God to Show Him the Way

Carl Gordon, who played Andrew Emerson, the hip father of Charles Dutton's character in the television show *Roc*, prayed to God to show him a career that he could love and help him never have a life full of regrets. When the "man upstairs" pointed him in the right direction, the talented actor, who began acting at age thirty-five, followed the inspiration and never looked back.

While working in the blanket department at the Brooklyn-based department store Abraham and Straus (A&S), Carl Gordon often frequented the cafeteria, where mostly older Hispanic and West Indian men daily sang sorrowful songs of their woes about lost dreams. Determined not to repeat their mistakes or have their type of regrets, he listened intently. "Over the years, I came to realize that I didn't ever want to look back at my life and say those things. And I made up my mind that whatever I wanted to do, I was going to try to do it."

However, there wasn't really any field that particularly piqued his interest. Early on, he had thought of becoming an electrician, but being in the air force changed all that. When sheet metal workers were needed by that branch of the armed services, Gordon reluctantly took a job in that area but was never satisfied. Upon leaving the service, he was hired in that field at Lockheed Aircraft until the company relocated. Not wanting to move to either Florida or California with them, he soon worked his way into a job at A&S, making only $42 a week.

After hearing those men in the cafeteria day after day, Gordon constantly thought of making a life-altering change. One night after a game of bowling, he decided to walk the forty blocks home and began thinking about his life. Going back to his childhood as far as possible, he took a good look at his predicament for the first time. When he was three-quarters of the way home, it began getting to him. "I was crying. And I stopped on the corner and said, 'God, what am I doing to cause all these problems in my life?' " He recalls the night when there would be a shift in his thinking. From then on, he would take responsibility and control over his destiny.

It would be eight long years before he would lift out of his adversity and begin a new direction. "I came home from work and was very depressed. I got on my knees and said, 'God, please. I don't know what it is I'm supposed to do with my life.' " He recalls the moment well. "Just as I said that . . . a little voice inside of me was saying, 'Go into acting!' I didn't know it then but the spirit of God was moving in me." It was amazing. Acting? "It had never entered my mind. No one in my family was in it or interested in it. And I had only seen one play in my life."

But God had made an impact and Gordon was serious about that message. Calling an old buddy who had a college friend with a family in the arts, he inquired about how to go into the field of acting. Shortly thereafter, his friend relayed some vital information: he should take acting classes from one of the top acting teachers, Gene Frankel, who has coached such greats as Maya Angelou, Anne Bancroft, Morgan Freeman, Louis Gossett Jr., James Earl Jones, Walter Matthau, Beau Bridges, Cicely Tyson, and others.

Immediately, Gordon signed up for lessons in Frankel's school and began training in the beginning acting class. Halfway through, he was good enough to be skipped to the intermediate level and came under the tutelage of Frankel himself. After three years of lessons, he began to get a considerable number of acting assignments. "I knew that this was what I was going to do. I had asked God to show me a career that I would love and could do for the rest of my life."

His first dramatic part would be in Douglass Turner Ward's memorable *Day of Absence*, produced by the Negro Ensemble Company. However, there was one troubling problem. By then, Gordon had moved on from A&S and was working full-time at Chase Manhattan Bank in their warehouse. Most people would have abandoned their dreams, which offered no real security, and stayed at a job that was very secure. "After auditioning for the play, I had a decision to make. Do I quit my job and do this?" He remembers the fear, stress, and trauma of this trying time. Divorced and living with his mother, he came up with a solution. "I told the bank that I had to go South with my mother for about six weeks. I told them that I was her only child and I had to help her. And they said OK."

When he stepped onto that stage in Chicago and heard the crowd's admiration, Gordon was changed forever. At this crossroads of his life, there was no more stalling. "After that show, I came back and told my mother, 'Either I'm a full-time actor or a part-time one!' And I quit my job at Chase."

Never looking back, he kept on acting for more than a quarter of a century before landing a choice Broadway role in August Wilson's *The Piano Lesson* and never regretted a moment. "When you love what you do in life, it is never hard. It's not that you don't have to work hard to get it to work for you, but it's just not hard work. When I used to work at those other jobs, I would stay home or wish that I could get a doctor's note so that I wouldn't have to go to work. Now, I just want to work and am unhappy when I'm not working."

Even so, Gordon was mostly acting on off-Broadway stages or doing extra work for films, and things sometimes became difficult. However, there were a great many prayers for his success as well as survival by his grandmother, who was his guiding light. "She was a very spiritual woman and her prayers were always answered. I am living proof of that!" he recalls. "Every time I would get in deep trouble, God would open up the door, send a job my way, and keep me from collapsing."

Through the twenty-seven years that it took for him to get the desired notice, he would never waiver. After landing the plum role in *The Piano Lesson*, Gordon would form a lasting bond with Charles Dutton, Rocky Carroll, Tommy Hollis, and S. Epatha Merkerson. He would also attract the attention of an agent for the first time in his career. As a favor to Dutton who asked him to audition for *Roc*, he did and received the role of Andrew.

Recently, he was seen in the Oprah Winfrey–produced television movie *The Wedding*, and has guest starred on the shows *The Practice* and *Malcolm and Eddie*.

Twenty-seven years is a long time to pursue a dream, but it was worth the wait for Gordon. Despite obstacles and uncertainty about his future, he had the courage to go on. "At first, there was a lot of ribbing from my friends who said things like 'I'm not going to pay money to see you act' or my family who said, 'When are you going to get a real job?' " Fortunately, he took the joking, mustered up the courage to follow his dreams, and hung in until it all came together. By doing so, he's a perfect example of someone who overcame all obstacles to accomplish his dreams.

Carl Gordon prayed to God for help. And he was delivered the chance of a lifetime at the age of thirty-five.

Count Your Blessings

In conjuction with going to God in prayer, you should thank him for all of your blessings, which can come in so many ways. If you look around us, there's so much for which to be thankful, and we take so much for granted. For example, did you ever think about the wonder of just waking up in the morning? Well, it never hit home with me until Russell Ennix, my beloved cousin, had a stroke, became comatose, and ultimately passed away. As I watched him lying in his hospital bed unable to wake up, I realized the wonder and beauty of simply getting up in the morning, something that most of us do not even think about it.

Count your blessings, which come from so many sources. One of Pamela Warner's came from her child.

She Was Blessed with Good Parenting Skills and a Special Child

God blessed her with a talented son and she took it from there. As a result, Pamela Warner, the mother of Malcolm-Jamal Warner (formerly Theodore Huxtable of *The Cosby Show* and presently star of UPN's *Malcolm and Eddie*) and president of Warner Management, has been the recipient of untold blessings. "I have been very blessed," she says. "Let me count the ways."

It all began when this talented and caring mother wanted to give her son, whom she named after Malcolm X, a creative outlet. "I truly feel that children should have more in their lives than going to school and coming home. So part of my parenting was to try and find other things that were stimulating for Malcolm. I had tried other things outside of school and nothing really kept his attention. His interest was not really there. So I tried acting, put him in a workshop when he was nine and it caught on."

Warner's son showed great talent. "He worked for several years doing children's theater and a couple of television shows," she recalls. "When he was thirteen, they were casting *The Cosby Show*. Malcolm went to his audition on Good Friday. Then he went back on Monday and won the audition." Immediately, Warner and son packed up and moved from California to New York.

The long-running *Cobsy Show* was the brainchild of Dr.

William Cosby and an immediate hit watched by millions every week. This show about an upper-middle-class African-American family with a physician father and an attorney mother captured our hearts and became an unexpected success. Warner remembers thinking that the show might have the same short-term success of other one- or two-season shows. "There was no expectation of it running that long. It didn't dawn on me that the show would be as successful as it was."

Ultimately Warner became fond of an industry where she could use her talents, and took over management of her son's career. "I love show business. I like being able to stimulate, guide, help, and be there for a person. It's sharing whatever experience I have to help them understand that they are not alone and other people have gone through whatever they are going through, too. I love exactly what I am doing," she says.

In much the same way, she feels that others can be led on their spiritual road to success. "Follow that dream. Let nothing or no one distract you from that. It is something that you must commit to and look at for the rest of your life. It is a long-term commitment and it doesn't happen overnight."

Today, her own commitment and blessings have taken her far. She has twelve clients, including Malcolm-Jamal, and is involved in many aspects of their development. Her job is all-inclusive: "Star management depends on the style of the manager." Warner describes a field in which responsibilities vary from getting jobs for clients to more extensive ones. "I tend to do everything . . . not only just prepare and get people ready for jobs. I'm all encompassing. Generally, a manager should give clients the one-on-one attention that agents just don't have the time or inclination to do. The nature of the business has changed so much that it's such a rat race for them, and they just don't have the time. And that's where a manager comes in. She or he gives that client the personal attention that they just don't get with an agent who may have fifty to one hundred clients."

Warner, who has a bachelor's degree in speech communications, feels that she is well suited to perform her duties. "My degree is really essential in this business. You need to understand that what a person is saying is not really what they're saying. It is really about understanding the subtext and knowing that it's not just the body language. But you must know all the nuances that go with communication other than the spoken word. There is nothing that I could have taken . . . degree-wise . . . that would have enhanced and assisted me in the business."

Warner is also a person with a strong spiritual base. "I have a very strong principle in my life: do unto others as you would have them do unto you. Always understand that honesty is the best way to go with people. You must be honest no matter how hard or painful it is for you. Hopefully, I am bringing something honest into someone's life, teaching them as I am learning, and helping to fulfill their lives. And everything that I do in business or otherwise is based on those things."

A mother who loved her child and wanted the best for him, Pamela Warner exposed him to acting and was blessed by her own life's work along the way. God answered her prayers for a wonderful child and gave her even more.

Can you cherish the many blessings that are bestowed upon you and begin to give praise for them? Even during adversity, can you see the beauty of life and God's gifts, and hear the message received from your various miracles?

Take a moment each day and give thanks. If you want success, say your affirmations, visualize your good, have faith, believe in God, pray, and count your blessings. And as Ephesians 6:10–11 proclaims, "Be strong in the Lord, and in the power of his might. Put on the whole armor of God." By doing so, you'll be better able to ask for and receive all of your good, and bless all that has been given to you!

Strategies for Affirming Your Success

1. Use affirmations on a constant basis.
2. Visualize your success.
3. Have faith.
4. Believe in your higher source.
5. Pray.
6. Give thanks and count your blessings.

‹ 5 ›

The Power of Prosperity Thinking

But my God shall supply all your needs
according to his riches in glory by Jesus Christ.

—Philippians 4:19

In addition to affirming success, it's now time for you to develop "prosperity thinking," another method that has been used by successful people for generations. But what constitutes this type of thinking? First, it requires that you mentally tune in to the abundance that the Universe can bestow upon you rather than focus on your lack. Second, it means developing the type of consciousness that will help make success happen.

Are You Poor or Wealthy in Abundance?

If you want to become successful, you must stop thinking of all the ways that you are "poor" and look at all the abundance in your life. Just look around you! Are you homeless? Do you eat three meals a day? Are you well clothed? Do you have a livelihood that provides for you?

While these are some ways that the Universe has blessed you with abundance, begin thinking about other ways. They could be health, finance, or peace of mind. Write down five ways in which you have received prosperity blessings. The following are examples of financial blessings:

1. I am blessed with everything that I need.
2. I am blessed to have a beautiful home that offers me comfort.
3. I am blessed to have all the talents that will increase my prosperity.
4. I have a wonderful career or business that allows me to prosper.
5. I know when one door closes for me, another one immediately opens.

Now, write down five more blessings of abundance that you would like to receive:

1. I would like to have more prosperity in my life.
2. I would like all of my financial responsibilities to be taken care of.
3. I would like to prosper more so that I can help my family.
4. I would like to prosper more so that I can help my community.
5. I would like to prosper more so that I can give back to a person or people who might need my financial help.

Tune In to Your Prosperity

Because to most, prosperity means financial blessings, start tuning in to your possible good by saying and believing the financial prosperity affirmations below or make up your own:

"I am prosperous!"

"I accept the money that flows to me from unexpected sources!"

"God is the universal source of my prosperity!"

"Prosperity is my birthright!"

"I have no lack nor see myself having any in the future."

"I pay my bills with love and happiness!"

"I know that my financial doors are always open for me!"

"I joyfully increase my income by creating a financial safety net for myself."

"I am not ashamed of having money."

"I am not fearful of prosperity."

"I am free to be all that I can be because my financial rewards are now being put in place!"

"I am becoming financially independent."

"I rejoice in all that the Universe has to bestow upon me!"

"I give knowing that I will receive!"

"I am claiming all my financial miracles."

"I desire prosperity and it is mine for the asking."

"I affirm my prosperity each and every day. I am thankful for all that I receive!"

"I give thanks for all my prosperity that is rapidly multiplying!"

"I know that all my financial affairs are being blessed and I am prospering beyond my wildest dreams."

"I have no room for lack in my life. I open up the channels for overflowing prosperity."

"I am sharing my prosperity with others. Because I know that it is more blessed to give than to receive!"

"I am awakening my mind to the prospect of prosperity."

As with all affirmations, say these day and night until you believe in the prosperity that is awaiting you. For if you believe that you are prosperous and hold on to that belief, the Universe will open up all kinds of financial channels to come your way.

Symbolize Your Prosperity and Spark Your Imagination

In addition to saying prosperity affirmations, use your imagination to symbolize all the prosperity and wealth that you want. A technique used by many successful people over the years, it's a wonderful way to manifest your good. By using all types of symbols, you can literally imagine yourself into success. For example, some people use visual images or pictures to symbolize what they want, such as homes, cars, or other material things, and put them on refrigerators or mirrors around their houses. Others use symbols like blank checks to help provide an open channel for their future good. For example, you can write yourself a check for a certain amount, put it in your wallet, and believe that you will get that sum of money. In no time, those exact dollars will appear, or you can do as the Church of Today suggests in its *The Master Mind Goal Achievers Journal* and use an Image Book in which to paste magazine or newspaper pictures and affirmations for getting what you desire.

Catherine Ponder writes about the power of this kind of symbolism in her book *The Dynamic Laws of Prosperity: Forces That Bring Riches to You*: "We are told in this modern age by authorities who are making a study of the mind that man can create anything he can imagine; that the mental images do make the conditions and experiences of man's life and affairs; that man's only limitation lies in the negative use of his imagination."

Perhaps, you can use a familiar symbol to bring about your prosperity. For years, television evangelists and preachers have asked viewers to send away for various items like prayer clothes. Although seemingly just a piece of cloth, the person who receives one feels that his or her prayers will be answered. In much the same way, you can take an ordinary household item like a beautiful box or vase, write down your prosperity wishes on a piece of paper and put them inside. And whenever you go past or bring this "symbol of success" into your mind, you will believe that these desires are manifesting.

Or you can use one of the most powerful ways to bring about

your prosperity. Write a binding contract between you and the Universal source of your prosperity. Make copies of the contract that follows and fill in your request. Review it on a daily basis and concentrate on receiving your good.

Contract Between You and the Universal Source of Supply

On this _____ of _____ in _____, I am making a contract between me and my Universal Source of Supply to have the following:

_____

_____

_____

_____

_____

I agree to do the following to make it happen:

1. _____
2. _____
3. _____
4. _____
5. _____

Every day, I will work on believing and manifesting my good.

Signed

_____

You can also use this type of mental imaging to help you get past obstacles that are blocking your success. I use the following technique to help me successfully complete my writing. After working on one of my books for many years, I was dead tired from spending so many days in the library, interviewing hundreds of people, and typing my fingers to the bone. Wanting to give up, I boo-hooed to my friend Joseph Lyle, who suggested a way that would spark my imagination and get the book completed. He told me to write down the following words on sheets of paper and put them up everywhere: "The book is finished, finish the book." I plastered the pieces of paper around my house, on the bathroom mirrors, refrigerator, front door, living room couch, bookcases, television, and stereo. Every time that I passed those papers, I imagined that my book was finished. Surprisingly, I finished it within two weeks.

Make a Plan for Prosperity

"Prosperity is your birthright." God is the all-powerful source who can shower you with untold prosperity. In the table that follows, make your five-year prosperity plans. If you believe in the possibilities, you can make it so. By planning for your prosperity, you're holding it in focus and opening up your financial channels. As all successful people know, writing down your prosperity goals can make them happen!

Five-Year Prosperity Game Plan

Year One

Prosperity Goals:
- _____
- _____
- _____

Total Amount Hoped For: _____
Date to Receive: _____

Year Two

Prosperity Goals:
- _____
- _____
- _____

Total Amount Hoped For: _____
Date to Receive: _____

Year Three

Prosperity Goals:
- _____
- _____
- _____

Total Amount Hoped For: _____
Date to Receive: _____

Year Four

Prosperity Goals:
- _____
- _____
- _____

Total Amount Hoped For: _____
Date to Receive: _____

Year Five

Prosperity Goals:
- _____
- _____
- _____

Total Amount Hoped For: _____
Date to Receive: _____

Think Positively, Think Prosperity

Many successful people are also advocates of positive thinking. It is the foundation for unlimited prosperity that comes when the subconscious mind believes in the possibilities. Think about how this might happen. Remember back to a time when you desired something badly. Perhaps you wanted to attract the attention of a special young man or woman. Or maybe you wanted to buy a new car. Or take a trip around the world, maybe to some faraway place. What did you do? You thought about it day and night. You prayed for it; you hoped for it. But more importantly, you believed that you would have or do it. And you know that it happened. You did get what you wanted!

I recall a time when I wanted to go to a career seminar given by Richard Nelson Bolles, the author of the best-selling *What Color Is Your Parachute?* Back then, I was just making ends meet but knew that this workshop would change my life. As soon as I saw the listing for it, I thought of nothing but attending. Day and night, I gave my entire thoughts and energy over to going to Chicago where it was to be held. And do you know what happened? Miraculously, the money came from a very unexpected source and I went to the program. It did change my life by giving me information about career planning that was parlayed into writing my column for *Essence* magazine, my books, and many more things. And it proved to me that there was real power in positive thinking.

Can you begin thinking positively and opening your financial channels for your good? Believe and there will be a way made for you! Look at the positive and prosperity thinkers in our race:

- Maggie Walker, the daughter of a former slave, joined the Independent Order of St. Luke, a Black fraternal insurance society in 1867 and became editor of the *St. Luke Herald* in 1901. A couple of years later, she took over the helm as the first president of the St. Luke Penny Savings, making her the first woman president of a bank in the

United States. A prosperity thinker, she once said, "Let us put our money together; let us use our money; let us put our money out at usury among ourselves and reap the benefit ourselves."

- Colin Powell, the child of Jamaican immigrants, rose to become chairman of the Joint Chiefs of Staff and a person many Americans want to see as President of the United States. A role model for everyone, including the children of the South Bronx, where he spent his youth, his thoughts were powerful enough to take him far.

Can you open up your thinking for your financial good like Maggie Walker and Powell? If so, you can take charge of your destiny!

Decide to Have It All

Change your thoughts and make yourself successful as well as happy. Contrary to popular belief, you can have prosperity and happiness. You can have it all. Susan Taylor is an example of someone who does.

◉<>◉

She Gave Herself Permission to Be Successful and Happy, Too

She's talented, intelligent, beautiful, and heads the largest magazine for African-American women. Exemplifying spirituality, Susan Taylor's formula for success is a unique blend of positive thinking coupled with peace of mind. "I've created a successful life because I have learned how to create happiness for myself," says the stylish editor-in-chief of *Essence* magazine. "People think that my life is successful because they are looking at it from afar and measuring it by what we've been told to equate with success . . . high profile, great job, great income. But I know people who have all of those things and who are unhappy."

While she is someone who now holistically approaches success and prosperity, things didn't always go so smoothly in her life. Taylor's climb to the top came after many trials. After landing some freelance writing assignments for the new *Essence* magazine in 1970, she found herself managing a great deal in her personal life. Her first marriage was dissolving; there was Shana-Nequai, a small daughter, to raise, a cosmetics company named Nequai Cosmetics to run, and bills to pay. When things became overwhelming, she found herself suffering from what some might call stress.

During a walk home one day, she happened upon a church. Inside, she would hear a life-altering message about an individual's power to take charge of his or her circumstances and the words offered an answer to Taylor's dilemma.

With this new discovery, she became determined to put her life in order and turn things around. *Essence* offered her a full-time position as beauty editor. Just twenty-four years old and full of hope, she wanted to take it. But there was a conflict of interest with running her beauty business. Still, she knew that the *Essence* offer was a great opportunity and there was always time to return to the business. So, enthusiastically, she took the assignment. "I said, 'I'm going to let the company go and I'm going to take this job! I'm going to expand this position at the magazine which I have grown to love.' And I believed that I could really make a difference."

One year later, her gamble paid off with a promotion to fashion and beauty editor. In that capacity, Taylor made more than a difference by impacting all of our lives. Through her efforts, the magazine's covers reflected women within the entire African-American color spectrum. From coffee to mahogany to seneca to café au lait, the women on *Essence*'s covers and pages looked just like us. And she made sure that we saw African-American women with all types of hair textures from kinky to straight, lip sizes spanning the gamut from pencil thin to full, and bodies from model thin to plump and round. And this essential touch helped make the magazine a further success.

When Marcia Gillespie stepped down as editor-in-chief in 1981, Ed Lewis, the publisher, tapped Taylor to become the publication's next leader. Since then, she has guided the magazine's growth to a monthly readership of 5.2 million. Her monthly column, "In the Spirit," is well read and cherished. Under her guidance, the magazine has also reached out to male readers with its annual issue on men and the monthly column "Brothers." And she hosted and was executive producer of *Essence*, the country's first nationally syndicated African-American–oriented magazine show. Phenomenally successful, it ran for four seasons and reached more than sixty U.S. markets as well as several in the Caribbean and Africa. For a splendid job well done in those leadership roles, she was appointed a vice president of Essence Communications, the parent company that owns the magazine, in 1986, and was made senior vice president in 1993.

While steering the publication that has become an inspiration for so many women of color throughout the world, Susan Taylor has also become a personal symbol of achievement. Despite the busy rigors of running a major publication, she took time to return to school, and received a bachelor's degree from Fordham University. Also a tireless champion of community activities, her work includes helping organizations such as the Edwin Gould Services for Children, an adoption and foster-care agency. And she has committed herself to the empowerment of poor and disadvantaged women and teenage mothers. For her achievements, she has received several honorary doctorate degrees from such institutions as Lincoln University, Delaware State University, and Spelman College.

An accomplished author, Taylor has penned the bestselling *In the Spirit* and *Lessons in Living*, and a third, *A Confirmation: The Spiritual Wisdom that Has Shaped Our Lives,* was cowritten with her husband Khephra Burns. Through the success of her books and work at the magazine, she is also a much-sought-after speaker on the lecture circuit.

Taylor feels that the key ingredient in her tremendous success is her love for what she does. "I think the most important thing to do is to decide that you are going to work at something you love doing. And that is the starting point to me. There are so many people who are guided into areas that they don't love or are not suited for their temperaments. They might have been coaxed into them because of hearing they were growth fields or where great money can be made, or someone who they admire was in that profession," she says. "Coming to work every day, doing something that you love, and trying every day to do it a little better will bring you the happiness as well as the material rewards that you are looking for." And that is sound advice for anyone seeking prosperity and success.

Susan Taylor epitomizes the successful African-American who has created not only the financial rewards but also the happiness that should go along with it. She shows us that when priorities are set, you can have it all. It's a matter of your prosperity thinking!

Like Taylor, can you have it all? Yes! There's a wonderful, prosperous Universe that is just waiting to fulfill your dreams. Sharpen your thinking through prosperity affirmations, symbolize and imagine your success, decide to have it all, be fulfilled, and the prosperity will come! You can count on it!

Strategies for Prosperity Thinking

1. Use prosperity affirmations to bring about your success.
2. Use symbols that reflect your success to spark your imagination.
3. Change your thoughts, change your life, and decide to have it all—success, prosperity, happiness, and peace of mind.
4. Be fulfilled and the prosperity will come!

‹II›

Taking Care of Your Future Dreams

‹6›

Standing on the Banks of Jordan: Release the Fear

Drop by drop the ocean is filled!

—Swahili proverb

Fear can cripple and paralyze you. It can make you tremble, break out in a cold sweat, and cause your knees to buckle. No matter who you are or where you come from, you've probably experienced some kind of fear at one point in your life. With the power to leave you trembling, it can creep inside your brain, drench you with terror, stop you in your tracks, and keep you from accomplishing or achieving your goals. But if you want success, you must learn how to control fear and not let it get the best of you!

You all probably remember your first encounter with something fearful. I can readily think of my most scary moment. Back in the mid-eighties, a woman named Randy Sher, who is now a good friend, invited me to Detroit to an event called Strategies, where women participated in workshops on success and career development. Since I was a seasoned speaker by then, I gladly accepted the offer. Thinking that this event would be business as usual, I planned to go to Michigan, give the lecture, razzle and dazzle a couple hundred women, and fly back home.

On the day of my workshop, I quite confidently strolled over to Cobo Hall where it took place, found my lecture hall, and sat on the stage. As I looked around the enormous room, I thought nothing of the more than a thousand chairs that were set up auditorium style. In my mind, I wrongly assumed that those large number of seats were for the next speaker.

In a matter of minutes, a bell rang that signaled the start of my workshop and more than a thousand women cheerily bounced into the room to take their seats. As I saw this huge audience swelling before my eyes, I became jittery and quite nervous because I had only spoken to a couple of hundred people prior to that event, and this large group startled me.

The woman who introduced me began rattling off my credentials: "Beatryce Nivens is a well-known author . . ." My heart started pounding. Wait! Stop! I've never done this before. "She is author of . . ." The woman began breezing through her introduction. Uh! Someone's made a big mistake here! How on earth was I supposed to talk to that many women? As a flush of fear overtook me, a panic attack gripped me. Was I going to make a stumbling, bungling idiot out of myself?

"Let's give her a warm round of applause," the woman finished. Slowly, I stood up, walked to the podium, stared into that large sea of happy faces, and a million negative thoughts entered my mind. Surely I wasn't going to pull this off! But in a flash of one second, I realized that I was not getting anywhere with this kind of fearful thinking and had to recover.

As I looked back into that audience, a solution came to me. Quickly, I thought back to my other lectures and audiences and knew that I could really wow two or three hundred people. So, why not pretend that there were only a couple of hundred in this room? Drawing an imaginary box around about two hundred women who sat dead center in front of me, I directed my lecture and spoke to them. Occasionally, my eyes moved around the lecture hall and I acknowledged the rest. And from the raves, I know that they loved my talk. By staring fear in the face, I overcame it. And today, I can easily speak before one or two thousand people.

Just as I did, you must control fear. If you want to become a success in life, you must overcome all of its inhibiting and debilitating effects in order to move on.

But how did fear seep into our lives in the first place? Most of us learned early to stay within our comfort zones and not tempt fear. For example, you'll see very little fear in babies. As babies make it out of their cribs, however, and begin exploring the world, their well-meaning parents, neighbors, and society drill fear into their heads. From as far back as we can remember, we heard the words "Don't run, you might fall!" "Don't go outside, it's dark and dangerous!" "Don't play so rough, you might get hurt!" "You can't do this or that because . . ." and more fear resulted. Then came the nos. Finally, there were the words that caused our bodies to tremble: "Terrible things happen to bad little girls and boys who don't listen to their parents!" As we listened, we became more and more afraid of our surroundings and life in general. Don't get me wrong, people were just trying to protect us. But sometimes it created havoc and fear within us.

Because of all this fear programming, many of us became boxed into little parameters that were acceptable to those in charge. We learned to play by the rules and those restrictions taught us how to fear. And those fears may have accompanied us into adulthood. It's time to get in touch with the fear that may be blocking our success.

To do so, first determine the fears that you have by looking at the table on the next page. On the left are listed some common fears. Ask yourself whether you have any of those fears and rate them from 1 to 5 with "1" being the greatest and "5" the least.

As you look through this list, think of which fears affect you the most. If you can be honest, you'll be better able to work on eliminating them, because acknowledgment is the first step in dealing with any problem. By acknowledging it, you'll be able to take a look at each facet of your fear and come up with solutions to overcome it.

Although eliminating fear can be difficult, let me remind you of an excellent story about how it can happen. I'm sure we're all familiar with the Bible story of David and Goliath. In it, Goliath of Gath was a big, menacing giant who threw around his considerable weight and height, and intimidated an entire people. Everyone was frightened of him and shivered whenever he came into view. Dismayed by this particularly big bully and his Philistine army that were gaining on them, King Saul offered

Fear Factor

I have a fear of growing old.	1 2 3 4 5	I have no fear of growing old.
I fear loss of my self-esteem.	1 2 3 4 5	I have no fear of loss of self-esteem.
I fear poverty.	1 2 3 4 5	I have no fear of poverty.
I fear being wealthy.	1 2 3 4 5	I have no fear of being wealthy.
I fear living.	1 2 3 4 5	I have no fear of living.
I fear dying.	1 2 3 4 5	I have no fear of dying.
I fear financial loss.	1 2 3 4 5	I have no fear of financial loss.
I fear losing control.	1 2 3 4 5	I have no fear of losing control.
I fear being in poor health.	1 2 3 4 5	I have no fear of being in poor health.
I fear getting cancer.	1 2 3 4 5	I have no fear of getting cancer.
I fear making a mistake.	1 2 3 4 5	I have no fear of making a mistake.
I fear change.	1 2 3 4 5	I have no fear of change.
I fear losing my job.	1 2 3 4 5	I have no fear of losing my job.
I fear getting a new job.	1 2 3 4 5	I have no fear of getting a new job.
I have a fear of returning to school.	1 2 3 4 5	I have no fear of returning to school.
I have a fear of not going to school.	1 2 3 4 5	I have no fear of not going to school.
I fear intimacy.	1 2 3 4 5	I have no fear of intimacy.
I fear being left alone.	1 2 3 4 5	I have no fear of being left alone.
I fear getting married.	1 2 3 4 5	I have no fear of getting married.
I fear getting divorced.	1 2 3 4 5	I have no fear of getting divorced.

I fear being in accidents.	1 2 3 4 5	I have no fear of being in accidents.
I fear the future.	1 2 3 4 5	I have no fear of the future.
I fear the past.	1 2 3 4 5	I have no fear of the past.
I fear being helpless.	1 2 3 4 5	I have no fear of being helpless.
I fear making decisions.	1 2 3 4 5	I have no fear of making decisions.
I fear the disapproval of others.	1 2 3 4 5	I have no fear of the disapproval of others.
I have a fear of success.	1 2 3 4 5	I have no fear of success.
I have a fear of failure.	1 2 3 4 5	I have no fear of failure.

giant riches and the hand of his daughter to whoever could kill the looming monster. Although many tried, no one could quite master the task until young David decided to tackle it. Looking fear in the eye and armed only with five stones, a sling, and faith, he fearlessly approached the giant.

Upon seeing David, who wore no armor, Goliath probably laughed at the young boy who had the audacity to think of conquering him. How could this little wisp of a thing do any harm to such a big man? But using his belief in God and power over fear, David put one of those stones in his sling, aimed it, and shot it at the huge giant, who fell to the earth. With one rock and faith in God, he brought down the giant who had spread fear across the land.

This story strikes me as a colorful way to depict our own ability to crush fear with a stone's blow. In much the same way as David, you can slay your giant fears with five powerful rocks of change: heal your inner fear, taking matters into your own hands, controlling your fears, reprogramming them, and using affirmations and visualizations to conquer them.

Rock #1: Heal Your Inner Fears

Begin the process of healing yourself from your fears by trying to understand why you have developed them. For example, many of you have a common fear of speaking in public. How did this begin? For many of you, it may have developed in your youth. Perhaps upon reciting your lesson in school, the other children laughed at you for your lack of knowledge or hesitancy in speaking before others. Or maybe a teacher criticized your speaking abilities. Or if you stuttered, the other children may have subjected you to snickering and humiliation. And, unfortunately, this resulted in fear.

When you tried speaking in front of the class again, it became painful and difficult as you dredged up memories of your first encounter. You tightened up at the thought of speaking again in public and kept your mouth shut. Even today, as those old pictures resurface, you relive the humiliation and become shocked into fear. And this is locked into your memory bank, preventing you from moving forward. But to do so you must stare fear in the face.

Take time and think back to the origins of your fear. Once you do so, think of how to overcome it. For example, you can think that you're no longer a child and the humiliation of speaking in public won't affect you in the same ways.

Rock #2: Take Matters into Your Own Hands

If you really want to overcome fear, you must overcome negative thoughts, forget about what others might think about you, and take matters into your own hands. Only then will you conquer it!

◉<>◉

She Took Matters into Her Own Hands

The year was 1970. I stepped out of my late aunt Beatryce Nivens Whitley's house in Cleveland, Ohio, to return to my job at Denison University. As I left, the cutest little girl tugged on my sleeve and told me: "Cousin, don't you ever forget me!" Her name is Kym E. Whitley, and I never have forgotten her or that moment. Today, she is all grown up and co-starred as the occasionally high-strung manager of the family-owned Los Angeles law firm in the television show *Sparks*, a MTM production for broadcast on UPN.

But acting wasn't always her calling. Like many of our family members, Whitley enrolled at Fisk University in Nashville, Tennessee. Becoming an art major, she planned to eventually enter the field of architecture. After all, her father, William, and James, his twin brother, are renowned Black architects and the owners of an architectural firm. Her late aunt, Joyce, was an urban planner who joined her brothers in their business. And Whitley's brothers, Kyle and Scott, and first cousin, Kent, are architects in the company. So she was naturally expected to join the family business.

While many of our cousins are humorous and could easily pursue careers in show business, Whitley was among the first to do so. Heading for Los Angeles, she took matters into her own hands to make a name for herself. In a field where many actors take years to get noticed, she created her own opportunity. "When I heard Shelly Garrett's play *Beauty Shop* advertised on the radio, I knew that I had to be a part of it. When I tried, there were no available parts. So I wrote one and presented it to Mr. Garrett. He loved it and the part of Sister Rosemary, the church lady, was born."

Whitley would go on to appear in national commercials. She played the role of Jackee Harry's twin sister in the NBC movie of the week *Double Your Pleasure*. And she has guest starred on numerous television shows including *Married*

With Children, *The Parent 'Hood*, and *Martin*, and was a series regular on Nickelodeon's *My Brother and Men* and *All That*. She is also a director and stand-up comic.

Although many another might be ill-at-ease and downright afraid of approaching a play's producer and writing her own part, Whitley did. Her advice for those who want to become successful? "The gift that God has given you is where you will truly find success. While I was interested in going into the field of architecture, I always had performed for my family in our living room. Then I did so with my friends. So it was always in me."

Can you, like Whitley, take matters into your own hands? If so, your fears just might vanish. Dare yourself!

Rock #3: Control Your Fear

Learn to control your fears by imagining the worst-case scenario. If you did what you fear, what is the worst thing that could happen? Ask yourself: Will I literally die? Will I stop breathing? Will life on the planet as I know it cease or end? Of course, the answers are probably no. But when you imagine the worst, and then realize it's probably not that bad, your fears can sometimes be allayed.

Now conjure up in your mind what else might happen or possibly go wrong. If you gave a speech in front of an audience, would you pass out from fright and cause everyone to call an ambulance? If you tried getting a new job in a new field, would you lose your voice at the interview? If you started a new business, would there be no customers? And if you went to a networking event, would no one talk to you? Go ahead! Imagine the worst-case scenario!

Then, ask yourself the following questions: Would I recover? Would I get past it? Would the damage cause any long-lasting problems? What would really happen to me? Perhaps you would suffer from a little loss of self-esteem. Or there might even be a little embarrassment. But you would get over it! And thinking of it in that light might help you get past the fear. You might see that things probably won't be as bad as you thought.

Rock #4: Reprogram Your Fears

What are you telling yourself about your fears? Are you constantly reinforcing them in your mind by saying things like "I'm afraid of failure." "I'm afraid of embarrassment." "I'm afraid of poverty or being homeless." "I'm afraid of dying." By constantly focusing on the fear, you're helping it come to pass because those things that are harped upon usually happen. Remember our discussion of the power of the subconscious mind and its ability to deliver exactly what you are thinking?

If you think about the drastic results of not controlling your fears, you can see the havoc that it can cause in your life. When you think about a fear, tell yourself that you are gaining control over it, and it's disappearing. Say it and believe it. And build up the courage to make it happen.

Rock #5: Use Affirmations and Visualizations to Help You Control Fear

Affirmations are important helpmates in the battle of combating the crippling effects of fear. Use them to help you reprogram your fearful thoughts. By affirming and reaffirming your belief in overcoming the fear, you're helping to flush out the negativity. Try one of these affirmations: "I have overcome my fear and am moving on to achieving all that is mine in the Universe." "Today is the last day of my past life. Tomorrow, I am free from fear and am living fully." "I have no fear of _____."

Visualizations can also help. Visualize your fear and then see yourself successfully conquering it. For example, if you fear leaving your old job and starting a new career, visualize the positive outcome. See yourself getting that new position and being happier in it. By visualizing and accentuating the positive, you'll begin to overcome the fear of the unknown. With the help of mind over matter, you can step beyond the fear. You may want to go back to chapter 4 and review the visualization exercises.

Get Beyond the Fear

Fear is a powerful deterrent to success. It can hold you back and keep you on the road to failure. But it can be overcome. You can overpower it by staring it in the face, taking matters into your own hands, controlling it, reprogramming your thoughts, and using affirmations and visualizations to help. If you do, you'll be well on your way to changing your life and living without fear.

And as you try to muster up the courage to fight your fear demons, remember that we are a people who have known fear, wrestled with it, and conquered it. We have so many examples of brave ones who never let fear hold them back:

- Harriet Tubman knew no fear as she dodged overseers and bounty hunters while rescuing slaves and navigating them through the Underground Railroad. Though suffering from headaches that often made her unconscious, she pushed on, maneuvering through the night, going to get her people and taking them to freedom's path.
- Zora Neale Hurston had no time to be fearful when she was thrust into the world at a young age to fend for herself. Traveling in the Gilbert and Sullivan circus, she overcame many adversities to go to college and eventually became one of the Harlem Renaissance's most distinguished writers and author of the classic *Their Eyes Were Watching God*.
- When Jackie Robinson broke through the color barrier in baseball, he had to overcome the bitterness of many whites toward him. He persevered by looking at the benefits of his gallant struggle. He survived the obstacles and took his place in sports history.
- Tired from a long day as a seamstress and only wanting to rest her feet while she rode home on a city bus, Rosa Parks

looked past what some might fear—jail. Refusing to give up her seat for a white rider, she bucked the archaic southern system of segregation and chose imprisonment over bondage. By doing so, she helped kick off the civil rights movement.

- Fannie Lou Hamer, a black sharecropper who overcame her fear of a system that had oppressed and brutalized her, led her fellow Black members of the Mississippi Freedom Party to take their rightful place as delegates at the Democratic National Convention. She was savagely beaten for her attempts at voting and helping others with their rights, but her strength never wavered.

- Fisk University student John Lewis, now a congressman from Georgia, faced a brutal white mob who wanted nothing more than to kill his group of Freedom Riders who butted their heads against interstate segregation. Beaten but relentless, they went from one southern city to another fighting for our rights

- The Little Rock Nine overcame fear, anger, and hurt to walk past brutal mobs who were threatening and violent. They were nine children staring fear in the face. And there were others: Autherine Lucy, who integrated the University of Alabama; James Meredith, the lone student to battle for his rights to attend the University of Mississippi; the courageous and determined Charlayne Hunter-Gault and Hamilton Holmes, who integrated the University of Georgia.

Like all those before us, step beyond your fear and move forward to success! If you do, you'll find many rewards.

Strategies for Unleashing the Power and Dealing with Fear

1. Heal your inner fears.
2. Control your fears.
3. Reprogram your fears.
4. Use affirmations and visualizations.

‹ 7 ›

Blast out of Your Comfort Zone: Taking the Risk

The opportunity that God sends does not wake up him who is asleep!

—Senegalese proverb

Each and every morning when you wake up, you're taking a risk. If you step into the bathtub for a morning bath, you risk slipping, falling, or breaking your leg. If you get on an elevator, it might plummet six stories to the basement. If you stroll out of your house, a piece of the roof might fall down and hit you in the head. On the way to work, your car, bus, or subway may get into an accident, and you may be injured and need hospitalization. As horrible as all this sounds, you still get out of bed, do your daily routines, move on with your life, and never even think of the risks involved in everyday living. When it comes to taking risks that can bring about your success, however, many of you become frightened, rigid, and unable to act. Why? Because these types of risks take you outside of your comfort zone.

Psychologist Craig Polite explains why this often happens. "People have internal thermostats. They operate within a certain range and it's very comfortable. But any time they ask themselves a question like 'Where should I be in life?' they start getting outside of that comfort range. And their internal thermostats kick in and say this is enough," he remarks. "However, to move into the more successful kinds of areas of life and to have results that are not expected, it really requires getting out of that comfort range and getting into some unfamiliar territory." In order to do this, you must take some risks and most people would just rather not.

◉<>◉

She Took the Risk of Going into New Territory and It Led to Many Good Things

Jasmine Guy stars in the lead role of Velma Murphy in the premiere tour of *Chicago, the Musical*. But she is best known as upper-crust, snooty, and lovable Whitley Gilbert in the long-running former hit *A Different World*. Learning at a young age to get out of her comfort zone, she dreamed of taking the dance world by storm—she knew by age twelve what she wanted to be.

With her parents' approval, Guy began attending a performing arts high school in Atlanta, Georgia. After graduation, she took the risk of leaving the security of her home and journeyed to New York. Once there, she landed a spot in the junior company of the prestigious Alvin Ailey Dance Company. She soon set her sights on acting on stage as well as in film and television. Taking lessons on her day off, she began the grueling process of finding an agent who would represent her. "That was the first big hurdle . . . especially for me, coming out of a concert dance world," she remembers. To help, she ambitiously sent out mailings to fifty people every six months with follow-up letters, postcards, and pictures.

Her diligence paid off. She did get an agent and began doing small soap opera and television roles. Soon she would move on to larger, more prestigious parts in Broadway musicals like *Leader of the Pack*, the revival of *The Wiz*, and *Beehive*, in which she thrilled audiences with her portrayals of Diana Ross, Tina Turner, and Annette Funicello. However, the turning point came when she landed a role in Spike Lee's film *School Daze*. This exposure ultimately led to her getting the role of Whitley, a southern belle with expensive tastes, in *A Different World*.

Using her knowledge of the women from her own southern roots, she developed a whining, pretentious accent, and turned the character into a memorable one. The hit show would prove a good experience for Guy. "The show opened so many doors for us. I think that playing Whitley helped me break through certain barriers. *A Different World* legitimized my acting and gave me a chance to act in a comedy, which I had not been seen in before," she says.

It also gave her an opportunity to explore other areas. With the help of director and mentor Debbie Allen, she was able to try her hand at directing and writing some episodes. "So I was able to really learn the business and have insights that I never would have had without being a regular on that show."

A Different World would provide other valuable opportunities, including gaining knowledge and insight from some show-business veterans. "It's been good for me to talk to those who have come through *A Different World* . . . Diahann Carroll . . . a trailblazer . . . the first Black woman with her own show on television, and Patti LaBelle," she says. "And in between scenes, we would just talk. And their knowledge has been very good for me. They have survived this business and a lot of people have not."

When the history-making weekly show ended, Guy was able to capitalize on the experience and land roles on other shows, such as *Melrose Place*, where she portrayed Caitlin Mills, an efficiency expert who went head to head with Heather Locklear's Amanda. And there was *Queen*, Alex Haley's long-awaited sequel to *Roots*, Eddie Murphy's film *Harlem Nights*, and *Stomping at the Savoy*. She was also in the 62nd Annual Academy Awards Show, choreographed by Debbie Allen, who persuaded Guy to don her dance shoes again.

Although ambitious and talented, the performer still faces many obstacles in her career. "The biggest one is the lack of opportunity . . . the lack of vehicles . . . the lack of roles," she stresses. "Just trying to stay actively working has been difficult because there aren't a lot of Black writers who are doing projects. And the few who get them done, everyone goes up for them." Casting directors and others in a position to give her roles say she is too light, too smart, or too short. Similar barriers have plagued many African-American actresses for decades.

To help ease this problem, Guy took another risk and started her own production company, Black and White Productions. Getting an exclusive production deal with Tristar Television, she can now help create vehicles for herself as well as bring more African-American films to the screen. Through the agreement, she will do projects for network television, cable, and syndication. One recent project is the exclusive option for *All Kinds of Blue*, an urban drama by Sheri Bailey about three African-American women and their cycles of addiction.

While she is an advocate for taking risks, Jasmine Guy feels that one should develop his or her skills in order to make the risk more successful. "Your natural ability and God-given talent should be a foundation. As in most fields, there still has to be some kind of technique, experience, and knowledge to get you through," she suggests. "So get your skills together. When people can afford the luxury of being trained, I think that they should really go for that."

Jasmine Guy was blessed with the ability to parlay one of her talents into another, and is very conscious of the role she plays. "If you have been blessed enough to have a sense of purpose to know what you were given to do . . . this is why God put me in this position. There is also a responsibility to it," she says. "It is not a hobby. It's not an ego trip for most people. And I have never felt that way." With her sense of responsibility and purpose, she has spoken out about the problems that African-American actors face.

◉<>◉

For many television seasons, Jasmine Guy as Whitley Gilbert made us laugh and cry. To get to the enviable position of having steady work for so many years, she took risk after risk and succeeded. As Dr. Polite says, she stepped out of her comfort zone and forged new opportunities for herself. Will you have the courage to take the same kinds of risks?

The Fear Factor

In addition to not wanting to move out of their comfort zones, many people don't take risks because of fear. They look at a certain risk or goal, feel they won't be successful, and become frightened. Instead of trying to overcome this fear, they dismiss the risk and move back into their comfortable lives.

Dr. Polite attributes this hesitation to fear of failure. "It's the idea that they may not be able to pull this off or 'What will people say?' or 'What will people think of me?' This is why people make commitments to themselves and don't do it publicly. It's a sense of embarrassment."

One of my clients, who was a very intelligent woman, had achieved a great deal in her profession and had a steady work history at one company. But when her firm gave her a pink slip during a downsizing, she was forced to seek other employment at age thirty-seven. When we talked, it became apparent that she had made some very fine contributions to her former employer and could easily find another position, even one at a higher level. However, she was afraid to pursue such a position. When one came her way, she was too petrified to even go to the interview.

Immediately, I knew that she was crippled by the fear of failure. If she worked at a higher level, she thought she would fail, or perhaps people would view her as an incompetent fraud. She didn't want to take the risk and passed up this golden opportunity. As a result, she became further wedged into her same old humdrum life. And she isn't alone. How many of you would rather remain completely frozen to the same spot rather than rock the boat in your life?

Begin Breaking the Cycle by Activating a Game Plan

As with anything else in life, you can blast out of your comfort zone, break the cycle of fear, and teach yourself the art of risk taking. Begin by activating a game plan. As you do, you'll minimize the risk normally associated with such actions.

Use the following seven steps to help make your transition from non–risk taker to risk taker a smooth one: knowing the different types of risks, making the plan, finding out all you can about the risk, building up courage by looking at old victories, seeing the benefits, getting support, and doing it.

Step #1: Decide on the Best Type of Risk to Take

Risks fall within three categories. First is the bold and daring risk, which is reckless and wild with no rhyme or reason. We've all heard about the person who risked everything and lost every penny while gambling on a long shot. Or the one who bet all of her rent or mortgage money or inheritance on a favorite race horse or the lottery. What about the person who put all of his money into some high-risk stocks with every indication that he would lose? Or someone who participated in a very dangerous sport that endangered or ended her life? Risks that are senseless and taken without reason should be avoided.

Another type of risk is the fifty-fifty one. Although it requires thorough examination of the options as well as planning and learning everything about taking it, there's still a fifty-fifty chance of succeeding. Although there's a good chance that a savvy risk taker might be successful by minimizing things, it still involves too much risk.

Perhaps the best and safest type of risk is the strategic one that requires research, studying the opportunities and possibilities, considering all of the pertinent factors, and planning it out. In this way, you've done everything to truly minimize the risk, which increases your chances for success.

Step #2: Make the Plan

Begin your strategic risk taking by planning and organizing. Look at the following table and start devising your plan. What type of risk will you be taking? What results do you want? What will be your short- and long-term plans? What obstacles may get in the way? How will you deal with them? Now, ask the same questions in regard to your backup plans B and C.

Major Plan for Risk Taking

Type of Risk: _____

Expected Results (What Do You Hope to Achieve?)

_____

Short-Term Plans: _____

_____

Long-Term Plans: _____

_____

Possible Obstacles: _____

How I Can Overcome Those Obstacles: _____

   Backup Plan B:_____

_____

   Backup Plan C: _____

_____

Target Date of Starting Risk: _____

Positive Affirmation for the Risk: _____

Step #3: Find Out All You Can About the Risk

Learn all about your future risk by researching the different options. This can be done in a variety of ways. For example, if you want to take the risk of improving yourself by returning to school, thoroughly research all the different programs at schools in your area and determine the best one for you. Or if you want to take the risk of moving ahead in your company, outline all the contributions you have made to your company and begin networking with higher-ups who can help.

Next, select a number of successful people whom you admire and study their past risks. Go to the library or bookstore and get their autobiographies. Or obtain back copies of *Ebony*, *Essence*, *Black Enterprise*, *Emerge*, *Upscale*, or *Ebony Man*, and read about their lives. Or study the profiles in this book. As you read about your selected role models, see the motivation behind taking their risks, the difficulties in achieving them, and the positive outcomes.

If possible, write to these successful people and ask them about their lives and their risk-taking habits. You'd be surprised how many people are receptive to this strategy and eager to help you. Find out their reasons for taking the risks, the roadblocks, turning points, gains, and sacrifices. By talking to other successful risk takers, you'll not only learn a great deal about their risks but also be inspired to take your own.

Afterward, determine what type of knowledge, abilities, or skills you need to make your risk successful. Do you have to go back to school? Do you have to have some short-term training? Do you have to learn a special technique?

Step #4: Build Courage

Whether you realize it or not, you have probably taken many risks and been successful. Go back and rediscover them. Start by looking at your past victories or successful risks. And by thoroughly analyzing and recalling them, you'll gain more courage and confidence about taking another risk. Ask yourself these questions about your prior risk taking:

- What was the risk?
- Did I initially fear taking it?
- How did I resolve the issue of fear?
- What were the positive outcomes?
- What did I do to make the outcome so successful?

- Did I prepare to take the risk?
- How did I feel about the successful results?
- How did the risk taking change my life? What were the benefits?
- Can I take the same type of risk or one like it again?

Study your answers and see how successful you were in the past. I'm sure that it will give you a little more confidence about taking another risk!

●<>●

Her Risks Took Her into the World of Books and Authors

Marie Dutton Brown took incremental risks to become one of today's leading African-American literary agents. With a wide range of clients including *Essence*'s Susan Taylor, TransAfrica's Randall Robinson, Donald Bogel (*Dorothy Dandridge*), Herb Boyd, and Robert Allen (*Brotherman*), artist and writer Tom Feelings, artist Faith Ringgold, Gwendolyn Parker (*Trespassing*), Vy Higgensen of *Mama, I Want to Sing*, Tonya Bolden, Sharon Robinson (Jackie Robinson's daughter), and Elza Boyd, she's doing exactly what she loves.

Once one of the most powerful Black women in publishing as a senior editor at Doubleday, she reluctantly took some risks that benefited her in the long run. While attending Pennsylvania State University, Brown majored in psychology in the college's school of education. After graduation, she taught junior high school social studies and ultimately became coordinator of intergroup education. As one of her responsibilities, she designed and implemented human relations workshops for the school system and invited Loretta Barrett, a former editor at Doubleday, to speak about multiethnic books. A subsequent luncheon meeting between the two led to a trainee position for Brown at the large publishing house.

After remaining with the company for two years, she married, relocated to California, worked in a bookstore, and had a daughter. During a subsequent move to Washington, D.C., she remained in touch with the Doubleday staff and was offered an associate editor position with the company.

Taking the risk, she returned to New York in 1972, began her new job, and steadily rose through the ranks in the company. Positioning herself to bring many African-American authors into the Doubleday family, she also became a mentor to many Blacks who worked in the industry. By 1981, however, another opportunity came along and she left the publishing giant to become editor-in-chief of *Elan* magazine. Although she was instrumental in creating a publication with a substantial circulation base, she had little control over the economics of the business. Despite its initial success, the publication ceased doing business after a few issues.

Later, Marie Brown returned to the world she loved and worked in a bookstore. At the same time, she was doing some part-time literary agenting work and was encouraged by people to pursue becoming a full-time literary agent. Although she wanted to take the risk of starting a business, she understandably had some apprehensions. "I did have fears and was resistant. I was staying in that bookstore out of a sense of security," she recalls. "And then as the business became more than I could handle part-time, I had to make a commitment. But it was scary. Because as small as the paycheck was from the bookstore, I was still getting one."

Gradually, she built up the desire to go out on her own. "I just started up. What worked very well for me was my knowledge of the publishing business and that I had actually worked in corporate America. It was not as an agent but in another facet of the business. So it wasn't as scary as it could have been. I did understand what I needed in terms of tools and resources," Brown says. "Having been in corporate

America, I knew that you didn't have to have a penthouse office or one on Madison Avenue. I knew that I could do it as other literary agents and publishers had done it out of their homes."

And it's sometimes our overindulgence that makes taking a risk so unsuccessful, particularly when venturing into business. "Many times we go into business and are thinking too much about what other people are going to say about our work spaces. But there are a lot of megamillionaires who have never come out of their homes or garages or wherever they set up their businesses," Brown cautions. "I've seen people spend their whole capital investments. Maybe they've received a hundred thousand dollars but have rented in one of these places costing seventy-five hundred a month. It doesn't take a math genius to figure out that you are not going to be around long unless you are generating a lot of income to pay for the rent, staff, and services."

While she started out small and eventually built up her business, she feels that now her business is on target. However, it was certainly a step-by-step process. "You have to focus on the small successes. You have to look at it and value it," she reminds us. "You have to keep your eye on your mark and acknowledge your own successes."

Because Marie Brown took risks into positions and areas that she knew, she feels that it minimized the risk. "It is better the more you know about the business that you are getting into. And that can come in many ways. You can take courses or go to the library. You can find someone in the field who can give you one or two hours of their time. Get some on-the-job training," she advises. "It requires a lot of energy, faith, and a great deal of ingenuity. And the last thing is hard work. All of us who work for ourselves work hard. And then the success comes."

Marie Brown took the initial risk of moving from the educational field into publishing. She built an impressive career and moved on. Although some of her risks were scary, she learned a great deal from the process. And that learning has culminated in her beginning a new venture as a literary agent. Now the guiding force for many appreciative authors who depend on her skill and literary talents, she has become invaluable to Black writers. And we thank her for her diligence, risk taking, and all that she has given back to us.

●<>●

Step #5: Weigh the Benefits

If there was nothing to gain, you would not take risks but remain complacent. You want to know the benefits. What's in it for you? Will you have better health? Will you get a promotion and more money in your paycheck? Will you get to move and live in a more beautiful environment? Will you shore up your financial future? Can you send your children to college? It's important to see the benefits because they can become your driving force. To the extent that you want the benefit, you'll take the risk to get it.

Take a look at the "Gains from Risk Taking" chart below, and determine the possible gains from taking your risks.

Gains from Risk Taking

Gains from Positive Risk Taking	Negatives from Avoiding Risk
1. More self-acceptance	1. Loss of self-esteem and self-worth
2. Opening yourself up to many new adventures	2. Remaining glued to the same position
3. Getting the self-satisfaction of rewards for taking the risk	3. Never reaping new rewards or benefits
4. Doing something that makes you happy	4. Doing what others won't even if it makes you miserable
5. Being in charge of your life	5. Being victimized by life
6. Feeling vulnerable but still doing it	6. Feeling safe but being inactive

7. Learning about new things and opportunities	7. Shutting down the learning process
8. Having an open mind	8. Having a closed mind
9. Learning a great deal about yourself in the process	9. Stopping at the first sign of defeat
10. Having the ability to live to the fullest	10. Having lots of regrets eat away at you

She Has Reaped Success from Risks

Terrie Williams, advisor to the stars and owner of the Terrie Williams Agency, believes in taking risks and has benefited tremendously by doing so. The cum laude graduate of Brandeis University, who has a master of science degree in social work from Columbia University, took her first risk while working as a medical social worker at the prestigious New York Hospital. In a situation that many would cherish, she should have had it all, but there was just one thing wrong. Burnt out from working with terminally ill patients, she wanted out. "I was being paid good money for the field of social work. I had Blue Cross/Blue Shield, unemployment benefits, and could see a doctor at any time without cost," she remembers.

Seeing the handwriting on the wall, Williams became determined to switch fields and began taking courses in public relations at the YWCA. Exploring the possibilities in such a diverse field, she took the plunge. "I left the security of the hospital to go to work for the Black Filmmaker Foundation, a newly founded organization that was funded by the New York State Council of the Arts and the Rockefeller Foundation." She recalls leaving the hospital's security on Friday and starting the new position on Monday. With only faith and determination to carve out a new life, she had little to anchor her risk upon. There was no office for the organization, which had literally just begun, and she had to work from her home. There wasn't even the real knowledge that she would get a steady paycheck.

And Williams's risk was a particularly difficult one for someone who is shy. In a field that demands meeting and greeting the public on a constant basis, she had to adapt to the world of public relations. "Once I knew that I was disenchanted with the field of social work and wanted new and better things, I could no longer afford to be shy." She recalls pushing herself to get out and mingle. "I began to force myself to have lunch with someone once a week."

Through her position over the years, she worked hard and subsequently came to the attention of Ed Lewis, the publisher of *Essence* magazine, who wanted her to head the public relations office of Essence Communications. It was the chance of a lifetime and Williams readily accepted the offer.

Once at Essence, another world opened up for her. She had the opportunity to meet and work with some of the most important African-American figures and celebrities. Carrying over her work ethic, she became known as someone who could get the job done. And at age thirty, she was rewarded by being named the youngest vice president in the history of the company. "I gave a lot of myself, cared about my environment, and left no stone unturned. I just believe in doing that. And when you give 110 percent, have integrity and loyalty, are smart, and care about people, you are justly rewarded in life. Maybe it doesn't happen at the place where you are working. But you cannot deny the fact that you will be rewarded if you work hard. If not there, what you have gained while you were at that place will undoubtedly help you reach your goal."

And that hard work would form the foundation for success in her own agency. Despite her love for Essence and the staff's admiration of her, she wanted to take one more risk and start her own public relations firm. It would be a big step, and Williams wondered how to make it happen. Fortunately, she's a person who nurtures her contacts and one from her old hospital days provided the opportunity. During her stint at New York Hospital she had met the great jazz legend Miles Davis, and remained friends with him. When the musician celebrated his sixtieth birthday, he invited Williams, who found herself in the company of celebrities including superstar Eddie Murphy.

Through the grapevine, she had heard that the star was looking for a public relations advisor. Knowing that this could be that special chance to get him as a client, she didn't approach him. Standing on protocol that didn't allow her to go up and ask him point-blank to consider her, she cultivated relationships with those around him.

Time passed, Williams stayed in contact with Murphy's people, and heard again that the star was in search of a public relations advisor. It was time to make the move. She sent him a package detailing her credentials and accomplishments. Impressed, the actor retained her services and the Terrie Williams Agency was launched in 1987.

At this point, it was time for her to take the biggest risk. Owning her own business would mean leaving the security of Essence, a place where she was loved and was comfortable. Still, this opportunity was too great to pass up. "I was scared, didn't have the money, and didn't have agency experience. What gave me grounding and confidence to move forward was the signal that the Creator sent me. To be able to launch a company with Eddie Murphy as your first client was a clear sign that I was supposed to do that. How could you say no?" she asks. "I said, 'OK Lord. This is what you handed me and I know that you are going to show me how to do it.' And it made me forget all those other things that could have been obstacles to some extent, and move ahead." In her usual thoughtful and professional way, she remained loyal to Essence, which became one of her first clients, and stayed for a brief period to find and groom a successor.

Other clients included Anita Baker, Janet Jackson, Kathleen Battle, Bobby Brown, Heavy D, filmmaker Matty Rich, Sally Jesse Raphael, Sinbad, Johnnie Cochran, astronaut Dr. Mae Jemison, former Washington, D.C., Mayor Sharon

Pratt Kelly, Take 6, Jackie Joyner-Kersee, Wesley Snipes, Martin Lawrence, Stephen King, Keith Sweat, and Dave Winfield. The agency also has corporate clients including HBO, the Disney Channel, Motown Cafe, Consolidated Edison, Time Warner, Nabisco, Schieffelin & Somerset, the NBA, Miramax Films, and PBS. She has also handled publicity for television shows and books.

For her outstanding work, she has been awarded the New York Women in Communications Matrix Award in Public Relations, the D. Parke Gibson Award for Public Relations/Public Affairs from the Public Relations Society of America (the first and only woman of color to be so honored by PRSA in its twenty-eight-year history), PRSA National Minority Committee Award for Excellence in Multicultural Communications, Black Women in Publishing Public Relations Award, and a National Foundation of Teaching Entrepreneurship Award. She has also been the subject of feature stories in numerous publications, including the *Washington Post, Boston Globe, Crain's New York Business, New York Daily News, Essence, People, Adweek,* and *Spin.*

Williams is also the author of *The Personal Touch: What You Really Need to Succeed in Today's Fast-Paced Business World.* And she is a frequent lecturer at colleges, universities, civic groups, professional sports teams, and women's and African-American professional organizations. Not only a believer in risk taking, she also feels strongly that perseverance is one key to success. She says, "Stay in the race! The only difference between those who make it and those who don't is that you have the perseverance to stay in the race. If you stay on the planet long enough and just kind of hang in there, you can have anything you want."

Even though she has gained a great deal from risk taking, Williams realizes that it's not easy to blast out of your comfort zone. However, she feels it's a must. "You don't do a thing in life unless you take a risk. To know that you are alive and healthy and going places, you need to live with a knot in your stomach, which means that you are scared.

Whenever you have that, it means that you are going on to bigger and better things," she points out. "So even though it doesn't always feel comfortable to have it, it's a good thing, because it means that you're going places. If you don't have it, it means that you're six feet under or going through life being pathetic."

And her risk taking has taken Terrie Williams all the way to the top in her profession as owner of one of the most prestigious public relations agencies in the corporate entertainment industry. She had a desire to change her life, risked all, and greatly benefited in the long run.

Step #6: Get Support

Some people can go through all the planning and self-encouragement and still aren't able to actually take the risk. In that case, you might want to consider getting help by joining a support group. Often, fellow group members can be wonderful allies in assisting you to gain more self-confidence to take risks. So take advantage of this wonderful support.

Step #7: Do It!

Now you're ready to take the risk. To do it, you must feel really uncomfortable about yourself and your life. You *must* find a new job, return for more schooling, make more money, start a business, move up the career ladder at your company, change careers, get a new home or car, get married and have children, relocate to another city and get out of your rut, lose weight, stop smoking or using alcohol, or just change your life or improve your well-being. Because if you don't, you'll burst! When you're in this space, you'll be able to take the risk.

If you don't succeed at first, don't worry. Keep on trying until you get it right. Like Williams suggests, perseverance is the key. If you hang in there, you'll be much happier.

He Kept on Until Landing His First Book Contract at Seventeen Years of Age

Lawrence Otis Graham, attorney, commentator on race and ethnicity, and the author of *Member of the Club: Reflections on Life in a Racially Polarized World*, took his first risk in his teens by writing *Ten Point Plan for College Acceptance* at the young age of seventeen. He would eventually go on to write a book every year while at Princeton University and Harvard Law School.

It all began when he attempted to write a magazine piece. "My plan was to write an article for magazines like either *Boy's Life* or *Seventeen* on how to survive the college admissions interview," he recalls. "I guess my first mistake was telling them that I was seventeen years old. And then they asked, 'Have you been published already?' I told them that I was editor of my high school newspaper and they said that wasn't good enough."

Not dismayed, Graham decided to take a bigger risk and approach book publishers. "I took my article on the admissions interview and did some more research and made it into a chapter," he says. "Then I took a bus to New York, went to a phone booth with two rolls of dimes, looked in the Yellow Pages, and started calling book publishers. I was connected to receptionists, assistants, and some new editors. Finally, someone told me that I needed to find a literary agent."

With change left, he again turned to the Yellow Pages and began calling agents. After going down the list alphabetically and being turned down by many, he finally came to the Zs. "I reached an agent named Susan Zeckendorf. She said, 'Well, I'm a new agent. I've just started and you sound like you're ambitious. Come over!' So, I literally ran over to her office, gave her my pitch. I told her that the book would take a student through the process of writing an application, studying for the SATs, and preparing for the interview. And that's how I sold my first book."

Eleven books later, he has been profiled by the *New York Times*, *People*, *Fortune*, *Essence*, *USA Today*, the *Washington Post*, the *International Herald Tribune*, *Los Angeles Times*, *Time* magazine, and many other publications. In fact, *Mademoiselle* named him one of the 10 Most Interesting Young Men in America. And he has made more than 250 appearances on such television shows as *Oprah Winfrey*, *The Today Show*, *Good Morning America*, *Phil Donahue*, *Politically Incorrect*, *Ricki Lake*, and *A Current Affair*.

Member of the Club, which is optioned to become a Warner Brothers movie, was the result of his *New York Magazine* investigative story "Invisible Man: A $105,000-a-year Harvard-trained Lawyer Goes Undercover as a Busboy at Greenwich Country Club." It was while writing *The Best Companies for Minorities* that he came upon the idea. "Many of the people who I interviewed for *The Best Companies*, especially the Black executives, kept telling me that country clubs were important for business connections. And that's when I decided to do the undercover exposé." As a busboy, he was "invisible" to many of the white members, and thus privy to the racism that exists at many of these clubs. After the provocative article appeared, Graham decided to expand it into a full book. "The whole point of writing that book was to talk about what it's like being a successful Black person in America. It was to show the kind of indignities that we face," he stresses.

Graham followed *Member of the Club* with the recently published book about bias in the workplace, *Proversity: Getting Past Face Value*. And his upcoming one is *The History of America's Black Upper Class*.

In addition to writing, Graham is also a corporate attorney in New York and an adjunct professor at Fordham University, where he teaches the course "Minorities and Women in Corporate America." He is married to Pamela Thomas-Graham, is president of his own diversity consulting firm, Progressive Management Associates, Inc., and contributing editor at *U.S. News and World Report*. A popular lecturer, he has spoken throughout the United States and in Japan, and worked at the White House and the Ford Foundation.

Lawrence Otis Graham took a big risk writing a book at such a young age. Combining his writing with his legal training and business savvy, he's doing what makes him happiest. "What I have been able to do is create a career that ties together my writing and law. I was very fortunate that I found a hobby because my writing started off as just that. So while people were working in the dining hall or in the library as their college jobs, I was writing books," he points out. "It was an activity that took me off a college campus where I was isolated and insulated. It was something that introduced me to the real world."

Very successful in all of his pursuits, he suggests that others read the success stories of those who have made it. "I am always selecting role models. I subscribe to a monthly publication called *Current Biography* and I select two or three role models every six months. I read everything that I possibly can about the person. At one point it was Senator Carol Moseley-Braun. I read everything about her—how she formulates ideas, her ambition, the concerns that she had."

Himself a role model for young people and all of us who have dreams to pursue, Graham, who plans to run for Congress, has shown that ambition, persistence, and talent can take you a long way up the ladder of success.

Whether you have to persevere to make your risk happen or it occurs right away, the important thing is to take it. Because if you don't, you'll have many regrets later. There'll be loss of your self-worth and self-esteem. Your psyche may become damaged, and you'll never expand your horizons. So although it might seem warm and seductive in your little comfort zone, think of the possible harm that it's doing to you.

And if you have the courage to take the risk, you, like Guy, Brown, Williams, and Graham, may just find it all worthwhile.

Will you blast out of your comfort zone into a new life? Remember that it's now or never. And you know what to do!

Strategies for Blasting out of Your Comfort Zone

1. Decide on the best risk.
2. Make the plan.
3. Find out all you can about the risk.
4. Build courage by looking at old victories.
5. Weigh the benefits.
6. Get support.
7. Do it!

Put Your Principles into Action: Work Your Way to Prosperity

Whatsoever thy hand findeth to do, do it with thy might.

—Ecclesiastes 9:10

In Catherine Ponder's wonderful book *The Dynamic Laws of Prosperity*, there's a subchapter entitled "Work Is Divine." A wonderful, profound, and powerful way to look at our livelihoods, it asks us to think of work in a different way. Because God put us here for a specific purpose or mission, it stands to reason that we should think of our work as a divine expression of ourselves and something special in our lives.

Unfortunately, many of us still consider work as drudgery. For too many of us, it's still something to do while doodling away our lives until retirement comes. But if you want to become successful, you must change that way of thinking and strive to do something that can bring you joy as well as pay the bills.

Find Something You Love to Do

There's a very simple rule of universal success for each and every person: work at something you love and you'll find success. Just study any successful person and you'll find that they not only love their work but have a passion for it. And as you've read in the profiles of the successful African-Americans in this book, you've seen that most adore what they do.

Now, some of you might be thinking: "Love work? How can that be possible?" You might have another kind of understanding of work, that it isn't possible to love it. However, if you want to become successful and achieve all that's possible, you must have more than a passing interest in what you do for a living.

I want you to think about anything that you feel passionately about in life. How do you approach it? Don't you put your heart and soul into it? On the other hand, aren't you only lukewarm for those things that hold no interest? For example, think about trying to play golf without having any interest in it. Of course, you wouldn't get past the first swing. Try to lose weight without any interest in shedding the pounds and you'll probably eat more from sheer frustration. Try to get married when you really want to be alone and you'll probably remain single for the rest of your life. Not surprisingly, when there's no passion you sabotage your own efforts and usually fail! So predictably, the same is true of your work life. Love what you do and the rewards will come. Work at something that you don't love, and you'll probably die of boredom.

To help with this process of getting in touch with something that you love and are passionate about, do some soul searching. Write down five things that you love and are passionate about. Be honest. For example, you might write, "I love and am passionate about helping others" or "I love and am passionate about children" or "I love and am passionate about working with computers," etc.

- I love and am passionate about _____
- I love and am passionate about _____
- I love and am passionate about _____
- I love and am passionate about _____
- I love and am passionate about _____

Now if you had a choice, which three of the five would you love spending most of your day doing?

- _____
- _____
- _____

Although a first step or launching point, this exercise will begin to help you discover what to do in life.

Be Fulfilled and the Success Will Come

You must find something to fulfill your dreams. When you do this, unlimited success will come. So many of us pursue things that aren't fulfilling and offer no joy. When we don't get too far in life, we wonder why we're not prosperous. Well, it's a little like trying to study a subject in school that doesn't interest you. It's hard to do because you're just not motivated! And the same is true in life. If you look at most successful people, they're usually doing something fulfilling. They chose their endeavor because of the joy it brings rather than the possible financial rewards. And by so doing, they were able to claim all of the success available to them.

He's Ecstatic About His Work

Vondie Curtis Hall's success was a long time coming, but now he enjoys it all. As the actor who plays the role of Dr. Dennis Hancock on the acclaimed CBS drama *Chicago Hope*, he proves that happiness comes from doing what fulfills you.

As a child, his encouraging parents gave Hall the opportunity to pursue his creative loves. "They always told me: 'You can do anything' and that carried through," he recalls. And while pursuing his number-one love of acting and music, he took full advantage of all the educational opportunities that came his way by training at The Juilliard School and Richmond College in London, England. And this cumulative education, as well as his talent, set the stage for him to pursue either music or acting.

While waiting for his break, he performed in New York clubs, playing his guitar. But a real opportunity to gain the spotlight occurred when he made it to the stage in the long-running *Dreamgirls*. He also appeared in *Lena Horne: The Lady and Her Music*, *It's So Nice to Be Civilized*, the Negro Ensemble Company's *The War Party*, and *William and Walker*, for which he won the 1987 Audelco Award for Best Actor.

Like many other actors, he thought that a move to Los Angeles would boost his career. After journeying there to do the film *Die Hard 2*, he decided to remain and success came knocking at his door. People began to take notice of his incredible talents, and he was eventually cast in the award-winning drama series *Chicago Hope* in which he plays a compassionate physician who joins the hospital staff.

Curtis Hall has also costarred as Sugar LeDoux, Alfre Woodard's heartthrob suitor in the Oscar-nominated *Passion Fish*; the patient and supportive Uncle Brown in Spike Lee's *Crooklyn*; the militant activist in *The Drop Squad*; and the outraged picketer in *Falling Down*. He has also had roles in *Coming to America*, *The Mambo Kings*, *The Cotton Club*, *Romeo and Juliet*, and *Broken Arrow*. And he was nominated for an Emmy as Outstanding Guest Actor in a Drama Series for his performance in NBC's *ER*. He made his directing debut in May 1996 with *Gridlock'd* starring Tim Roth and the late Tupac Shakur. He has also formed Motor City Films, a new film company which has deals to write, produce and direct films for 20th Century-Fox, Warner Bros., and Touchstone Pictures.

He has shown that pursuing one's love can be not only fulfilling but also successful. "I define success as being happy with what I do and having the freedom of choice," he says of a profession that has brought him respect for his talent and abilities. Although there were many bumps along the way to his success, he has remained faithful and persistent. "I have a strong attitude and have always had a deep sense that I would become successful. I was single-minded in my efforts and sort of myopic. I never let anyone turn me around. Every day, I thought that I was getting closer to my goal."

Vondie Curtis Hall is an exemplary model of one who followed his heart and became successful in the process. His advice to all who want to follow their dreams is to "do it because you love it!" And by having this correct mind-set, he has proved that the right attitude and love of work can lead to everything that you might want in life!

Like Curtis Hall, can you pursue whatever will make you happy and fulfill you?

Pulling It All Together

You've been honest and written down your true loves and passions. You've also thought about what will fulfill you. Now, it's time to move from simply wanting or desiring something to making it happen. There are five steps to help in this process.

Step #1: Assess and Cherish Your Strengths

To help you gain some insight into what you might love to do, let's start by further getting in touch with what you might like to do. Often, you can take direction by looking at your strong points or things that you do well. Unfortunately, many of us downplay our strong points. After years of negative conditioning, we've bought in to a less than positive perception of ourselves. We feel that we're contributing very little to our work or society in general.

At my lectures, I would ask group after group of people about their strengths or strong points. Many would simply stare blankly ahead and look askance. Others couldn't think of a single one, or could come up with only two or three. When I delved further by having them do some exploratory exercises, we found that many of these people had a wide variety of strengths that were hidden or had gone unnoticed. Unfortunately, they had taken them for granted and paid little homage to the things that made them unique.

Do you feel the same way? Are you downplaying or de-emphasizing your strengths? If so, you must change that way of thinking. Ask yourself, What do I do that is great, special, or unique? Then ask, What am I most proud of? The table on page 140, which lists the major categories of possible strengths—dealing with people, leading others, communicating, and thinking—will guide you. Check off those that apply to you.

Afterward, look at the table on page 141. Use your strengths to consider what possible endeavors might be best for you. Since many successful careers have been built by people who recognize their strong points, capitalize on them. Now, let's look at how one person took strengths and rose to the top of her career.

◉<>◉

A Way with Words

Marcia Gillespie's strong points or strengths are communicating well both orally and in writing. She parlayed these strengths into a noteworthy and extraordinary career. Her accomplishments have taken her to the top: she sits at the helm of *Ms.* magazine as editor-in-chief. Once the guiding force of *Essence* magazine's editorial staff, this remarkable woman stands tall among the most gifted people in her field.

Long an advocate for social reform, Gillespie has championed issues concerning African-Americans, women, and feminists. Now as head of the only women's magazine of its kind and one with a readership in the United States,

Strengths

Dealing with Other People

Cultivating relationships
Open to others' opinions
Helping others
Being loving to others
Influencing others
Being a good listener
Managing conflicts
Entertaining others
Being empathetic to others
Being approachable
Being understanding
Being trustworthy
Being compassionate
Able to persuade others
Being sympathetic
Having good self-esteem
Being a good team player
Being supportive

Leading Others

Coaching
Mentoring
Team building
Resource expert
Overseeing
Managing a budget
Creating new ideas
Getting the job completed
Resolving conflicts
Implementing policy
Being resourceful
Risk taking
Organizing
Taking charge
Managing time
Managing projects
Managing people
Motivating others
Delegating

Communicating

Facilitating
Training
Writing reports
Public speaking
Editing
Speech writing
Communicating well orally
Communicating well in writing

Thinking

Technological thinking
Developing global strategies
Critical thinking
Problem solving
Analytical/complex thinking
Strategic planning
Computer proficiency
Prioritizing

Build Your Career on Your Strengths

Strengths

Helping others

Career Possibilities

trainer	city manager
facilitator	librarian
teacher	rehabilitation worker
motivational speaker	chiropractor
supervisor	optometrist
manager	dentist
entrepreneur	dental hygienist
mediator	medical laboratory worker
counselor	radiologic technician
public official	public relations worker
ombudsperson	podiatrist
consumer rights advocate	dietitian
lawyer	occupational therapist
paralegal	physical therapist
urban planner	pharmacist
recreation worker	college student personnel worker
psychologist	physician
nurse	physical assistant
respiratory therapist	social worker
health professional	minister
community service worker	financial planner

Strengths	Career Possibilities
Training	trainer coach lecturer speaker human resources specialist teacher
Computer proficiency	help desk support staffer computer consultant computer salesperson computer repair person trouble shooter systems analyst systems planner programmer computer sales manager computer store supervisor/manager computer engineer computer technical writer computer graphics designer
Communicating well in writing	articles writer novelist screenwriter playwright speech writer public relations specialist essayist journalist writing teacher corporate communications specialist technical writer freelance annual reports writer

Canada, the United Kingdom, Australia, and New Zealand, she continues fighting for the causes in which she believes.

After graduating with honors from Lake Forest College, Marcia Gillespie never knew where her destiny would lead. In fact, she was one of those typical college graduates who had little idea of a future career. "In college, I had toyed with the idea of being a historian and teaching on the college level." She remembers how publishing just sort of fell into her lap. "When I came back to New York, I needed a job. A friend's mom worked at the NAACP. She called to say that Time Life was hiring. So I raised my hand and was hired as a researcher. I had been there about six months and decided that publishing seemed interesting."

Four years later, she would make a career move that would ultimately change her life, impact the lives of thousands of African-American women, and thrust her into the public eye. Hired at *Essence* magazine as a managing editor, she was one of its early pioneers. By 1975, she became the editor-in-chief and made history. Conceiving its editorial philosophy and format, the new editor raised circulation from less than 50,000 to 750,000 with a total readership of more than two million.

As *Essence* became successful, Gillespie rose in stature and gained national attention. Lecturing and taking the magazine's message across the country, she became a celebrity in her own right. Although many were disappointed when she stepped down from her position in 1980, her close professional relationship with Susan Taylor helped to pave the way for the magazine's former beauty and fashion editor to take over her mentor's responsibilities. And this made for a smooth transition.

Afterward, Gillespie became an editorial consultant, serving as an adviser to editors and publishers. Her clients included *Life* magazine, The Educational Development Corporation, the Children's Defense Fund, *Essence*, and *Ms.* magazine Creative Communications (a Jamaican publishing group), and the University of the West Indies.

In the late eighties, Gillespie returned to the daily rigors of magazine work and was tapped to become executive editor of *Ms.* Two years later, she held the position of coordinator and managing editor of a book on the global impact of the AIDS epidemic for the United Nations Development Program under the auspices of the Ms. Foundation of Educational Communications. By 1992, she was back on board with the magazine, and was named the editor-in-chief of *Ms.* in 1993. "I've had a relationship with the magazine since 1980," she recalls. "Robin Morgan, who was the editor, and I have known each other for years, and she asked me to lunch in 1992. She was ready to step down and said that I was the only person who she wanted to see as the editor. With that, I met with Gloria Steinem and the publisher."

It's not easy running a twenty-six-year-old publication with a circulation of two hundred thousand. However, Marcia Gillespie has done an outstanding job. Her greatest accomplishments? "A great deal of it has been continuing the tradition of the magazine as well as hopefully making certain changes," she says. "I hope that I've made the magazine more inclusive. I hope that I've put in ethnic cultural diversity but also the differences within the feminist movement."

Assuming full editorial managerial responsibilities, she monitors all phases of the editorial process. Loving what she does, she advises the same for others. "You must be able to do work that you enjoy and of which you are proud at the end of the day," she stresses. "It's not necessarily about the paycheck. You can get a paycheck but not necessarily the satisfaction. We all work longer hours and put in more time. If you're going to put in that time and energy at something you don't like or are doing something that you can't really hold your head up about, that's a problem. It's about having fun. And I have a good time at work."

Despite the joy that work might bring, there's also another necessary side. "Be prepared to work hard. The words that you should never utter are: 'That's not my job!' or 'That's someone else's job!' " Gillespie reminds us. "If you want to be at the top of the ladder, you must know how to do the grunt work as well. When it's about getting the job done, everyone has to be able to pitch in and not stand on title."

Still, along with the hard work there must be priorities. "I won't take work home on the weekends. I'd rather come in early in the mornings," she comments about the need for her to read other things and inform herself on matters happening around the world.

And this dynamic editor also makes time for another agenda in her well-rounded life. "The biggest priority when you're looking at your life is your family. The only things that you can really depend on in life are God and your family," she says. But there's also a wonderful network of friends who give constant support to Gillespie. "I've been blessed with incredible sister friends who have always been there for me in terms of offering advice or a shoulder or being someone to laugh with." And this makes her life well-balanced.

She's been to the top at two magazines; she's affected our lives for the better. With her energetic and intellectual leadership, Marcia Gillespie reached out to make a better world and used her strong points to make it happen. She helped shaped the magazine for "Today's Black Woman." And her columns always enlightened us, giving us strength to go on. Today, she continues this effort at *Ms*. We salute her drive, passion, and high level of excellence!

Step #2: Cherish Your Contributions

Next, you should determine your specific and unique contributions. By doing so, you may find something that strikes a responsive chord inside of you and that can lead to a specific vocational choice.

What are you good at doing? What have you contributed? What distinguishes you from others in the workplace? Unfortunately, so many of us are brainwashed into believing that we don't matter at work. And when we take this attitude, we think very poorly of our contributions. Amazingly, there are far too many of us who haven't the slightest clue of how great we are. We sluggishly go through our work lives without once stopping and saying, "Hey! I did that! My work has helped out today!" Rather, we downplay our contributions and even forget about many of them. But if you want to become a success, get in touch with all that makes you special.

Ask yourself, What have I contributed to make my work environment more stable in the last year or five years? How many dollars have I made in the past six months or a year? How much time have I saved? What systems did I design? What cost-saving errors did I discover? Did I do any unique problem solving? Was I selected to participate in any industrywide forums or seminars? Have I been awarded with a letter of commendation or merit award? Have I been given any promotions?

All of us have made contributions! Whether you have fielded a hundred client calls per day or five hundred a week or two thousand a month, you've contributed tremendously to your organization. So, let's get in touch with your contributions. Look at the examples that follow. Use them to think about your own contributions.

CONTRIBUTIONS

Marketing and sales: Developed a discount marketing plan to keep competitors from edging out company. Resulted in retention of clients and $10 million in revenue.

Purchasing: Developed cost-effective strategies to purchase $20 million in goods. Saved company $3 million through negotiations with vendors.

Strategic planning: Developed series of corporate strategies to enter new markets. Resulted in $2 million in new business.

Banking management: Managed more than thirty corporate clients with loan portfolios of $120 million.

Human resources: Interviewed, placed, and trained more than 7,000 employees in central employment office.

Project director: Wrote grant for $400,000 career-transition program for unemployed.

Real estate brokerage and management: Designed sales incentive program for salespeople that increased overall company profits by 60 percent.

Real estate sales: Sold more than $1 million in residential real estate. Increased sales by 30 percent from previous year.

Information systems: Designed, installed, and evaluated system that increased document management by 75 percent.

Paralegal: Designed system and reorganized more than three hundred cases in litigation that resulted in 90 percent time savings to attorneys.

Counseling: Provided career and academic counseling to eighty-five students on caseload. Assisted 95 percent in getting into graduate, law, or medical school or permanent postcollege employment.

Engineering: Designed prototype that brought in $8 million to company.

Administrative assistant: Coordinated move of 75 managers and 150 other staffers to new facility. Increased effectiveness and organization of move by 80 percent.

Secretarial: Assisted director of three-hundred-employee district and organized word processing pool of eighty to take care of district's secretarial needs.

Customer service: Directed operations of large cable company's customer service department with 120 employees. Managed budget of $1.6 million.

Medical records management: Managed five employees responsible for forty thousand patient records in metropolitan hospital. Designed system that increased efficiency by 50 percent.

International marketing: Developed marketing strategies that increased company international business by 40 percent.

Step #3: Explore the Possibilities

Once you've done the preceding exercises and discovered your loves and passions, strong points, and contributions, you can use this information to explore possibilities in different fields. For example, let's say that your strong points include motivating others and resolving conflicts. Mediation could be one of the possibilities to explore. Or perhaps your strong points are in being a resource expert and communicating well in writing. If so, you might explore the arenas of speech writing or writing training or technical manuals. Again, refer to the table on page 141 for help.

The next step is to select one or two fields on which to focus. Afterward, start doing some investigating to find out about them. For instance, it does no good to just select the computer field, because there are literally hundreds of opportunities within the field. You must delve further.

You can do this by reading all you can about your choice. Browse in your local library or bookstore. Read magazine and newspaper articles about the field. Most importantly, talk to people in the field and find out about what they do. Fortunately, most people will take the time to help you. If you don't know anyone, ask for referrals.

Continue to explore all the possibilities, even after you're in your new position. Because career planning is life planning, you will continuously be challenged to explore and open opportunities. If you're flexible and enjoy new challenges, you'll be able to zoom to the top and enjoy the ride.

He Took Advantage of All of Life's Possibilities and Landed on Top

Born in Brooklyn's Bedford Stuyvesant, Franklin Thomas has taken advantage of all the opportunities in his life and emerged a winner at the top of his field. The former head of the prestigious Ford Foundation, which awarded $300 million in grants in 1995, he's the first African-American to lead such a worldwide organization.

He is the youngest of six children of immigrant parents: his mother was from Barbados and his father from Antigua. Early on, they taught him the value of an education, and he readily excelled in school. A good student and proficient athlete, he graduated from Lane High School and went to Columbia University on scholarship.

After graduating from college, he sought a solid opportunity in the United States Air Force and became a navigator in the Strategic Air Command from 1956 to 1960. As his four-year stint came to a close, he pondered whether to make a career in the air force or pursue additional educational opportunities. Determined to widen his academic horizons, Thomas elected to go to law school and was accepted to Columbia University School of Law. "There were a few people in the air force who reminded me that the fruits of life are really out on the limbs of trees and aren't really alongside the trunks. If you want the fruits of life, you really have to be willing to take risks in order to achieve them." He fondly remembers the career change that would propel him to the top. "And that's what life is about. It wasn't simply about the security."

Graduating from the law school in 1963, he took a position with the Federal Housing and Home Finance Agency. One year later, he was asked to become assistant U.S. attorney for the Southern District of New York. And in that capacity, Thomas did trial work as a criminal prosecutor. By

1965, he was known for his skill and excellence, and was tapped by the New York City police commissioner to become deputy police commissioner in charge of legal matters. It was a position he held for two years. "We did everything, including police discipline, interpreting case law, legislative work, liaison work to the mayor's office as well as the Corporation Counsel's office of New York," he points out.

Around that time, the urban rebellions of the sixties exploded. There was turmoil and violence in the streets. African-Americans demanded more participation in the American dream. To help ease the upheaval, there were attempts by fair-minded people to address the issue. In 1967, a group of Bedford Stuyvesant citizens, Senator Jacob Javits, Senator Robert Kennedy, as well as some businesspeople, came together to form The Bedford Stuyvesant Restoration Corporation, which would have a community-based board. Still in operation today, its primary focus and purpose was to operate in a nonprofit community development corporation capacity while simultaneously addressing and resolving problems affecting housing, employment, recreation, culture, and the arts.

Franklin Thomas was elected its president and chief executive officer. "I was born in Bedford Stuyvesant and it seemed like a perfect way to make a contribution back to the community I knew and loved," he says of the position in an organization that would positively impact the community for several decades. And for ten years he was the guiding light, remaining at the helm to help form and operate the corporation's mortgage finance and construction companies, renovate the neighborhood's housing, and create the Billie Holiday Theater.

In 1977, he resigned his duties at the corporation. Seeking an opportunity to work for himself and practice law, he opened the doors to his own firm. Simultaneously, he was asked to become a trustee of The Ford Foundation's board.

His affiliation with Ford would set into operation a remarkable career move. "When the president resigned in 1979, the trustees went on a search for his successor and asked me if I wanted to be interviewed. Although I wasn't looking for a job, I interviewed and they ultimately offered me the presidency," he says. However, it would still be months before Thomas could begin his duties due to prior obligations with his law firm.

For the foundation, the wait was worth it. Franklin Thomas has proved to be a capable leader with visionary foresight. "As president, I was the chief executive officer and member of the board. So with the board, we helped to develop policies on the recommendation of the staff. Once those policies were adopted, I was delegated to implement them," he says. The vast Ford Foundation operation has a staff of six hundred people in almost twenty offices around the globe, in such places as New York, Asia, Africa, and Latin America. "The foundation has a worldwide network of staff and offices. All grants are funded through returns on investments that are made here. Ultimately, I was responsible for investment of the foundation's assets, and they were a little over two billion dollars in 1979. They are now more than nine billion dollars."

Although his financial investment proficiency speaks for itself, Thomas's impact on people and their countries will have long-lasting effects. "I like to think of the foundation as the research and development arm of society. We tried new ideas. We bet heavily on people who were experiencing problems, and tried to help them address those problems. We tried to help governments see the value that people bring to the issues. And we were constantly trying to create a bridge between people close to where problems are experienced and those who are forming policy or are developing and implementing policy. So we were able to see the problem from each other's perspective and together fashion better solutions."

And it's this desire to initiate problem solving that is perhaps one of his greatest strengths. To expand this important aspect of his work, he'll use his talents and expertise in helping our brothers and sisters in South Africa. In the spring of 1996, Franklin Thomas left The Ford Foundation to devote his time to another labor of love. "I'm going to devote a block of my time to helping President Mandela and others in South Africa with their development needs. They have needs that are obviously even greater than those we have had in this country. And to be able to help them at this point is, I think, a great honor."

In fact, his view of success is measured through the amount of help that can be given to others. "I see it in the opportunities that you help create for others, and the observation of how well they use those opportunities to both enhance their own lives and feel an obligation to others. I really see it as an enabling function," he says. "This notion of rendering service to others is noble in its own right. But what's more noble about it, is that it is the key to a good life for you. If you have power and influence, the extent to which you use that to assist and enable others is the extent to which the power means something and enhances your life. It's the best secret around."

Franklin Thomas has spent most of his professional career in the nonprofit arena, helping others. As he looks back on his phenomenal rise to the top, he feels that his success has been grounded in having old-fashioned values and principles as well as never limiting himself. "It starts with self-worth but not arrogance. You shouldn't accept the notion that you can't be, or can't do, or can't understand something. In fact, if you have a reasonable amount of intelligence and you apply yourself in a disciplined way, you can accomplish much, much more than even you dreamed of," he states.

However, there's one more step that you must do! "Set your sights as high as you possibly can. Get out, try and read about, meet, and talk with as many people who are in the positions that you aspire to. Write them a letter. Find ways of communicating with them or others who know them, so you will see that they are not fundamentally different from you. And that takes some of the mystery out of life, and removes false barriers from in front of your eyes," he comments. "Once those are removed, you'd be amazed about what you can accomplish."

Franklin Thomas has shown us what great leadership abilities can accomplish. He has given so much of himself to those in need. A wonderful example of success, he shows each and every one of us how to excel.

Step #4: Detail the Course

Once you've done the preliminary footwork and targeted where you want to be, it's time to determine your goals. What do you see yourself doing in your work life over the course of the next years? How will you get there? What do you need to do? How can you get to where you're going if you don't know what it is? Make your goals and detail the course!

She Charted Her Own Course and Came Out on Top

Carolyn Baldwin is one of the top African-American women executives at the Coca-Cola Company in Atlanta, Georgia. She is vice president of the Coca-Cola Company and president of Coca-Cola Financial Corporation. Ms. Baldwin is a dedicated professional who works in a position she loves.

As far back as college, she began charting the path which would lead to her stellar career. An economics/business administration major at Fisk University, she took the risk of specializing in an area where few women had ventured. Undaunted, she walked into the college's freshman economics classes, proceeded to get A's on three exams, and was subsequently sold on the field. Because the mid-sixties was an exciting time at Fisk, Baldwin was able to capitalize on the college's emphasis on innovative educational programs. Taking advantage of one, she became involved in the Fisk Student Enterprises where students started their own businesses.

As she advanced in her studies, she remained primarily focused on the field of economics as a future career prospect. And as graduation approached, she applied to and was accepted at several major schools but chose the University of Chicago. The dean of the Graduate School of Business convinced her to consider pursuing the more marketable Master's of Business Administration (MBA) rather than a Ph.D. that was her initial interest. Agreeing, she entered the business program and graduated with an MBA in finance.

From there, she was recruited by Citibank and began its rigorous and competitive training program in New York City. In the four-and-a-half years at the bank, she ultimately became senior account officer. During this time, however, Baldwin had married and was the mother of a small child. In an attempt to find a more conducive atmosphere for him to grow up in, she relocated to Atlanta, Georgia. Approaching Coca-Cola for employment, she became one of the few walk-ins which the company hired. "I am truly one of those who came up from the bottom. My first job was senior financial analyst for Coca-Cola USA, the flagship division of the Company, working in the strategic planning area," she recalls. In the position for only four months, another opportunity came her way in corporate treasury. "They created a job called treasury specialist and I became the first one in this company."

By 1981, skill and talent would land her the position of assistant treasurer, which is an officer level position, and manager for the Latin American Treasury Services. Her responsibilities included cash management, bank relations, foreign exchange, accounts receivable, and borrowing for the Company. And it was in this capacity that she made significant career progress. With her prior multinational expertise from those days at Citibank, coupled with her belief in customer satisfaction, she was able to parlay this experience into a solid career move. What made the difference was her ability to take risks by requesting more and more responsibilities from her boss. "I started to expand the position from more of a financial to an operational one. Finally, in the end, it started growing until I was getting involved in significantly more than the treasury side of the business."

At the same time, Baldwin began to solidify her relationships with the bottlers in Latin America. "I have many contacts and relationships with not only our people in the Coca-Cola company's operations in Latin America, but with the bottlers as well, who are extremely influential people in that part of the world as well as all over."

Her foresight, ability to take risks, knowledge, and financial abilities paid off. She was promoted to president of the Coca-Cola Financial Corporation. "We loaned money to bottlers and sometimes suppliers to promote the sale of Coca-Cola. And we financed ventures all over the world to accomplish that," she says of the perfect matching of two strongest skills. "I had been a banker before, so I had banking expertise. In addition, I knew the Company's operations from my experience in Latin America. I understood the problems and issues that the Company's managers were facing in the fields, so I could assist them with financial progress and solutions."

By 1993, she was elected to the position of vice president of the Coca-Cola Company, chief of internal audits (Worldwide) and director of the corporate auditing department. While a new area for her, she welcomed the challenge. "Taking this job was a risk. If you look around the country, you will see that CPAs, accounting majors, and career auditors have filled chief internal auditor positions. I am not a CPA but have a MBA. But I have financial as well as operational experience," she notes. "I bring that into a function that has largely been confined to the financial side of it. Rather than having strictly a financial auditor-type in this job, the Company had someone with a breadth of experience of the whole company and its operations."

In this new position, Baldwin headed a fifty-four-person staff, many of whom are based strategically around the globe. "Some of them travel around the world and have no permanent base but go from one operation and country to the other. They may stay in a country for as little as three weeks or as long as three months," she says. "I also had a group that is based out of Atlanta, and they travel from here to various places in the United States. Sometimes, we send them abroad so that they can have some cross-functional training. I have a group of informational systems auditors and most of them are also headquartered here."

For those who aspire to reach the heights which Carolyn Baldwin has, she advises: "You have to get the best credentials that you can get because the competition is tough. With downsizing, you are going to have to have better credentials, like the MBA."

A believer in having the right attitude, Carolyn Baldwin also feels that successful career climbers need two attributes along with knowledge and skill. "You must also have the right attitude to succeed. Basically, there are so many obstacles and stumbling blocks that present themselves and would hamper you from achieving your goal. If you are not committed, you can be turned around. So you have to have the commitment and drive."

In her own career, Carolyn Baldwin has proven that hard work, commitment, and talent are key factors to success. Coupled with dynamic risk taking, she has dedicated herself to her career and company. A winner in the corporate arena, she is a motivation for anyone who wants to achieve.

Are you, like Baldwin, charting the course for the future?

Step #5: What's Holding You Back?

Can you ultimately be as successful as Curtis Hall, Gillespie, Thomas, and Baldwin? I know that you can. But if you've not yet achieved this mark of success, think of what may be holding you back. Although many of you may genuinely want a better life and desire something else to do, sometimes *you* can get in the way of your own success. You can think of a thousand reasons for not leaving an unsatisfying work situation and moving on to something that will bring you joy and satisfaction. But it's now time to begin taking the first step.

In the table below, you'll see some of the ways in which we hold ourselves back that lead to unpleasant and undesirable traits. There are many affirmations you can use to get beyond this negative programming. Try the ones in the righthand column or come up with your own.

Don't Hold Back

Things Holding You Back →	Leads To →	Affirmation
Fear of the unknown	Complacency, nonmovement, and refusal to take risks	I, (your name), believe in myself. There are no fears that hold me back. I go into the unknown as a willing subject.
Denial of self-worth	Apathy and laziness	I know my worth. I have and will give myself the benefit of being all that I can be in life.
Anger at being downsized or other work-related adversities	Being stuck in the moment of the happening or event and unable to get beyond it	I know that if one door is closed, there are many others that will open wide for me. There's nothing but abundance in the Universe waiting for me.

Things Holding You Back →	*Leads To* →	*Affirmation*
Laziness to move on to better opportunities or clinging to security	Willingness to hold on to something that makes you unhappy because of a paycheck; inertia, unhappiness, and profound sorrow; work-related illnesses.	I'm no longer content with having something that is unsatisfying. I seek work that is spiritually uplifting.
Killing yourself by working where you don't want to be.	Sickness, chronic illness, and shutting down, or even dying	I will provide for myself and my family by finding something that is fulfilling and joyful.

Time is ticking away. Life is short! In the end, don't have any regrets about your career and contributions. So what are you waiting for? Work your way to prosperity.

Strategies for Working Your Way to Prosperity

1. Find something you love to do!
2. Find something you are passionate about!
3. Assess your strong points and cherish them!
4. Cherish your contributions.
5. Explore the possibilities.
6. Detail the course.
7. Overcome what's holding you back!

‹ 9 ›

Empower Yourself: Success Strategies for the Entrepreneur

Why did I succeed when so many other Black publishers failed? The answer is simple. I was lucky, the timing was right, and I worked hard.

—John Johnson, *Succeeding Against the Odds*

Becoming a business owner is a great alternative to nine-to-five work. No more struggling with other commuters for a train or bus seat or piece of the road. No more getting up early and wolfing down a bagel and coffee. No more trudging into a thankless workplace. With entrepreneurship, you can achieve a lasting kind of success and gain financial independence.

If you've considered this option and are bitten by the entrepreneurial bug, you're in tune with many African-Americans who are stepping into business ownership. According to the U.S. Department of Commerce's Survey of Minority-Owned Business Enterprises, there were 620,912 Black firms with receipts of $32.2 billion in 1992. In this era of downsizing and other job upheaval, this alternative is rapidly gaining acceptance.

Although African-Americans have traditionally not treaded upon entrepreneurial ground in large numbers, we have had some significant business success stories in our community. From Madame C. J. Walker, who became a millionaire through owning a hair-care company, to modern-day Reginald Lewis, who built Beatrice International into a multibillion-dollar empire, there are many examples of our successful business ventures:

- He was a former slave but Alonzo F. Herndon began the Atlanta Life Insurance Company a few years after the turn of the century and built it into a multimillion-dollar business.
- S. B. Fuller grew up poor on a tenant farm but turned those circumstances around. After a career in insurance, he opened up Fuller Products and became the wealthiest African-American in this country at the time. Relying on his positive thinking and talents to run a major company, he skyrocketed above the adversity of his birth. Years later, Joe Dudley, one of his protégés, built the Dudley Products empire.
- Madame Sarah Washington's thoughts and ingenuity, like those of Madame C. J. Walker, took her all the way to millionaire status. As the woman who made Apex Hair Products a household name in the African-American community, she eventually owned the Apex Beauty Colleges and the *Apex News*. Born about twenty years after the end of slavery, she became one of our most successful entrepreneurs.
- Asa T. Spaulding headed North Carolina Mutual Insurance Company and helped transform it into one of our largest African-American businesses.
- To borrow $500 to start the *Negro Digest*, megaentrepreneur John Johnson asked his mother to put up her furniture for collateral. She did and the rest is history. From those beginnings, he eventually started *Ebony*, one of the premier African-American publications.
- Chemist George Johnson worked for Fuller Products but wanted to venture out on his own. Beginning Johnson Products, one of the most renowned African-American hair-care companies, he proceeded to become a leader in the field.
- The Gordy family of Detroit, Michigan, advanced Berry Gordy the money needed to launch Motown. With it, he created the record company that became a dynamic force in the music industry.
- Four men, including Edward Lewis and Clarence Smith,

came together to form *Essence* magazine, the first magazine for the Black woman. As one of our most cherished publications, it has had more than two decades of tremendous success.

• In 1970, Earl Graves Sr., the Brooklyn-born ex-army man and real estate salesperson, began the highly regarded *Black Enterprise* business-oriented magazine. Today, his company ranks seventy-third on the B.E. Industrial/Service 100.

While we have these business role models to emulate, becoming an entrepreneur isn't for everyone. It takes special skills and a certain temperament. To assess your potential, ask yourself the following questions:

Have I ever thought of owning my own business?

Can I take the risk of becoming an entrepreneur?

What is my business idea?

Am I enthusiastic enough about it?

Am I a person who can work hard?

Can I work on my own in an independent manner?

Am I disciplined?

Am I structured?

Can I persevere?

Am I creative?

Am I imaginative?

Can I make good business decisions?

Do I handle my finances well?

Can I work under enormous pressure?

Can I manage other people?

Can I win support from customers?

Can I use my education, skills, and training to put my best foot forward in operating the business?

Do I have a support network of people who are knowledgeable about my future business?

If you answered yes to these questions, you probably have the qualities and characteristics to become a full-fledged business owner. But before you begin your journey to become one, you must have the right start-up information. There are twelve principles to help:

Principle #1: Develop the Idea

In order to have a successful business, you must have a strong idea. Although some of you might search and search for suitable ideas, many great ones may be right in front of your eyes. Simply look around!

However, since the success or failure of a business can rest primarily upon the owner's knowledge, it may be better to go with something that you know and are passionate about. What do you know best? What are your areas of expertise? For example, an experienced teacher could find success in opening a nursery or private elementary school. A computer expert would find it much easier to maneuver through a computer business than a food one. A marketing specialist would probably find more satisfaction in opening a marketing research firm. A telecommunications specialist could become a successful consultant in that field. And an artistic person would be much more successful using his or her creativity in an art-related business.

Let's look at one person who looked around her environment—the fashion industry—and founded a business built upon her expertise.

Her Idea Spells Success

Six feet tall and beautiful, Audrey Smaltz is the owner of the Ground Crew, the fashion industry's first backstage management company. Responsible for dressing the models and coordinating backstage operations, she helps make sure that leading fashion designers' runway shows are a success. The Harlem-born former model and *Ebony* Fashion Fair commentator started this original concept based on her observation of the industry.

She came upon the idea for her business while in Europe. "When I was working for *Ebony* magazine as a fashion editor, we did not have invitations to many of the shows in those days. So, I would just go in the back door, stand backstage, and watch the whole operation. By doing so, I learned more about the clothes than if I was sitting or standing outside," she explains. "So, I was able to see the shows firsthand and had a chance to really know the designers and models. And while there, I noticed that the people who dressed the models in Europe were the seamstresses and those who worked for the companies. Years later when I started my own business, it hit me that this is what I should do!"

Smaltz was sure that she had come upon something big. Her company could provide professional assistance to handle the tedious job of backstage management for fashion designers. "I knew that the designers just had friends and family dressing the models, and these people did not really want to do that but instead wanted to be sitting out front, watching the fashion shows." She remembers trying to get the fashion designers to see the need for her services.

However, apparently her idea was too new and bold to catch on. "In early 1982, I sent out about a hundred letters telling designers about this unique business to dress the models for fashion shows." She recalls the lack of interest and the disappointingly low response. "Eventually, I sent out more letters. I told people that they needed the Ground Crew not just for fashion shows but for 'Market Week' to dress the models. Well this took many, many long hours to convince people. I was constantly on the telephone. No one needed the Ground Crew because they did it themselves."

Eventually, Smaltz gave potential clients a personal guarantee that she would be responsible for all items like shoes, earrings, and other necessities, and that no accessories would be missing. And this managed to perk interest with a few more people. But the interest wasn't enough to keep her business going. In the meanwhile, she produced shows for companies like Mattel and Sears, and continued the job of selling others on the importance of the Ground Crew.

Persevering in the uphill battle for acceptance, she subsequently attracted a few more clients, including Bergdorf Goodman, the classy, upscale store that asked her company to do the backstage dressing of its models for one of its shows. And people particularly liked what they saw in Smaltz's professionalism. "I was always there . . . me . . . making sure that everything was right. And people would notice that I had a system which I kept refining and refining."

And as timing and luck would have it, a reporter from the *Wall Street Journal* learned about the Ground Crew and asked to be included in its backstage operations for the Bergdorf show. Smaltz complied by donning the journalist in one of the company's signature black T-shirts and putting her to work. Later, a glowing article appeared in the prestigious publication and the rest is history. "That was 1987 and that story put me on the map. More jobs started coming in then! And everyone wanted to know about the Ground Crew."

Today, her company, which employs mostly African-Americans, is run from her midtown Manhattan penthouse off Fifth Avenue, around the corner from world-renowned Trump Towers. Her past and present client list reads like a Who's Who in Fashion and includes Donna Karan, Calvin Klein, Bill Blass, Oscar de la Renta, Gucci, J. Crew,

Adrienne Vittadini, Carolyn Roehm, Vera Wang, Nordstrom, The Limited, Lerner, Express, Victoria's Secret, and Bergdorf Goodman.

Now an institution in the fashion business, Smaltz's business sometimes employs three to four crews as well as seamstresses, tailors, and pressers to handle 175 to 200 fashion shows a year for both European and American designers. Constantly busy, the company sometimes does six to seven shows in one day.

Today, Smaltz can look back and see that her business idea and persistence to see it to fruition has paid off handsomely. "I'm doing exactly as I please and what I love doing," beams the woman who has been named three times to the International Best Dressed List, and is now also a frequent lecturer on dressing for success at colleges, universities, women's groups, and other organizations. A contributor to *Sister to Sister*, which was edited by Suzan D. Johnson-Cook, she is working on a soon-to-be released book called *Hip Fashion Tips for Women in the Spotlight*.

For the former fashion commentator who started the business because as she says "the designers on Seventh Avenue wouldn't let me in the front door so I just went around to the back door," there has been a long-fought, more-than-ten-year struggle to make her business a success. She took a risk on an unknown concept, built upon her knowledge of an industry, and turned it into a profitable business that is making history in the fashion world.

Do you, like Smaltz, have a unique idea that will take you to the top? If so, begin bringing it from concept to actualization.

Principle #2: Scan the Market and Make It Yours

Now you must do some market research. You may have a good idea but do others share your passion? But how do you really know? First, you must take the time to find out the wants and needs of your potential customers. To do so, some established entrepreneurs hire market research firms to query public views. However, the beginning business owner seldom has the resources to do this.

What are the alternatives? You can call together a group of consumers to test your idea like many large companies do. However, yours would be on a smaller scale. First, select people who aren't affiliated with you and can give unbiased reviews. Set up a consumer panel. Ask them to sample your product and then discuss how they liked it, what most appealed to them, possible suggested prices, and other issues. An ideal way to do this is to approach and poll some random members of a civic club, an African-American professional organization, or a church group. And you might consider compensating people for their time and efforts.

You can also try several alternative marketing approaches. For example, one business owner actually went from door to door with her product in hand. She asked people to sample it and took their opinions to heart. Another way is to do a sample mailing. Select a list of potential customers, mail them samples, and ask their opinions or see whether they respond with orders. For example, a new publisher who self-published many of his books sent order forms to potential customers. Without going to the expense of printing books that would stay in a warehouse, he was able to predict how many people were interested in the book before it was even published. Or there was the woman who wanted to write a book and first surveyed her market to find out what type of book they wanted. With the results, she wrote the book according to their needs, and consequently had large numbers of orders.

If you decide to do a target mailing to a large group of potential customers, you might consider purchasing lists from list brokers who gather names and addresses of consumers in a wide range of categories for a reasonable fee, e.g., new mothers, parents with school-age children, college students, recent purchasers of computers. To locate them, look in your business Yellow Pages under Advertising-List Brokers.

You can also do market research by reading trade journals, business magazines, and newspapers with large business sections. Often, they can offer you information on trends regarding consumers' tastes. To get help in this area, go to a business library in your area and consult the librarian.

Another way to do market research is to talk with owners in similar businesses. If you want to open a restaurant, talk to some restaurant owners in your neighborhood or city. If it's information that you need, your local chamber of commerce may be able to provide statistics or general information about specific businesses. In either instance, you may be able to size up the competition and see whether your business is feasible.

In addition, since many of you will attempt to reach the $360 billion Black consumer buying market, it's a good idea to know where the largest groups of Blacks are located, and then saturate those markets. According to *Target News*, a Chicago-based publication, the top twenty-five African-American markets by population are:

1. New York, New York
2. Chicago, Illinois
3. Detroit, Michigan
4. Philadelphia, Pennsylvania
5. Los Angeles, California
6. Houston, Texas
7. Baltimore, Maryland
8. Washington, D.C.
9. Memphis, Tennessee
10. New Orleans, Louisiana
11. Dallas, Texas
12. Atlanta, Georgia
13. Cleveland, Ohio
14. Milwaukee, Wisconsin
15. St. Louis, Missouri
16. Birmingham, Alabama
17. Indianapolis, Indiana
18. Oakland, California
19. Newark, New Jersey
20. Jacksonville, Florida
21. Boston, Massachusetts
22. Columbus, Ohio
23. Cincinnati, Ohio
24. Kansas City, Missouri
25. Charlotte, North Carolina

Select the areas that you want to target and begin doing some research. Ask yourself: What will be the best marketing strategies to reach and encourage potential customers to purchase? And to get optimum results, be sure to find out the following demographics:

- Who are the people in my potential market?
- Where do they live?
- What are their ages?
- What are their backgrounds?
- How do they spend their money? On what products? What services?
- How can I get my product or service to them?
- What innovative strategies can I develop to do this?

Principle #3: Bring in the Money

You have a great idea and marketing strategies, but now your business must be financed. Since no successful business has ever survived without proper financing, this is a very important step. But getting to first base with potential investors can be tough. So, how do you go about seeking out those who can possibly provide this needed assistance?

Often, many fledgling business owners turn to their banks to get loans for small business financing. While neighborhood banks or financial institutions may seem like the best potential lenders, these organizations generally have a poor record of lending to start-up businesses, and an even more dismal one to minority start-ups. Because they tend to be conservative and heavily scrutinize all aspects of a potential business start-up, you may not find much help in getting financed. However, if you decide to approach a bank, bear in mind that they'll be looking at the following:

- Do you have good character and references?
- How thorough are your ideas?
- What is your knowledge and expertise for running your business? Do you have a track record?
- What is your work history? Is it stable?
- Can you successfully manage a business?
- How much money do you need and is it justifiable?
- What is an adequate projection of your business's success given competition, market trends, and the economy?
- Can you meet your goals and pay back the loan?

- Are you financially stable and do you know how to manage your own money, credit cards, and debts?
- Do you handle your taxes well?

There are several alternatives to bank financing: government-backed lenders, venture capitalist financing, and private investor financing.

The first option, government-backed financing, can be provided through the U.S. Small Business Administration. The most popular of several loan programs for beginning entrepreneurs is the Low Documentation Loan Program, for loans under $100,000. With paperwork and documentation streamlined, this loan program offers a more efficient way of applying for financing. For more information, contact the Small Business Administration.

The second alternative is to try and get financing through a venture capitalist company. These organizations take chances or risks on businesses that more traditional lenders like banks frown upon. For example, let's say that you may want to start a magazine. However, given the number of magazines that start up and rapidly cease publication, they are generally not considered good business risks. On the other hand, a venture capital company may take a chance and invest in you.

In many cases, start-up entrepreneurs turn to private investors, including friends, relatives, and associates. If you have a good idea, some people may be willing to take a chance on financing your dream. Still, when dealing with private investors, you should approach them as you would any lender, even if they are friends or family. They also want to make sure that your business is a sound idea, so having a modified business plan will help.

If these three methods fail, another approach is to fund your own business. In starting their businesses, some owners use their credit cards or pension plans or former company profit-planning revenues. Others take out second mortgages on their houses. Still others sell cars, property, or other material possessions to make their dreams happen.

But regardless of the method that you use to get your business financed, make sure that you get enough financing. Since businesses often fail due to undercapitalization, you must be sure to get enough operating capital. If you need $100,000 to make your business successful, keep looking until you find that amount.

To help present yourself in a good light, it's imperative to have a business plan before approaching a financial institution. But what exactly does one entail? Generally, it's a ten- to more than one-hundred-page document that details your business ideas. In it, you should provide the following data: financing information, description of the company, risk factors, objectives, product or services, the market and competition, sales and marketing strategies, production process, distribution and service, facilities, management, expenses, and balance sheets and other financial information. For a sample business plan, look at the criteria on the next page.

As you can see, preparing a business plan takes research, thought, and effort. If you're having trouble developing yours, there are many organizations around the country to help. For example, the U.S. Department of Commerce's Minority Business Development Agency (MBDA), which is located at 14th and Constitution Avenue, N.W., Washington, D.C., funds a network of offices, many of which provide assistance in preparing business plans. There's also the U.S. Small Business Administration's Small Business Development Centers (SBDCs) which offer one-stop business assistance, and they can be contacted through the SBA at 409 Third Street, S.W., Washington, D.C. 20416. Or check your local librarian for other resources in your community.

Once your business plan is complete, it's time to get financing. Let's look at difficulties that one entrepreneur had in trying to finance his business.

Sample Business Plan

1. **Financing**
   - Amount requested
   - Purpose and use of funds
   - Structure of deal
   - Capitalization

2. **Description of the company**
   - Name and location
   - Nature of business
   - Product
   - Facilities
   - Market and competition
   - Competitive advantage
   - Investment appeal

3. **Risk factors**
   - Management expertise
   - Stage of product development
   - Market trends
   - Competition

4. **Business plan**
   - Objectives
   - The product or service

5. **The market**
   - Description
   - Competition
   - Trends

6. **Competition**
   - Size
   - Experience
   - Orientation
   - Changes

7. **Sales and marketing**
   - Strategy
   - Method
   - Pricing policy

8. **Production process**
   - Materials
   - Supply sources
   - Method

9. **Distribution and service**
   - Strategy
   - Method

10. **Facilities**
    - Location
    - Size
    - Age and condition
    - Planned capital improvements
    - Expansion opportunities

11. **Management**
    - Organization and personnel
    - Management structure
    - Description of directors
    - Responsibility of officers
    - Résumés of key members
    - Description of staff organization

12. **Expenses**
    - Fixed overhead
    - Variable
    - Provisions for increases

13. **Financial information**
    - Balance sheets
    - Income statements
    - Cash-flow analysis
    - Break-even analysis

- Explanation of projections
- Earnings and potential return to investors
- Payback

14. **Conclusions**
    - Assessment of opportunities
    - Status of the company

He Runs One of New York's Top Radio Stations but Had Trouble Financing It

Ask any African-American who lives in New York City and all its boroughs about WBLS-FM and WLIB-AM, and they will tell you that the premier radio stations broadcasting today's favorite music and up-to-the-minute, informative programs about African-American issues, are two of our community's treasures.

Pierre Sutton, the chairman of Inner City Broadcasting, the parent company of WBLS, fought and never gave up the struggle to make his company a success. It first began when he returned home from serving a tour in Vietnam during the late sixties, and became an entrepreneur. Forging a partnership with Percy Sutton, his renowned and highly respected father, along with a cousin and a friend, he resurrected the ailing *New York Courier*, a Harlem tabloid. "We started this newspaper out of a basement in a brownstone on 130th Street between Lenox and Fifth Avenues," he recalls. "We thought that it was a good alternative community newspaper." However, there was not sufficient advertising support at the time for a start-up newspaper in Harlem. Luckily, they were able to sell it to the *Amsterdam News*, a major African-American newspaper in the community. Afterward, Sutton began a company called Inner City Research and Analysis Corporation and hired local college students to conduct interviews that were later sold to major pollsters.

Later on, an opportunity came to purchase WLIB. "The man who owned the station had heard my father on the radio during the riots in 1968. And he told him that if he was ever of the mind to sell the station, he would come to my father first with the opportunity. So he came to my father," Sutton says. "And we went around to thirty or forty banks for financing, all of which turned us down."

Although Percy Sutton was then borough president of Manhattan and the Suttons had an impressive group of sixty-three shareholders, they couldn't find financing. "Our shareholders included Dr. Betty Shabazz (the late widow of Malcolm X), Judge Bruce Wright, singer Roberta Flack, Jesse Jackson, teachers, preachers, and other community pillars who had raised $253,000. Still, we couldn't get financing," he says. "One of our shareholders, Bill Tatum, who is now the publisher emeritus of the *Amsterdam News*, had as a camp counselor once saved the chairman of the board of Chemical Bank's son from a drowning accident. He went to him and we were given a loan."

With the help of bank financing, their business dreams came to fruition. "We were ultimately able to purchase WLIB for a price of $1.9 million and secured the option to buy WBLS for $1.1 million. While my father continued to serve as borough president of New York, I became the incorporating president of Inner City Broadcasting Corporation in 1971."

By the time that the elder Sutton had thrown his hat in the ring during an unsuccessful bid for mayor of New York in 1979, the company owned WBLS. It was that FM radio station that set the pace and created the format that many stations use today. And it gave style and innovation to Black radio.

When Inner City wanted to expand to purchase a station in Michigan, they returned to Chemical but the chairman who had given the first loan was no longer there. "I said, 'Look! I'm number one in New York. If you give me more money, I can do this in other places,' " Pierre Sutton remembers. Still, he was turned down. "I went to Citibank and they gave me the money. With it, I bought the Detroit station for $1.5 million. In Los Angeles, I purchased an AM-FM combination for $5.6 million." And in addition, the company owns two stations, KRE-AM and KBCX-FM, in San Francisco that were purchased for $1.8 million.

However, Sutton's young age (twenty-seven), which made him the youngest broadcasting group head in the country, would prove to be a problem with investors and board members in a sort of younger to older generation conflict. Seeking a solution, he called for his father's assistance. "I said to him that 'I need you to be chairman of the board.' And he actually turned me down. Finally, he agreed and we worked together until six years ago when he retired."

Now, the company, which is listed as number 83 on *Black Enterprise*'s Top 100 list of businesses, owns another station in Texas, and a cable television station. It reopened the world-famous Apollo Theatre, and is responsible for the production of *It's Showtime at the Apollo.*

While busy running his communications empire, Pierre Sutton is also the chairman of the 250-member National Association of Black-Owned Broadcasters, which dispenses vital information regarding the Federal Communications Commission as well as the communications industry. He is constantly in Washington lobbying on behalf of issues that affect African-American broadcasters. "There was a time in broadcasting when there were rules. You had to ascertain what the community's needs were. And then create programming to meet those needs. You had a license term for three years and if at the end of that term you didn't do what you said that you were going to, then you had a fair chance of having your license challenged and lost. Those days are gone," he comments about disappearing benchmarks. "They're changing the rules. They've increased the license term and made it more difficult for licenses to be taken away. With this newfound security in broadcasting, the large money has started to run into the arena."

Finding time for community pursuits, he's on the board of the Child Care Action Campaign and the Foundation for Minority Interests in Media. And Sutton is also involved with many community-based organizations.

Sutton's success philosophy is based on perseverance. "It's not that I'm brighter than anyone else, I just don't give up. Ten out of eleven times, you'll be beaten down. If you give up, you have lost. If you don't give up, you can never lose," he says. "A lot of people just stop right when it gets really hard. But right around that little corner could have been success."

In an age when running a business and keeping it afloat is increasingly difficult, Pierre Sutton has proved that his business skills and forward thinking are keys to success. As he takes his company into the next century, he remains a leader in the African-American business community.

Principle #4: Structure Your Business*

Once you have the financing, you should give some thought to what type of structure your business will have. Will it be a single proprietorship, partnership, or corporation?

If you choose a single proprietorship, the main advantage is that you as the single owner will have complete freedom to

---

* This information first appeared as "Principle Three: Structure the Business" in *The Black Woman's Career Guide* by Beatryce Nivens (Doubleday, 1992).

make business decisions. Another advantage is that once the money rolls in, it's yours alone, minus the operating expenses.

The disadvantages of single proprietorship are more complex. First, you must shoulder the burden of the business alone. Second, until the business is financially solvent, you'll have to shoulder the financial burden of the company and may not be compensated for several years. Without additional sources of income, you may personally go under financially. Third, if the business fails, you're personally liable for all debts. Fourth, you must pay all federal, state, and city income taxes and social security deductions.

In partnerships, you can share the burden of running a business with one or more people. In these business marriages, you may have a full or limited sharing depending on legal agreements. In some states, all the partners in a general partnership must pay federal and state personal income taxes, as well as taxes for unincorporated businesses. On the other hand, you may choose a limited partnership where you can have partners who only put up the cash and are liable only for that amount of money.

The advantages of partnerships are that you, as an individual, may not be an expert in all areas, and the contribution of another's expertise may be helpful. The disadvantages of partnerships are that sometimes too many cooks spoil the soup. As in all "marriages," breakups can be imminent unless there is harmony.

Unlike individual proprietorships or partnerships, corporations are entities unto themselves. They are created by the state as a privilege. Corporate liabilities are shouldered by the corporation instead of the owner or owners. The corporation must pay filing fees and organization taxes; it must also have a board of directors by draft bylaws. Corporations may sell shares to stockholders to raise their beginning capital, but stockholders can invest in a corporation without having to be involved in the day-to-day operations.

With all three of these business forms, you should get advice from your attorney to explore fully the best form for you.

Principle #5: Promote Your Business

One strategy that you may use to get to your potential market is to promote your business. Although many businesspeople feel that paying for promotion is a luxury, it's really an absolute necessity.

While some business owners hire public relations professionals or firms to handle their promotion, the majority of start-ups won't be able to budget this item. So what can you do? First, think about the uniqueness of your product, service, or business. Is this something that a wide audience of people might be interested in? If so, you can try doing your own promotion. Begin by contacting your local television and radio stations. If your business is newsworthy, these media organizations may be quite willing to have you appear on their shows. And the same is true of newspapers. If you have an interesting product or service, contact the paper's editor for a possible story about your business or product.

To get maximum exposure in the Black community, you might consider buying ads in some of the popular African-American publications like *Ebony*, *Essence*, *Black Enterprise*, *Emerge*, *Body and Soul*, and others. In addition, don't forget to put your ads in the Black newspapers that are read by large portions of the community.

You may also elect to do radio or television advertising. While expensive, it's an effective way to reach hundreds or thousands of potential consumers. If you're interested in this option, contact the advertising sales executives at your local radio or television station.

Principle #6: Do Business on the Internet

One of the best ways to promote and market your business is through the Internet. With as little as a computer, modem, telephone access, and a provider service like America Online, CompuServe, and others, you can be well on your way to doing business in cyberspace. Believed by some to be a great asset to all business owners, this type of opportunity has the potential to allow African-American businesses to really flourish both nationally and internationally.

By setting up a web site and featuring your business on it, you'll be able to reach hundreds of thousands of customers. While this can make your business take off, there can be one particular drawback. If you don't have enough product or can't provide services fast enough, you have the potential of going under. I remember that one business owner was shocked at the number of orders that he received through the Internet. Really scrambling to fulfill these requests, he was fortunately able to eventually handle the overflow. So make sure that you're ready to take on such a large market.

For more information about doing business on the Internet, contact the Association of On-line Professionals at (703) 924-9692.

Principle #7: Do Global Business

Another way to expand your business is to look to Africa and other places in the African Diaspora for opportunities. With unlimited potential, doing business with one or more of the fifty-four countries in Africa alone can provide excellent benefits to your company.

And the stakes are high. According to the U.S. Department of Commerce's U.S.-African Trade Profile, for example, "South Africa alone purchased $2.2 billion of U.S. exports in 1994," making "South Africa a larger market for U.S. exports than all the countries of Eastern Europe combined." And ranking second was Nigeria with Angola third.

What are some of the exports that African countries are purchasing? A *Business America* article entitled "South Africa: Big Emerging Market" (January 1995) suggested that the largest exports included the following categories: industrial chemicals, computers and peripherals, computer software, and other products.

If your company can provide these or other needed products, you may begin to take advantage of doing business in this fast-growing African market.

And, of course, as an African-American, you're in a unique position to do business with your African brothers and sisters on the continent. There's a common bond between us, and they need our expertise in many areas. Although there may be cultural differences or different ways that we do business, we are needed and welcomed there.

But doing business in African and other countries has its complexities. For instance, some locals require that you set up a local residency, and/or restrict certain types of businesses for foreigners. So if you're interested in doing business in foreign countries, it's a good idea to contact the U.S. Department of Commerce for information. In addition, their International Trade Administration (ITA) has created export assistance centers. Or you may try to obtain necessary information from the embassies of individual countries. And you may contact some of the African-American business organizations like the National Minority Business Council, which led a trade mission to South Africa in the fall of 1995. They can be contacted by writing to NMBC at 235 East 42nd Street, New York, NY 10017.

Politics is another thing to consider when doing foreign business in these countries. With so much upheaval and turmoil in some parts of the African continent, you'll want to assess the political situation before attempting to do business. Do thorough research by talking to others and reading newspaper and magazine articles as well as business journals.

Principle #8: Take Advantage of Minority Purchasing Programs

Many progressive and enlightened companies have minority purchasing programs. Through them, African-American and other minority entrepreneurs are linked with corporations and given opportunities to sell their products and services. Without such established programs, Black business owners may never have this avenue of exchange.

Heading this effort is the National Minority Supplier Development Council, which is instrumental in bringing together these two entities: corporations and minority businesses. Under the leadership of Harriet Michel, it certifies minority businesses for this unique opportunity. Over the years, it has been an excellent conduit for this exchange and has increased the numbers of minority businesses—15,000—who have participated in these corporate programs. And at the same time, their 3,500-member corporations have spent billions in procurement purchases from the businesses who have profited from the windfall.

To take advantage of the council's programs, contact them at 15 West 39th Street, 9th Floor, New York, NY 10018; the telephone number is (212) 944-2430.

Principle #9: Get a Piece of Someone Else's Dream

While some of you may start a unique business and see it expand to provide services or products to Africa and other countries, others will decide to buy an existing business or a franchise. However, there are advantages and disadvantages to doing both.

One advantage of buying an already existing business is that you're coming into it at an established point. If the business is lucrative, you're buying a winner and can continue to build upon that success. In addition, you'll be given the existing customers, building or office, equipment, and contacts. On the other hand, if the business is less than lucrative, you can be left "holding the bag." So avoid any surprises or problems, and thoroughly research the business you wish to purchase.

Many of you may consider purchasing a franchise. In this form of business, you'll pay to be affiliated with an established enterprise. As with buying an existing business, there are pros and cons to consider with this type of opportunity. One of the advantages is that you get training and support for your business as well as the franchisor's experience. However, a major disadvantage is that some franchises may not be reputable or financially sound or the owners may not give what was promised. To avoid this, do thorough research and investigate your prospective franchise. Many business-oriented books have lists of reputable franchises. In addition, talk to others who have purchased franchises with the company.

She Mastered the Art of Franchising

Seasoned entrepreneur Carole H. Riley is known to the Harlem community as the former owner of four McDonald's restaurants. Recently, she sold those businesses and purchased forty-five Pizza Huts in the Upstate New York area.

Riley spent her early days dreaming of becoming a business owner. Born in Columbia, South Carolina, and raised in New Orleans as well as Atlanta, she graduated from Spelman College in 1978 and received an MBA from Atlanta University. "I always wanted to do something entrepreneurial even when I was in college and graduate school. But being that young and having no capital or experience, I wasn't sure what direction to pursue," she remembers. "So I went and entered corporate America to get some exposure and experience."

For the next ten years, she worked as an advertising sales executive at Time, Inc., magazine company doing stints at *People* and *Money* magazines. "I entered Time Warner knowing what my advancement may or may not be. And I felt that entrepreneurship would give me control over my own destiny based on how hard I wanted to work, how smart I was, and how much luck I had," she says.

Just prior to leaving Time, she had already pursued the option of purchasing a McDonald's franchise and decided to enter its training program. As a candidate, she was required to do more than two years of extensive training and evaluation that involved twenty to thirty hours per week of commitment including in-store training and classroom sessions.

To accomplish this, Riley still worked full-time but rose at 4:00 A.M. and did her franchise-related, on-the-job training until 8:30 just prior to work. In addition, she worked nights, weekends, holidays, and vacations. "It's part of the franchise training program for individuals who wish to become owner/operators but did not necessarily rise through the ranks in a corporate store or work in a McDonald's environment. For example, I didn't start as a crew person in high school and work my way up from manager to owner/operator. I came from the outside. So, in order to gain the same amount of knowledge as everyone else who was ingrained with McDonald's operation, I had to learn everything from *A* to *Z* about running a restaurant," she points out. "In order to do that, the corporation requires that you spend two thousand hours physically working in a McDonald's restaurant and pursuing the course work, including basic operations, management, concentrated courses on refrigeration, grill operation, production, and training. You are also given exposure to who you will be working with including customers and employees."

Like all franchise owners, Riley was required to raise start-up capital. "The cost of owning a McDonald's franchise varied in range depending upon what part of the country you're in. Other factors included what type of restaurant, whether it was a large or small one, whether you're in a low-cost area for business, etc. If you had a new store, the price was different from taking over an existing one from someone else," Riley stresses. "If you were to call McDonald's and ask how much it takes to get into a franchise unencumbered, their answer would be 'at least a hundred thousand dollars.'"

When asked how the average African-American could raise this amount of money, she quickly responded in the positive. "The initial money comes from your own resources, so you have to have some capital. My resources came from my profit-sharing and stock plan because I didn't have that kind of money sitting in my banking account," she stresses. "Many of the franchisees who went into the training program when I did left corporate America or had been downsized, and had severance packages or profit packages or 401K to initially qualify."

She also received help from the corporation's parent company. "The McDonald's network can provide you with resources in terms of a network of banks for loans. However, they don't influence the banks one way or another. But over the years, the McDonald's franchises have had a good reputation with most bankers and institutions. So they are more inclined to work with you," she explains.

In 1992, Carole H. Riley realized her dream and opened two McDonald's restaurants. Working under its corporate umbrella was a tremendous help. "The golden arches are an American icon. Everyone around the country and world knows what McDonald's represents. And the company gives you a foundation that includes a franchise that appeals to a national and international public. For example, I don't think that I could have sold two million dollars' worth of hamburgers by advertising 'Carole's Hamburgers,' " she says. "Because people understand that when they come into a McDonald's restaurant, they expect to get a certain standard of quality, service, cleanliness, and value. That was the company founder's philosophy: QSC and V!"

Carrying on that tradition, Riley created restaurants that became community showcases in Harlem. Along with Kelli Givens, her vice president/administrator and executive director, she established businesses that were clean, efficient, and hospitable. Their Afrocentric interior design, which Givens, who's a graphic artist, was largely responsible for, added to the ambience. There was "The Apollo Wall of Fame" as well as artwork lining the walls by famous African-American artists, including Romare Bearden, Allen Stringfellow, and Ernie Barnes, and commissioned statues by George Mingo. Music videos and educational reels were played throughout the restaurant. In addition, the employees were decked out in Kente cloth–inspired uniforms.

Riley enjoyed success because the Harlem community steadily patronized her business, and she believed in reciprocation. Each year, the entrepreneur makes funds available for a young Harlem woman to attend Spelman College. "What I did was establish a scholarship fund called Strivers in Excellence in memory of my father, the late Dr. Edward R. Riley Jr. Since Spelman is very near and dear to me, this was also a way to give back to the Harlem and Black community," she says. But her philanthropic work benefited many organizations in the community. Through the auspices of her business, she has given to the Harlem Dowling Children's Service, the Boy's Choir of Harlem, the Urban League, and other groups. On Thanksgiving, there was community outreach through a program to feed the homeless. And for music lovers, there was a Sunday brunch known as "McPraising," which featured live gospel music.

Now as owner of the Horizon Collective, Inc., a holding company for Horizon Foods of the Adirondacks, she serves as president and chief executive officer of each company. Givens is executive vice president/chief operating officer. Under its auspices, they operate a total of forty-five Pizza Huts in Upstate New York cities including Albany, Utica, and Binghamton as well as Springfield, Massachusetts. As with the Harlem businesses, they will continue their focus on community activities. "Based on our McDonald's experience, we understand the importance of being involved in the community, and are committed to continuing this philosophy in our Pizza Hut markets."

The recipient of many awards, Carole H. Riley proudly accepted the McDonald's Corporation's 1992 Outside Appearance Award and Outstanding Decor Award. She was given the 1992 National Image Award from NAUMDA (the National Association of Uniform Manufacturers and Distributors Association) for her employees' Afrocentric uniform designs, and they were displayed at the Folk and Craft Museum in Los Angeles and the Smithsonian Institute's Experimental Gallery. There have also been other awards from *Dollars and Sense* magazine and the National Association of Business and Professional Women (New York chapters), as well as the 1994 Access Award from the Manhattan borough president's Advisory Group on Disabilities. In addition, she has been written about in the *New York Times*, the *Wall Street Journal*, *Black Enterprise*, the *Christian Science*

Monitor, *Crain's New York Business*, the *Daily News*, the *Amsterdam News*, and others.

Carole H. Riley's success story began with a dream of owning a business. With a great deal of persistence and hard work, she was able to actualize her goals. For others who want to find similar business success, she advises: "Prepare yourself, educate yourself, and have a plan. You also have to understand that it's a lot of work. If you don't have the drive, patience, and commitment to be in business, you won't make it."

A remarkable entrepreneur who has stepped into business ownership through first purchasing a franchise, she has proven that we all make our own successes with talent and determination.

●<>●

Principle #10: Manage with Insight

Whether you're a successful franchise or independent businessperson, you must learn to manage your business properly. First, you must set priorities. What are your specific business goals? What's most important to the welfare of your business? What will keep your business afloat? If you think about these questions, you'll be well on your way to good management. And if you prioritize your business needs, you'll eliminate many of the everyday problems that can arise.

Next, you must also set deadlines, given your goals. Decide what you want to accomplish and by when. Once you do, attack the problems at hand and steadily move toward completing your work. Don't get into the trap of letting things just happen in your business. Rather, remember that success happens because of well-thought-out plans and actions. So plan your action and work those plans.

As many successful entrepreneurs know, you must systematically go about conducting your business. To do so, design a specific and successful way to do things and don't deviate. Determine your method of operation and keep on that path.

And above all, surround yourself with employees and managers who think like you do. Are you all on the same page of thought? If you're thinking one way and your employees are thinking another way, your business success will be hampered. Hire and keep only those with positive attitudes who have a stake in and are dedicated to what you're doing. You want people who care about you, your business, and your customers. Always remember that your employees are a reflection of you. In a small business, this is particularly important. If you choose the wrong people, it can be detrimental with business/customer relations.

And that brings me to the most important ingredient in business—your customers. Never take them for granted because they are the lifeblood of your company. If your customers appreciate you, they'll refer others and come back themselves. If they are unhappy, they'll go elsewhere. And if you're in the service business, you definitely can't afford to have unhappy clients.

Principle #11: Have a Vision for Your Business

There are businesses that pop up today and are gone tomorrow. And there are businesses that last a lifetime. The difference usually is the owner's vision. In today's competitive and global business atmosphere, an entrepreneur must be able to look ahead and see the possibilities. He or she must look beyond the ordinary and see the extraordinary. Robert Johnson, the founder and owner of Black Entertainment Television, is one such person. Here is his story.

⊚<>⊚

He Built an Empire with Incredible Vision

Robert Johnson, the chairman, president, and chief executive officer of BET Holdings, had a vision to start a cable network that would primarily target African-American consumers. Today, that parent company's core business, known as Black Entertainment Television (BET), reaches over 50 million cable households as of January 1996, according to A. C. Nielsen. In the publishing arena, its magazines, which are geared to the African-American audience, include *Emerge,* a hard news and issues magazine, and the *BET Weekend Magazine,* which currently serves over 1.2 million readers.

Johnson has also expanded the television conglomerate into other areas: BET International distributes programming overseas and BET's Syndication Division has developed and syndicated programs like the Emmy-nominated *A Tribute to Black Music Legends* and *YSB*'s *Bookin' It Back to School,* BET Jazz, which is a new 24-hour, basic cable network that was started in early 1996; in 1997, BET Pay-per-View, a low-cost mini–pay cable television service was launched.

Johnson, a native of Mississippi, who grew up in Freeport, Illinois, has a bachelor's degree from the University of Illinois and a master's in International Affairs from the Woodrow Wilson School of Public and International Affairs at Princeton University. He has held positions at the Washington Urban League and the Corporation for Public Broadcasting, and was the press secretary for the Honorable Walter E. Fauntroy (the congressional delegate from the District of Columbia).

However, it was his work as vice president of government relations for the National Cable Television Association (NCTA), a trade association representing more than fifteen hundred cable television companies, that sparked his interest in owning his own cable company. "I had a desire to run a business of my own. At the time, I was in the industry when the technology was evolving so that you could do satellite-delivered channels like BET. It was being in an industry where people like Ted Turner and the owners of ESPN as well as Home Box Office (HBO) were starting their businesses," he recalls. "And I had been exposed to a number of groups that felt there should be a media opportunity to regularly showcase Black creativity, information, and ideas. There were organizations like the Cable Television Information Center and the Booker T. Washington Foundation that were talking about ways of getting Black images on the screen on a consistent basis."

The idea for Black Entertainment Television took root, and he approached John Malone, Ph.D., president of Tele-Communications, for funding. "When I started BET, I didn't have any money, but I knew how to explain to people what I was doing. So I took my idea to people who were in the business or related to the business that I wanted to go into," he says. "John Malone, whose company was the third-largest cable operator in the country and now is the largest, understood what I was talking about. He could buy into this idea of putting money behind it, and did put the first half-million dollars into it. So it would be helpful if the people who you are talking to have some understanding of what your business is about. It's hard to tell someone something when they have absolutely no understanding of it."

Johnson feels that you have to then convince others of a business's validity. "Whether it's a bank, your cousin, or uncle who you're going to for the money, you must convince them that you will take their money and make something of it. Sometimes people give you money because you're nice. They say: 'OK. Here's the money. I think you can do it!' But that's rare," he comments. "But if you're looking for more than pocket change, people want to know and believe that you're going to do your best to make it work. So you have to have something in you to convince the person. John Malone, for instance, might have thought that I might lose this half-million dollars, but he knew I was going to do my best to succeed so he took the risk."

Johnson took his start-up financing and did his best to make things happen. With foresight and determination, he created an empire that is number 10 on the B.E. Industrial/Service 100 List with sales over $170 million and a cable station that goes into twenty-five hundred markets. "With any kind of business, you have to start out with a vision of what you want it to be. We wanted to be the preeminent Black media company. So naturally, you look for business activities that make you sort of dominant," he explains. "We saw that no one had a jazz channel, but there's a tremendous interest in it on a global basis, and we did a jazz channel. There was no one distributing Black products via newspapers in major urban markets. And we said: 'Let's do that.' We said, 'Let's do a joint venture with Microsoft and do an Internet service.' We looked at opportunities that no one was doing. If it was consistent with our media strategy of taking BET into all areas of information and entertainment, we considered it. And you must have the willingness to take risks."

He also feels that staff selection is important. "And then you must have around you people who you feel can help you carry out your vision. Hire people who are brighter than or as bright as you. Give them as much decision-making authority as you can. Give them as much resource support." His management staff has been with the company for an average of ten or twelve years. "And let them be comfortable with risk taking. Don't make them so afraid that they don't ever make a decision because they think that they'll fail," he cautions. "As long as it's a risk based on a considered judgment, what's in the best interest of the business and all the knowledge that they can marshal, go with them."

What advice does he give to beginning entrepreneurs who want to create a business empire? "First of all, you have to believe that you can do it no matter what anyone else says. You have to put on blinders to people who say that it can't be done. Secondly, you have to be willing to dedicate yourself to the agenda of running a business," he advises. "You have to be able to have a vision. While the network guys saw news as a thirty-minute show that was hosted by a guy named Dan Rather, Ted Turner looked at it and saw something completely different. He looked and saw twenty-four-hour news. Someone might look at something and say it's a mountain. But Walt Disney looked at it and said it was a theme park. And that's what vision is . . . the ability to look over the next hill. And that's the kind of vision that you have to have!"

Robert Johnson took his knowledge and desire for entrepreneurship and created a formidable empire.

Principle #12: Leave a Legacy

As an African-American business owner, you're in a unique position to leave a great legacy to your children, their children, and your community. By building your empire, you'll be giving back to many. And if you decide to run a family-owned business, give your offspring a chance to step into your shoes.

He Stands on the Shoulders of His Father and Grandfather

The legacy of H. J. Russell and Company, Atlanta's best-known construction and real estate company, which ranks number 5 on the *Black Enterprise* Top 100 List, was passed down to H. Jerome Russell. With the big shoes of his father, Herman J. Russell Senior, to fill, he's now the president and chief operating officer of the newly reorganized and consolidated company, which has $154.7 million in sales. "We have been in business for forty-five years. My grandfather started the company when he was a young man and my father took it over," the younger Russell says proudly.

Under Russell's father, the business expanded into other areas. "My father built the company by being a contractor. Now we do general construction, real estate brokerage and development, as well as property management," he says. "We've been blessed to be involved in many major construction projects like Georgia Dome, Federal Center, Clark-Atlanta University, the Atlanta Hartfield Airport, Home Depot, and others." His father is still very active in the family-run business, which is considered one of Atlanta's and the country's premier African-American businesses.

A native of Atlanta, H. Jerome Russell is a graduate of Georgia State University and holds a degree in business administration and management. His father never pressured him to go into the family business. After college, his first position was as assistant to the general manager at City and Suburban Distributors in Chicago. One year later, he returned home and began working as a brand manager for City Beverage Company, another family business, which is a $15 million beverage distribution company. He was soon promoted to executive vice president and general manager. Responsible for sixty employees in that capacity, he formulated marketing strategies that helped build market share and profitability. In 1989, he was appointed president. Later, he and his brother purchased City Beverage from their father.

Always on the outlook for new opportunities, H. Jerome Russell set his sights on real estate development, becoming a project manager for his company Gibraltar Land, Inc., in 1990. Successfully overseeing the development of a $1.3 million retail center and $4.1 million residential hotel, he was appointed president of the Russell Property Management, Russell Properties, and Gibraltar Land companies in 1992. By then, he was given the added distinction of being on H. J. Russell & Company's board.

An astute businessman, the thirty-three-year-old who has impacted the growth of his family's vast empire, feels that many ingredients have spelled success for him and advises other entrepreneurs to use them. "Once you identify the business that you want to run, you should know it inside out." He stresses the need to understand your market. "Let's say that you want to start a dry cleaning business within a certain three-mile radius. You need to understand what dry cleaners are within that radius and why people go to those dry cleaners. You need to understand the economics of it, what makes it work and what makes it profitable."

Russell also says that African-Americans should pursue

certain types of businesses. "Focus on core businesses. We as African-Americans spend a lot of money buying different products. So try to focus on a business where we may be spending large sums of money. For example, we need to move toward dry cleaners, hair-care products, and retail-type stores. In our particular communities, you have Asians and Indians who are coming in and running those types of core businesses. I'd like to see us in more of them."

Once you're in business, he suggests that planning is key. He feels that entrepreneurs must have foresight. "You have to have a vision of where you want your business to go. Have a road map and game plan to achieve that vision," Russell advises. "Once you understand that, you have to be committed to it, pour your guts and soul into it. And you must be willing to be everything . . . the operator, accountant, etc."

Russell also feels that your business inner circle is key. "Make sure you surround yourself with the best people both internally and externally," he says. "By externally, I mean consultants, lawyers, advisers, and accountants. By internally, I mean people who you bring into the organization. That is real critical. Then if you have people involved in your organization, make sure that they are part of the process and can grow with it."

Running a high-powered business is no easy task, but H. Jerome Russell has mastered it. With the legacy left by his father, he has helped build an impressive empire from which many aspiring entrepreneurs can learn a great deal.

As all the African-American business owners profiled in this section will tell you, your dream isn't impossible. With vision, determination, and old-fashioned hard work, these individuals who are inspiring examples of successful entrepreneurship prove it's possible.

Strategies for Maximizing Business Success

1. Develop the idea.
2. Scan the market and make it yours.
3. Bring in the money.
4. Structure the business.
5. Promote your business.
6. Do business on the Internet.
7. Do global business.
8. Take advantage of minority purchasing programs.
9. Get a piece of someone else's dream.
10. Manage with insight.
11. Have a vision for your business.
12. Leave a legacy.

‹III›

Taking Care
of You

‹ 10 ›

Honor Your Temple:
Take Care of Yourself

You can't eat everything you see!
—Bessie Delany, coauthor of *Having Our Say*

Although many of us may think of success as having material things like huge paychecks, large houses, and fancy cars, there's so much more to it. For without good health, we won't be able to enjoy any of it.

Just look at the dreary statistics. In Barbara Dixon's excellent book *Good Health for African-Americans*, she lists some startling facts:

- Black people can expect to live six years less than the average American.
- Black men, in particular, will die younger.
- Our risk of getting *cancer* is 32 percent higher than average.
- Our risk of having a *stroke* is 82 percent greater than average.
- Our likelihood of *kidney failure* is 176 percent higher; *diabetes*, 132 percent higher; and AIDS, 250 percent higher.

While all of this is extremely troubling news, Dixon wrote, "All of this death and disease is totally unnecessary." By knowing the causes of some of these illnesses and how to prevent them, we're more likely to avoid getting them or to survive if we do.

Causes and Prevention

Let's explore the causes and possible prevention of hypertension, heart disease, and cancer, the three major killers of African-Americans.

Hypertension

"African-Americans have a higher rate of hypertension, which is defined as a blood pressure of 160/90 in an adult. Gone unchecked, it can lead to stroke," says Dr. Donna M. Mendes, a graduate of and assistant clinical professor of surgery at Columbia University's College of Physicians and Surgeons, and attending surgeon at St. Luke's Roosevelt Hospital in Manhattan. "In the general population, another cause of stroke is a narrowing of the blood vessels from the carotid artery in the neck, which decreases blood flow to the brain. In recent studies, we've seen that if the narrowing of these blood vessels is 70 percent or more, the patient has an increased risk of stroke."

What are the danger signs? Mendes points to the following and explains that if you're experiencing any of them, you should immediately be evaluated by a physician:

- Weakness on one side of the body
- Slurring of speech
- Inability to hold something in your hand because it suddenly becomes weak
- Severe headache
- Vomiting

What can you do? "Even though hypertension is a predominant finding in African-Americans, the cause of it remains unknown," remarks Dr. Mendes. "And consequently, Blacks must assume the responsibility of ensuring that their [blood pressure] is normal or well controlled with medicine. So yearly physicals are a must because this disease is a painless one. You can have it and not be aware of it. If it goes unchecked, you can ultimately develop renal failure, a stroke, or worsening heart disease."

Heart Disease

With an alarming rate of heart disease among African-Americans, we need to know what causes it as well as how to prevent it to help us avoid its debilitating effects, which often include premature death.

In searching for these answers, let's first explore the cause of heart disease. "Essentially, it occurs when the heart muscle itself is not pumping properly because the blood vessels that flow blood to the heart have narrowed," Dr. Mendes explains. "This can be due to many factors. Specifically, cigarette smoking, hypertension, diabetes, and a high-fat diet are some of the causes."

What can you do to help prevent heart disease? Dr. Mendes suggests the following:

- Although cigarette smoking is unfortunately rampant in our population, it's clearly one thing that we can change. Stop smoking!
- Change your diet. We were all raised to eat large portions of fat-laden meats and starches with a significant amount of butter or mayonnaise. We all considered this good. But as we grew older, we realized how this can ultimately decrease our longevity.
- There is good (HDL) and bad (LDL) cholesterol. If you exercise more, you can increase the good cholesterol and decrease the bad.

(For more information on heart disease, contact the American Heart Association at 122 East 42nd Street, 18th Floor, New York, NY 10168, or call them at 1-800-242-8721.)

Cancer

Nearly everyone knows someone who has cancer or has died from it. Thought to be caused by a variety of factors, including cigarette smoking, environmental factors, food additives and preservatives, and genes, it's a disease that adversely affects

African-Americans. Unfortunately, we have not only a higher rate of getting cancer but also less chance of surviving it for five years.

What are the warning signs? According to the American Cancer Society, they are:

- Change in bowel or bladder habits
- A sore that does not heal
- Unusual bleeding or discharge
- Thickening or lump in breast or elsewhere
- Indigestion or difficulty in swallowing
- Obvious change in a wart or mole
- Nagging cough or hoarseness

If you have one or more of these warning signs, see your doctor immediately. The longer you delay, the more advanced the disease will become. Remember that your body is a wonderful mechanism that often tells you what's wrong. So take the time to listen!

What can you do about cancer? The first line of attack is to have a yearly checkup. Next, you should restrict your diet and follow the one recommended by the American Cancer Society. For more information on this diet and other cancer material, call them at 1-800-227-2345.

Manage Your Diet

Since diet seems to play an important role in your health, it's time to take steps to having a better one. In 1967, the Honorable Elijah Muhammad wrote a splendid book entitled *How to Eat to Live*. In it, he said something that might have been considered before its time: "The only way that we can have life, keep life and prolong life is by what we eat and how often we eat it!"

Unfortunately, the ravages and hardships of slavery provided African-Americans with a generational legacy of poor eating habits. Always relegated to eating the leftovers from our masters' tables, we acquired some potentially unhealthy and harmful diets. For example, instead of eating the pork chops, we were forced to eat the intestines of the pig, which we all know as chitterlings. It wasn't until recently that we realized the potential danger of eating this meat, which has long been a favorite along with other parts of the pig, including its feet. Just think about what happens in a pig's digestive organs or, even worse, where its dirty, germy feet have been. Would you want to ingest it? And what about the smell of chitterlings cooking? I remember running like crazy from our house when my mother was making them. But just the same, I smacked my lips and put it in my stomach at dinnertime.

As African-Americans, we're also fond of eating highly spiced food, usually cooked in grease or lard, in hefty portions without giving it a second thought. Would you slap a wad of grease into your pan, cook it, and eat it? Of course not. But we never think about all that grease being absorbed into the food that we do cook.

Our love for soul food and traditional attachment to it doesn't have to be unhealthy: it can be nutritiously prepared. Without even missing the ham hock or other pork, for example, I make some delicious collard greens with garlic, cooking oil from the health food store, vinegar, and a dab of salad dressing with no preservatives.

Even though old habits are hard to break, we must try to eat better for the benefit of our health. "Our parents and grandparents felt the foods that they served were good for us. And at the time, they were trying their best," says Dr. Mendes, who strongly suggests that we take a good, hard look at our diets. "Begin increasing your chicken and fish, and decreasing the amount of red meat as well as the [total] quantity [of food] that you eat. By doing so, you are going to ensure that you lead a healthier lifestyle and feel better."

To help you start moving toward a better diet, there are certain foods that you should avoid. *Nutrition and Your Health, Dietary Guidelines for Americans*, a fifty-series package that is available from the U.S. Government Printing Office (P.O. Box

371954, Pittsburgh, PA 15250-7954) recommends that you cut back or eliminate the following:

- Fat
- Saturated fats (red meats, butter, cheese, egg yolks, etc.)
- Meat intake; substitute soybeans, whole wheat, oatmeal, etc.
- Refined sugars and flours
- Nitrate-linked foods with additives, such as smoked or cured meats and fish, ham, and luncheon meats
- Salt
- Coffee and tea
- Alcohol and cigarettes
- Whole milk; substitute skim milk

Some people go one step further, abandon meat altogether, and become vegetarians, even though there is great resistance to this lifestyle. I once heard a young man who was talking about vegetarianism announce in a rather strong baritone: "I'd rather die than eat grass for the rest of my life!" Knowing that he was completely wrong, I just shook my head. Having once enjoyed the vegetarian lifestyle, I knew that you don't have to eat "grass" but can enjoy deliciously prepared, nutritious meals.

However, the benefits of being a vegetarian go beyond taste. Elza Boyd, author of *In Our Own Words: A Treasury of Quotations from the African-American Community* and *Proud Heritage: 11,001 Names for Your African-American Baby*, has been a vegetarian since the seventies and explains why she began eating this way. "I decided to become a vegetarian for political reasons. I was always involved in the movement, especially the Black Power end of it. Simultaneously, I was introduced to Elijah Muhammad's book *How to Eat to Live*. I then began to find information about the politics of diet and the health implications of diet. And I felt compelled to make the change. But I did it gradually," she says.

Almost immediately, Boyd found the change beneficial. "One of the most rewarding things about being a vegetarian is that the health benefits have been amazing. At the time of becoming one, I was under a doctor's care because of getting this or that infection. I had the flu in the spring, the flu in the fall. I had sinus problems. Once I became a vegetarian, however, I stopped having sinusitis and didn't get the flu. It was the most amazing thing. I was no longer under a doctor's care and only went in for physicals after that."

Although many people feel that they can't become vegetarians, Boyd says that this attitude can be overcome. "I think that meat eating to the extent we do it in America is as much a habit and an addiction as anything else. You simply don't need that much protein. So, we have to start breaking that addiction like we would work on our smoking addictions and other habits. When you do, it will mean fewer doctor bills, lower restaurant and grocery bills, as well as better health. Now, I consider being a vegetarian as a part of my medical care."

Many of you may want to become vegetarians but try and fail. To avoid this, Boyd recommends that you do it one step at a time. "First, think about why you want to do it and have some really good reasons for doing it. Then go into a health food store and read books. Take your time. And do it very gradually. I did it that way over a four-year period. First, I gave up pork. Then it was beef, lamb, chicken, and eventually turkey over time. The last thing that I gave up was seafood. And I just automatically gave up eggs without even thinking about it."

Whether you decide to become a vegetarian or just want to eat better, you need to do this for your health. By eating healthier, you're ensuring a longer life.

Exercise

Because many of us work in sedentary jobs or are complete "couch potatoes" at home, it's time to get into a regimented exercise routine to better our health. First, go to your physician and have him or her determine your health status and just how much exercise you can do. Then gradually ease into any kind of program, including the following: walking; aerobic dancing and step aerobics; bicycling; playing sports like basketball, racquetball, and tennis; jogging; hiking; swimming; and working out in a gym.

Once you begin exercising, you'll immediately feel the benefits. Keep these tips in mind:

- Choose an exercise that you enjoy. Do something that doesn't seem like work.
- Set exercise goals and stick to them. Start off slow and gradually increase the amount of time you spend exercising.
- Try to choose an exercise site near your home or another convenient spot; otherwise, you might sign up for an exercise activity and never quite make it there.
- Commit yourself to exercise! And once you do, don't let anything deter you!

Strategies to Take Care of Yourself

1. Have a yearly physical.
2. If you have hypertension, make sure to take your medicine.
3. Stop smoking.
4. If you are prone to heart disease, have your physician closely monitor you.
5. Manage your diet.
6. Exercise.

‹ 11 ›

Manage Stress

Everyone has probably said "I'm stressed out!" at one time or another. However, stress is much more serious than most of us think. It can lead to debilitating diseases and even cause death. But what exactly is stress? In *Stress Without Distress*, Dr. Hans Selye, a pioneer and major researcher in the field, says that stress is "the non-specific response of the body to any demand placed upon it. . . . It is immaterial whether the agent or situation we face is pleasant or unpleasant; all that counts is the intensity of the demand for readjustment or adaptation."

You can look at it another way. Whether you experience good or bad stress depends on your way of handling it so that it does or doesn't create problems. As Dr. Robert Woolfolk and Dr. Frank C. Richardson commented in their book, *Stress, Sanity and Survival*: "It is primarily our perceptions or appraisals of events that make them stressful." For when we don't handle stress well, we create problems. And problems caused by chronic stress can lead to a variety of illnesses, according to Woolfolk and Richardson: "ulcers, hypertension, coronary disease, many allergies, migraines, tension headaches and numerous other physical maladies." In other words, we need to manage our stress.

But how can you effectively manage stress? First, you must discover what things in both your work and personal life are causing stress. Take a look at what follows, and ask yourself about possible stressors in these areas. Then select your top-ten stressors in each area and rank them.

The Top-Ten Stressors in My Life

Answer the following questions and select the top-ten stressors in both your personal and work life:

Work Life

1. Do I consider my job stressful?
2. Do I have too much work to do?
3. Do I have too little work, which leaves me bored?
4. Do I have too much responsibility?
5. Do I have too little responsibility?
6. Is my work hazardous?
7. Do I manage or supervise others?
8. Do I get along with my subordinates?
9. Do I have poor relationships with my coworkers?
10. Do I consider my workplace one with toxic people who are engaged in toxic relationships?
11. Is there tension on my job due to downsizing, reengineering, layoffs?
12. Am I afraid of losing my job?
13. Is there a chance that my department unit will be phased out?
14. Is my company or industry experiencing a downturn in business?
15. Do I have too much work to do because of downsizing, reengineering, layoffs?
16. Is my company experiencing change or a new way of doing things?
17. Will I need new training or lose my job?
18. Are my job duties changing?
19. Do I have tight deadlines to meet at my job?
20. Am I dissatisfied at my job?
21. Are my job duties clearly defined?
22. Do I know what's expected of me?

23. Do I know how to survive and keep my job?
24. Am I driven at work?
25. Am I a perfectionist?
26. Am I an underachiever at work?
27. Do I avoid work?
28. Am I disorganized?
29. Can I follow through on assignments?
30. Do I have to take work home evenings and weekends to get work accomplished?
31. Are there promotional opportunities at my job?
32. If I'm a supervisor, do I delegate responsibilities to others?
33. Do I have a thankless job?
34. Am I losing my job?
35. Am I changing careers?
36. Am I retiring?

Considering my answers, which situations do I consider the top-ten stressors in my work life?

1. _____
2. _____
3. _____
4. _____
5. _____
6. _____
7. _____
8. _____
9. _____
10. _____

Personal Life

1. Am I overwhelmed by problems in my personal life?
2. Do I have problems with my mate or significant other?
3. Do we have serious arguments?
4. Are those problems serious enough for divorce or separation?

5. Do I have problems with my children?
6. Do I have problems with my parents?
7. Do I have problems with my siblings?
8. Do I have problems with my friends?
9. Do I have problems with my neighbors?
10. Do I have problems with my mate's parents or family?
11. When I have problems, do I eat too much?
12. When I have problems, do I smoke too much?
13. When I have problems, do I take prescription or other types of drugs?
14. Do I have problems managing my money?
15. Do I have a lot of bills?
16. Are bill collectors harassing me?
17. Am I in danger of losing my home or apartment?
18. Are my children leaving home for the first time?
19. Are my children returning after they've left?
20. Am I moving or relocating?
21. Am I taking care of an elderly parent?
22. Am I taking care of a sick child?
23. Does my child have any disabilities that require special attention?
24. Am I a single mother?
25. Am I a single father?
26. Has there been a death in my family recently?
27. Has anyone close died recently?
28. Am I going to have another child?
29. Am I doing too much in my personal life?
30. Am I doing too little in my personal life?
31. Do I have any fun?
32. Is life boring?
33. Do I have trouble sleeping?
34. Do I have trouble concentrating?

What situations do you consider the top-ten stressors in your personal life?

1. _____
2. _____

3. _____
4. _____
5. _____
6. _____
7. _____
8. _____
9. _____
10. _____

Do you feel that you have a better handle on what's causing your stress? If so, let's see how you can better cope with and manage these factors in your life. We will discuss six methods used to manage stress: progressive relaxation, meditation, a stress log, quiet time, therapeutic massage, and vacations.

Progressive Relaxation

By listening to a progressive relaxation tape, which can be found in health food stores or New Age–oriented bookstores, you'll be able to totally relax your body and its muscles. By beginning with your toes and working upward to your head, progressive relaxation can often help reduce stress.

There are many good tapes that provide progressive relaxation exercises. Every night I listen to a thirty-minute progressive relaxation tape and am amazed at the benefits. Besides helping me to sleep, I feel relaxed upon awaking the next day. And if you try this powerful stress-reducing method, you'll soon begin to feel its beneficial effects.

Meditation

Back in the sixties, Maharishi Mahesh Yogi brought transcendental meditation to the Western world, and many who were in search of peace and better lives, including celebrities, flocked to embrace his teachings. In his book *Meditations of Maharishi Mahesh Yogi*, he says: "Meditation I define as the method of drawing the attention towards the inner glory of life."

Many people have found meditation to be extremely helpful and a wonderful way to reduce stress. I am one of them who signed up to become a student of the Maharishi. Back in the mid-seventies, I had a stressful full-time job counseling more than a hundred students, as well as a part-time job in another town. In my spare hours, I was traveling around to college campuses, giving poetry readings. Without my knowing it, my body was tired and "stressed out." Immediately after meditating, I found myself unable to handle my second job or the poetry readings. I just couldn't do it. It seemed as if all the tiredness in my body was brought to the surface, and I spent a great deal of time yawning. After a few weeks of resting, my body seemed to thank me for stopping the long-standing abuse of it and rewarded me with a great sense of serenity and less stress.

As I was instructed, meditation works best when you meditate twice daily for twenty minutes in the morning upon waking and at night before sleep. If you choose an established meditation system, you may be given a mantra, which is sound(s) or syllables to say while meditating. However, some people who meditate on their own simply use the word *Om*. By saying your mantra over and over, your body is put into a deep state of relaxation. You get in touch with inner peace and tranquillity and also reduce your stress.

Although there are many types of meditations, you must choose one that works for you. Go to a health food store, bookstore, or library and do some research about the various types. Or talk to people who actively meditate to find out about which meditation will be most helpful to you.

Stress Log

Some people find it helpful to keep a stress log. When you record your stress episodes, you'll usually start to see a pattern emerge. For example, you may feel extremely stressful when you go to work. Perhaps an irritating supervisor is constantly berating you or looking over your shoulder to make sure that you do your job, or you are overloaded with writing reports. If you understand the stressors in your life, you can better deal with them.

Next, you can develop coping mechanisms. Perhaps you

might decide to deal with your job stress by transferring to another department, or learning to tune out the person who is annoying you. Another coping mechanism is to try walking in that person's shoes. Why is he so miserable? Why is he giving you such a hard time? Maybe he doesn't have friends or has a hard personal life, or is under constant stress from *his* boss. You even may be able to sympathize with him. And he may feel your compassion and, in return, get off your back!

Begin writing down stressful events that happen during your day. Afterward, try keeping a daily stress log to determine what you can do about them if you keep track of all stressors in your life.

Quiet Time

We all need time to ourselves. However, we seldom seem to take the necessary time in our busy lives, and then wonder why we experience stress. But if you set aside a few minutes every day to have a special quiet time, you can avoid being "stressed out."

Essence magazine's Susan Taylor has a daily morning ritual that gives her quiet time and prepares her for the day. "What I've learned is that we have to put on what I call our spiritual armor every single day. It's not enough just to go to church on Sunday and believe that you are going to have the spiritual food that you need to sustain you throughout the week. So I try to begin every day with quiet, introspective, meditative time," she says. "It's a time when I remind myself to put myself in charge and not let the world and pressures in my world erode my happiness, stress me out, and overwhelm me."

It works for her. "I find that when I do that consistently, take that quiet and introspective time to do my little morning ritual, and take some time to work out, this is a major stress reducer. And when I do, the pressures in my world are held at bay and I find my life easy and enjoyable."

Her ritual consists of a forty-five-minute period. "It's getting up when the alarm goes off so that you are not pushing that snooze button for five and ten minutes to get more sleep that doesn't do you any good. I lie on my back for five minutes, put myself in charge, and do deep, rhythmic breathing. I decide that I'm going to take off the agenda anything that is overwhelming, unnecessary, and doesn't need to be attended to that day. I affirm that I'm not going to scream or shout at my family or anyone in my life. And no matter what is happening, I'm not going to lose my cool because the divinity is within and I can handle it. That's the first few minutes," she stresses. "Then I get up and do a twenty-minute workout, jogging in place in my living room while I have on the morning news or am reading the newspaper. Or since I'm right down the block from Central Park, I might go for a good twenty- or twenty-five-minute jog. Then it's ten minutes in the bathtub listening to the divinity within so that I can take my direction for the day and for my life from that inner wisdom."

Why does Taylor do this routine without fail? "It's the wisest investment that anyone can make. I always tell myself that if I don't have the discipline to give myself forty-five minutes out of the twenty-four hours, then I don't deserve to be running a magazine and managing other people."

Whether you have a daily ritual like Taylor or create your own, do take a special time during the day for yourself. And when you do, you'll find yourself better able to handle stress!

Therapeutic Massage

When I first had a therapeutic massage, it felt like I had crawled back in the womb. As my masseur kneaded my muscles, it seemed like my body's stress was just evaporating into the air. And if you want to treat yourself, you should also try this great stress reducer.

It's important, however, to choose the best massage therapist. For the best results, ask friends or associates for referrals to a therapist. When you find the right person, make sure that you tell him or her your goals and what type of benefits you want from massage.

Vacations

Each one of us should rest his or her body occasionally and go on vacation. When you go to a different locale and relax for a week or more out of a year, you're more likely to get rid of built-up stress from an active work year and become refreshed. If you don't, you simply won't be as effective in your daily life, because of the uninterrupted stress.

While some people pride themselves on never taking a vacation or sick day, they may win points with their bosses, but wreak havoc with their health. Think of your body as a machine. If you treat it like a workhorse, it's going to slow down or even stop in time. So forget about being a hero at work. It's time to take care of yourself!

Other Ways to Manage Stress

Let's explore three more ways to relieve daily stress.

Vent and Talk Openly About Your Problems

Many people are very secretive about their problems. They bottle up their woes inside and become more and more affected by damaging stress. If you can, talk with a trusted friend and discuss what's bothering you and stressing you out. Talk frankly and emote. Cry, yell, scream, but get it all out. And when you do, you'll feel a great deal better. However, if you continue to hold things in, you're setting yourself up for a lot of heartache as well as stress-related illnesses.

Relax and Have Fun

Some of you are workaholics, never stopping to take a breather or enjoy life. In fact, your work is everything and there's simply no time for frivolous activities. But when you work, work, work, you're depriving yourself of relaxation and continuously stressing your body. And if you keep on going, you'll end up either sick or severely burnt out.

Remember that God put us here to enjoy our environment. Think about the last time that you took a moment to see and enjoy the earth's beauty around you. When was the last time that you saw a sunset or a rainbow? Although we've been programmed to gear our lives toward acquiring material things, there's so much more to life than that. Can you stop for a moment and appreciate all that's around you?

Learn to Cope

In our daily lives, we're subjected to a great deal of stress. But it's how we adapt or handle it that's important. Learn to have a happy-go-lucky attitude about life. Don't let little things that don't matter get to you. Avoid negative people and toxic situations. Or if you have to be exposed to them, don't let them get under your skin. Learn to let go and live. And when you do, your stress will slowly evaporate.

If you have a great deal of stress in your life, you must get control over it and learn to cope effectively. If you don't, you'll find yourself open to all kinds of opportunistic stress-related illnesses as well as personal grief. So take control of your life and manage the stress in it. And while you're at it, take good care of yourself.

Strategies to Take Care of Your Stress

1. Understand your top ten stressors.
2. Do daily progressive relaxation exercises.
3. Meditate.
4. Keep a stress log.
5. Have some quiet time.
6. Get a therapeutic massage.
7. Take a vacation.
8. Vent and talk openly about your problems.
9. Relax and have fun.
10. Learn to cope.

‹ 12 ›

Manage Your Time

Time Flies!
—Dr. William "Bill" Cosby

Our inability to manage time can be one of the biggest stressors in life. In our daily routines, we have so many things to do, places to go, and people to see that we're constantly on the move, trying to cram a great deal into every second. Unfortunately, there are only so many minutes and hours in a day. And if we don't control our time effectively, it will control us. To avoid this, it's a good idea to stop, reflect on how you use time, and begin to manage it better.

Self-assessment

Perhaps many of your time-management problems can be alleviated by assessing how you spend your time.

How Do You Spend Your Workweek?

First, determine how you spend your time at work. Write down what you do on a daily basis. Just take a typical day and start becoming aware of how you're spending it by accounting for every hour. For example, how is your morning spent? Do you come in at nine and head straight for the coffee machine or bagel cart? Or do you begin perusing your work-related magazines or journals? Or do you spend ten or fifteen minutes or more talking to colleagues when you first come to work? Are there meetings that last all morning? How much time do you spend at lunch? An hour or more? Or do you even take a lunch hour? Next, take a look at how you spend your afternoons, and actually calculate how much real time is spent on working.

By looking at how you spend your time, you may begin to notice problem areas. If you do, ask yourself some serious questions. For example, are you spending too much time talking on the phone? Are you letting other interruptions keep you away from doing your work? Are meetings gobbling up too much of your precious time? Are you disorganized and utilizing too much time looking for things on a cluttered desk or in a hopelessly messy file cabinet? Be honest. By getting in touch with how you spend your time, you're well on the road to managing it better.

How Do You Spend the Rest of Your Time?

By the same token, you need to take a look at the rest of your life to see how time affects it. Ask yourself the following questions:

- What roles do I have to play in my life? Am I a mother or father? civic or professional group officer or member? active church member? community volunteer? caregiver to elderly or sick parents? part-time business owner? part-time student?
- How much time do I give to each? For example, you may spend eight hours at work but must come home and have to mother or father for hours at night and on the weekends. So how much time is spent on parenting or other activities in your life?

Again, actually count out and total the number of hours spent on each activity. If you take a hard look at both your personal and work time, you'll be in better touch with your time-management problems and can begin to correct them.

More Self-assessment

Let's do another self-assessment exercise that will help you better understand that time-management problems are self-induced, work-related, or life-related. Look at the list below and try to determine which areas most affect you.

Self-assessment

Self-induced

- Is my day spent productively? If not, what am I doing to waste time?
- Do I spend a great deal of time on the phone?
- Am I a perfectionist?
- Do I delegate responsibilities to others or insist on doing things myself?
- Do I set goals to accomplish things and follow through?
- Do I feel overwhelmed by all the things that I have to do?

Work-Related

- Do I go to a lot of meetings?
- Do I get a lot of phone calls?
- Do I spend a lot of time fraternizing with office colleagues?
- Do I do a lot of paperwork?
- Am I deluged with mail?
- Is there a lot of reading material on my desk that I never get to see?
- Do I spend a great deal of time searching for things?
- Do I have a good filing system?
- Are there deadlines on my job?
- Do I always say yes to every request?

Life Barriers

- Do I have too many things to do in my life?
- What are my responsibilities (work, home, family, school, etc.)?
- Am I trying to be a superhuman person?

Self-induced: While you might not like to admit it, many time wasters in your life are self-induced. Instead of controlling your time, you may wander aimlessly about doing things, just hoping for the best. You know that there are many things to be done but you simply procrastinate and never get around to accomplishing any of it. You let little interruptions cripple your intentions. Do you stare out the window and do anything but the task at hand? Are you doing busywork instead of actual work to keep yourself occupied? If so, it's time to take stock.

What about your personal way of dealing with work? For instance, are you a perfectionist? Or are you the one who must do everything? When finishing and following through on projects, do you make goals so that things get done? Or do you just hope for a miracle? And when you can't do everything, do you feel overwhelmed?

If you've answered yes to any of these questions, most of your time-management issues are self-induced. You either procrastinate about getting the job done or find other more enjoyable activities to fill up your day. Stop right now and decide to change, or continue to be plagued with these self-induced time-management problems.

Work-related: Many time-related issues can be determined by your work environment. Too often companies create their own brand of time-management nightmares. For example, are there too many meetings at your work place? Although having employee or departmental meetings on a regular basis can be positive, some organizations have so many meetings that their employees can't get their jobs done effectively. One organization I worked for had twice-weekly departmental meetings. We had to attend whether or not there was anything to discuss. I thought that most of these gatherings were a waste of time and wondered when my superiors would see the value of letting us work instead of meet. Unfortunately, they never did, and this institution continues to function ineffectively.

Besides time-wasting meetings, there are other issues that cause work-related time-management problems. Are there interruptions at your job? Do too many client-related phone calls overwhelm you? In this type of environment, you're bound to have difficulties doing your job.

Some companies have departments or divisions that are "paper driven"—their very survival is based on their ability to justify their existence through forms. Unfortunately, this can contribute to your inability to properly complete work assignments. Are you required to do a lot of paperwork in your unit? Do you have to take home your paperwork just to keep on top of things? Although there is sometimes a need for documentation, it can also be a terrible waste of time when done to excess.

Some companies or departments are always in a crisis. On a regular basis, there's bad news from higher-ups regarding budget crises, downsizing, layoffs, and other things that tend to make employees nervous. If this occurs too often, you and your fellow workers tend to become nonproductive, strangled by the fear of losing your jobs. You spend your time worrying instead of contributing.

Another detrimental time waster is too much fraternizing among employees. How often do you socialize with your colleagues in the office? Does your company allow it? Many people waste half of their workday by talking to their coworkers. They walk from office to office, chatting with everyone in sight. Instead of doing work for which they are paid, they waste time gossiping about office politics or their personal lives. And, unfortunately, many companies look the other way.

Life-related: Are you trying to do too many things in your life? What are your responsibilities? Are you trying to be the perfect mother or father, household provider, employee, part-time student—and all at the same time? Sometimes there are so many roles to perform in your life that you can simply get overwhelmed trying to be a superhuman person. You never seem to have enough time, which tends to stress you out. And as we have seen in the preceding chapter, stress can be damaging to your health and general well-being. So it's wise to try to manage your different roles. With a little thought and planning, having multiple responsibilities can be successfully accomplished.

Time Robbers

As you can see from doing this kind of self-assessment, many general areas affect your time-management habits. Take a look at twelve major culprits that rob you of time and cause havoc in your life.

1. Failure to Set Goals

Although we've discussed goal setting earlier, planning in terms of time management is a habit that you must adopt! If you're a poor manager of time, you've probably failed to set goals. Rather than determining where you're going, you move ahead without any rhyme, reason, or direction, and find yourself unable to successfully do anything. If you have a project to complete, you just dive in without first considering what you want to achieve and how. But in order to successfully manage your time and do your work, you must set some short-term and long-term time-related goals.

To begin this goal setting, ask yourself some questions. For example, what do you want to accomplish in a short period of time: right now, in a week, in a month, in six months? Then determine what needs to be done on a long-term basis—a year or five or ten years from now. Copy the form on the next page and write down your short-term and long-term time and work goals. By doing this, you'll be able to provide some direction as to where you're going.

Short-term and Long-term Time-Management Goals

Short Term

1. What are my short-term goals?

   _____

   _____

   _____

2. When do I want to achieve them?

   _____

   _____

   _____

3. How will I accomplish them?

   _____

   _____

   _____

Long Term

1. What are my long-term goals?

   _____

   _____

   _____

2. When do I want to achieve them?

   _____

   _____

   _____

3. How will I accomplish them?

   _____

   _____

   _____

2. Lack of Planning

Many people who don't set goals also don't plan. And you're bound to fail without an adequate plan. Instead of merely beginning your work without targeting a specific goal, try planning what you want to do and having some clear objective of where you're going. In this way, you're more likely to be successful. As with goals, there are two types of planning: short-term and long-term.

Short-term planning: This type of planning deals with work to be accomplished within a short period of time. Let's say that you have a report to complete in two months. In order to do this, you must do the research, including gathering statistics, talking to people in your department, getting input, and doing the actual writing. Or perhaps you must put together a meeting on time management for the fifteen staff people in your department, which is the example used in the following chart. You will need to hire outside consultants to lead the meeting, and have only thirty days to do it. Look at the chart, and see how you might accomplish this. Outlining a day-by-day plan of what needs to be done will help you do the job in the allotted time.

Long-term planning: You can use the same format as the previous table for long-term time-management planning. Just put down weeks or months instead of days. By using this approach, you'll be able to see the big picture of what needs to be completed in a much longer time frame. Ask yourself these questions: What are the tasks? When do they have to be accomplished? How will they get done successfully?

Once you've answered these questions and know overall what has to be done, begin chopping your tasks into smaller time frames. Let's say you may have to do a comprehensive company sales trend report that's due at the end of the calendar year. Determine what needs to be done during the first, second, third, and fourth quarters. What follow-through is necessary during that time? What has to be done by the end of the year to successfully complete the report?

Things That I Must Accomplish to Complete Project A

Name of Project: Time-management meeting for 15 staff people.

Due Date: Thirty days from now!

List of What Must Be Done on Daily Basis (Days One to Thirty)

Days One to Three: Assess what is needed for the meeting's agenda.

Days Four to Five: Determine what consultants will be hired to lead meeting and discuss with manager. Go over budget for meeting.

Days Six to Eight: After OK, begin contacting consultants to determine their availability and send them formal letters.

Day Nine: Call and arrange for room or auditorium for meeting.

Days Ten to Eleven: Decide what materials will be needed.

Days Twelve to Thirteen: Go to corporate library to research materials.

Day Fourteen: Meet with staff to discuss future meeting and get their input. Spend afternoon further researching materials to be used.

Day Fifteen: Send materials to word processing and reprographics.

Day Sixteen: Write formal memo to staff and invite them to meeting.

Days Seventeen to Eighteen: Confirm consultants' attendance at meeting by phone. Have them fax any written materials that they'll be using.

Days Nineteen to Twenty: Type consultants' bios and agenda. Send to word processing and check on whether consultants' materials are complete.

Day Twenty-one: Review budget with manager again to see if meeting costs are on target.

Day Twenty-two: Meet with audiovisual people and caterers. Decide on whether to provide bagels and coffee and what menu will be for lunch. Reaffirm meeting place with room schedulers.

Day Twenty-three: Make arrangements to pick up consultants at airport.

Days Twenty-four to Twenty-five: Have name tags for meeting participants made. Get material back from word processing and stuff folders.

Day Twenty-six: Prepare welcoming speech for meeting.

Day Twenty-seven: Go over last-minute details with manager.

Day Twenty-eight: Contact consultants for last-minute details and confirmation of travel and pick-up arrangements. Contact audiovisual department to reconfirm.

Day Twenty-nine: Make sure that all details are taken care of.

Day Thirty: The event.

If you do both short-term and long-term planning, you'll know where you're going, why, how you'll get there, and when. If you don't incorporate these plans into work, you'll be just like a ship without a compass or destination. Be sure to make a detailed plan!

3. Perfectionism

Although good time management leads to more efficiency and productivity, there's an extreme side of it known as perfectionism. Although we don't live in a perfect world and perfectionism often leads to poor time management, some of you continue to strive to be "perfect." As a perfectionist, you're never satisfied with what you do, so you can never quite get the job done. Redoing and redoing the task, you continue until you're past deadlines, or just abandon the project altogether. Perfectionism is not about pursuing excellence; rather, it's a form of insecurity or a way to avoid criticism.

There's nothing wrong with someone who wants to achieve excellence in his work, and does the best job for the boss. Yet, a perfectionist is never happy with his work. A paragraph may need changing; more statistics may be needed. Sometimes, perfectionists will actually destroy their work and begin over and over again.

Perfectionism can kill careers. While you're so busy being perfect, others are passing you by and moving up the ladder of success. So get in touch with this problem and learn to overcome it by doing something only one time. Then reread, approve it or make minor changes, and let it go!

4. Inability to Delegate

The inability to delegate can also be a form of perfectionism. By wanting things done perfectly or in your own particular style, you can't or won't allow others to help out. This type of behavior sets you up for burnout and failure. So, particularly in your work situation, you must trust others to handle some of the load, and allow them to do so. You may be right in your belief that no one can do it like you; however, if you're a supervisor, this attitude may alienate your workers and make them feel hostile or inadequate. And even though things in your department may be done correctly by you and you alone, you're bound to get low marks as a manager.

Correct your inability to delegate by determining what has to be done and asking others to assist. When you do, you'll be more apt to get the task done without having to assume the entire burden yourself. In addition, you'll build up a functional team and improve your department's productivity.

5. Doing Too Many Things at Once

Some of you are wasting time by trying to do too many things at once. You've failed to prioritize your work assignments and feel that everything's important. To avoid stress, you must select the activities that are most important and concentrate on them.

In order to set priorities, you must determine what's essential or what must be done first. If you take the case of setting up a time-management meeting discussed above, think about the following questions: What would be the first priority? Would it be contacting and hiring the consultants who will lead the meeting? If so, this would be considered priority one. Next, a place must be found for the meeting or one can't be held—that would be priority two. Lower on your list of priorities would be things that are desired or may make the meeting better but are not necessarily needed; these would be priorities three and four. Use the form below to start prioritizing your projects right away.

Prioritize Your Time

Number One Priorities

a. _____

b. _____

c. _____

d. _____

e. _____

Number Two Priorities

a. _____

b. _____

c. _____

d. _____

e. _____

Number Three Priorities

a. _____

b. _____

c. _____

d. _____

e. _____

Number Four Priorities

a. _____

b. _____

c. _____

d. _____

e. _____

6. Failure to Limit Correspondence

Many of you might be deluged with mail at home and in your office, and have a virtual mountain of "junk mail." As it piles up, you become overwhelmed with too much of it, stack it on your desk or kitchen counter, and never seem to get around to reading it, even though you swear to get to it one day. But if you haven't read it in a day or two, you probably never will. To help manage this, try reading your mail immediately and if you don't need it, put it in the nearest wastepaper basket. If you want to save some of it for further use, keep it in a "references" or "pending" file.

You may also be having problems with other types of mail, including magazines, newspapers, and business journals. I know many people who keep stacks of newspapers and magazines, hoping to get to read them one day. Unfortunately, as with junk mail, that day never comes, and they're left with cluttered homes or offices. To avoid this, immediately read a magazine or newspaper. If there's an article that you want to save, clip it and put it in your file cabinet under "articles."

7. Desk Clutter

A disorganized desk is another common clutter problem that leads to poor time management. If your desk looks like a wilderness or has everything on it but the kitchen sink, you probably can't find important documents when they're needed, and this causes you to waste too much of your precious time. So get rid of the clutter and start becoming more organized.

8. Ineffective Filing Systems

Although an efficient and effective filing system can eliminate most desk clutter and some time-management problems, many of us don't take the time to develop one. How many hours have you wasted searching and searching for misfiled items? I know that when I haven't taken the time to adequately organize my files, I lose a lot of time just trying to locate things. By simply taking some file folders, labeling them, and alphabetizing your files, however, you'll begin to gain control and cease losing time looking for missing things. File regularly, keep your files current, and from time to time weed out the unnecessary papers in your file.

9. Inability to Meet Deadlines

Self-imposed deadlines will help you to better complete your work assignments on time. Without them, you can torpedo any attempt to get things done. Begin by simply trying to make a deadline. Write it prominently on your calendar and keep to it. Make sure to review your calendar often with an eye to upcoming deadlines. Once you do, you'll be surprised at your increased efficiency.

10. Lack of Follow-through

Some of us have trouble meeting deadlines; others have difficulty with follow-through or completing a task. Although you might do a great deal of work, a lack of focus on detail and follow-through prevents you from actualizing your goals. And since you'll be judged on the results, you must begin doing the follow-through to get the desired outcome. To successfully do this, you must have a plan. By making sure that every aspect of the task is accounted for and completed, you're more likely to succeed.

11. Lack of Work Breaks

Don't think that mastering all of these time-management problems means that you're going to be working all the time! If you work, work, work, and don't take breaks, you won't be as effective or efficient: you'll eventually become tired, lose your concentration, and develop blocks to doing your work.

After taking a break, you're more likely to be refreshed and better able to complete your tasks. Try walking to the lobby or taking a brief stroll outside. Or you can go to lunch and have a great meal. Stop at a neighborhood store and treat yourself to a gift. But whatever you do, take a break!

12. Inability to Say No

Are you always accommodating everyone's requests without any regard to your own time constraints? Do you volunteer for activities when your plate is already full? Are you pushing yourself to the limits with too many things to do? If so, you have an inability to say no. As a result, you're bound to experience the frustration of poor time management and will eventually become overwhelmed.

If you have this problem, try getting in touch with why. Do you want to be indispensable? Are you insecure and feel that you can't turn down another's request for fear of being disliked? Or do you perceive of yourself as a superhuman who can do all things and be everything to everyone? Regardless of your reasons for not being able to say no, learn to simply turn down requests that aren't in your best interests. When you do, you won't overtax your mind and body or become useless to everyone, including yourself.

Tools That Beat the Time Robbers

Here are five tools that can help you gain better control of your time and overcome time robbers.

1. To-do Lists

The best way to get control of your time is to make lists. With them, you're able to detail which tasks need to be done. After each one's completed, you can check it off and move on to the next item. I know that I couldn't live without my lists. When I'm doing something that requires the utmost organization, I find these lists to be invaluable—and so will you.

Although you can buy ready-made lists, you can also make your own. Use a piece of paper or your calendar and write down in chronological order everything that needs to be done. As you finish each item, cross it off. In this way, your project will be organized and you won't feel overwhelmed by the tasks.

2. Calendar

Every astute time manager has a daily, weekly, or monthly calendar that allows him or her to manage projects and appointments. Your calendar can be in book form, or hung on a wall, or sitting on your desk. To use it correctly, be sure to include everything: meetings, client visits, work time, luncheons, doctor or dentist appointments, children's school activities, after-work social affairs, etc. Begin each morning by perusing your calendar to see what's in store for the day and plan accordingly. Every night, look to see what will happen the following day.

Also use your calendar to manage your appointment scheduling. Because too many of us make appointments without giving it any real thought, this can lead to poor time management and frustration. If you consciously take the time to properly schedule your appointments, you'll be better able to manage your work life. For example, all of your out-of-the-office appointments could be slated for the same day, which would leave the rest of the week for other matters.

3. Technology

Although annoying, your phone-mail system can be your best time-management friend. When you're in the office and have work to do, simply put on your phone mail, and you won't miss important calls.

E-mail can also help you manage your time. Instead of calling people or having them call you, which can interrupt your work, you can e-mail them. Then set aside a certain time every day to retrieve and answer all of your e-mail.

The computer is also a great aid to time management. Because it allows you to edit, check your spelling and grammar, use a thesaurus, cut and paste, copy, insert files and charts or graphics into reports, and do other time-saving things, you're bound to be more efficient. You don't have to use correction fluid, retype, or toss away copy. And it allows you to store or file all kinds of material that might have ended up on your desk.

4. Computerized Address Book

As a person who has hundreds of telephone numbers to keep track of, I used to waste a lot of time searching for specific ones. With a computerized address book, I can locate these important numbers in a fraction of the time. If you invest in one, you'll also see immediate benefits. Browse your neighborhood electronics or department store and price them. And be sure to get one that is compatible with your computer.

5. A Good Old-fashioned Garbage Can

When in doubt, throw it away! Handle your correspondence or periodicals only once. Either file them or put them in the garbage!

If you manage your time, you can live a happier and less frustrated life. Don't watch time fly—grab control of it! And when you do, your career and personal life will converge toward success.

Strategies for Managing Your Time

1. Assess how you spend your time.
2. Determine whether your time-management problems are self-induced, work-related, or life-related.
3. Set time goals.
4. Plan your time accordingly.
5. Don't be a perfectionist.
6. Delegate responsibilities.
7. Don't do too many things at once.
8. Manage your correspondence and periodicals.
9. Unclutter your desk.
10. Create a good filing system and use it.
11. Make and keep deadlines.
12. Follow through on assignments.
13. Take work breaks.
14. Learn how to say no.
15. Make to-do lists.
16. Get a calendar and use it effectively.
17. Use e-mail and other technology to your advantage.
18. Get a computerized address book.
19. Use your garbage can more often!

< 13 >

Give Back

Give to him that asketh thee. and from him that would borrow of thee turn not thou away.

—Matthew 5:42

In the sixties, we used to say, "Each one, teach one!" Today, our focus should also be "each one, help one!" If you look around, you'll see that we're surrounded with abundance, living in one of the richest countries on earth. Yet, do we have charity in our hearts?

When you see a homeless person, do you turn your back and refuse a penny or dime or quarter? Do you think, Oh, this person doesn't really need it. He'll just use it for drugs or alcohol. This is the fifth person who asked me today! Is that the *charitable spirit*? A penny? A dime? A quarter for your brother or sister who is struggling, living in conditions of squalor and hopelessness? Will so little change financially make or break you? Will you live as the Bible teaches us, "Give and ye shall receive!"

I remember going to an outdoor concert for the homeless in New York's Times Square. Stevie Wonder, the guest artist, performed his songs, including "Take the Time Out!" which celebrates one's humanity. In it, he tells us to love people whether they are homeless or rich. As people rocked to the beat and hugged one another in universal harmony, a homeless man made his way through the crowd. With his hand held out, he asked us to share the spirit of which we sang. To my surprise, many people stopped singing, stepped out of the man's way, and refused to give him a cent. Others were openly hostile. "Get away from me," I heard one person say. Another one chimed in, "No! I don't have any money!" In utter amazement, I thought, What is wrong with this picture? Wasn't it ironic that people were singing and hugging one another in the spirit of humanity but had none for a homeless person? And I thought, There but by the grace of God, go I!

The Bible says, "Whatsoever a man soweth that shall he also reap" or, as my grandmother used to say, "What goes around, comes around!" If you're uncharitable, life will be uncharitable to you.

Sharing the Wealth

Most successful people know that sharing of their resources will multiply their wealth. Denzel Washington, Whitney Houston, Michael Jackson, Magic Johnson, Eddie Murphy, Michael Jordan, John and Eunice Johnson of Johnson Publications, and *Black Enterprise*'s Earl Graves Sr. are just a few of our successful African-Americans who have shared their wealth. Every day, there's a story about some successful Black person's contributions to our community. Camille and Bill Cosby gave one of the most generous gifts when they presented Spelman College with $20 million. And no one can forget their million-dollar-plus gift to Fisk University when the institution was experiencing financial difficulties. Oprah Winfrey has made many wonderful contributions, especially in the area of breaking the shackles of many families on public assistance and her "Angel's Network."

However, it was the $150,000 gift from Oseola McCarty to the University of Southern Mississippi that tugged most at our national heartstrings. After years of saving money at her laundry work, this valiant giver presented much of her life's savings to fund scholarships for Black students. In her own special way, she wanted to give something to better the lives of others. And for her efforts, President Clinton gave her a prestigious medal and she received as well an award from *Essence* magazine.

●<>●

He Makes It Possible for Others to Succeed

For fourteen years, Ted Lange, who costarred as Isaac Washington in *The Love Boat*, has given back to the African-American community. The accomplished actor is a director with such credits as the television shows *Moesha* and *The Wayan Brothers*, and a screenwriter as well as playwright. His latest play, *Lemon Meringue Façade*, opened this past January, and his *Four Queens—No Trump* won the NAACP Image Award for Best Play in 1997.

However, few people outside of Hollywood know that he financed an acting competition to help struggling actors in Los Angeles. This showcase has helped launch the careers of many African-American actors. A trained Shakespearean actor who studied at the Royal Academy of Dramatic Arts in London, he named the competition after Ira Aldridge, the great African-American Shakespearean actor. He explains why he began the project: "The Ira Aldridge Acting Competition was born out of my own frustrations as an actor when I first came to Los Angeles. I didn't know anyone. I didn't know how to audition and I didn't know any agents or casting directors. The competition alleviates all this for those starting out. If you go to the Ira Aldridge, you get your foot in the door." In fact, it does a great deal more.

Actors go through several competitions before making it into the finals. If they make the last cut, they're able to give their performances in front of the judges: Hollywood's top casting agents and actors. However, winning isn't the only benefit. Lange explains, "Say you don't get to the finals, you're there with other actors. It's a communal thing where you meet other people and exchange. And that's really important because people don't congregate in Los Angeles. It's really difficult." And so the contest is about "networking! It's about information!"

There are added advantages to participating in the contest. "The people who don't win can come back again. I've

known people who didn't win and were able to get jobs anyway. Even if you don't win first prize, people see you and
the people who see you are in a position to help. It's networking. It's about information," he reminds us.

When asked about his generosity in providing this wonderful opportunity for others, Lange thinks back to a time
when he had difficulties: "The actor Percy Rodriguez, who
lived in my apartment building, and I were talking one time.
And I was telling him about how tough it was. He said that I
would make it. But he reminded me that usually when a person makes it, they never give back. He told me, 'I just hope
if you ever make it, or when you make it, you remember
how you feel right now. A lot of people feel that same way.'
That always stuck with me. So when I was in position and I
had some money, I did." And through the years, there are
many actors who are thankful that he reached back.

Give Back by Deed

Many African-Americans give back by deed; perhaps you
can, too.

- Our brilliant scholar W. E. B. Du Bois met with a group in
  1909 to protest increasing violence toward Blacks and thus
  planted the seed for the beginning of the NAACP.
- Carter G. Woodson, the father of "Black History Week,"
  fought for a national recognition of African-Americans' contributions. The highly esteemed "Black History Month" is
  the culmination of his work in the Association for the
  Study of Negro Life and History.
- At the invitation of First Lady Eleanor Roosevelt, Marian
  Anderson sang to a crowd of more than seventy thousand
  when the Daughters of the American Revolution refused
  to give her the opportunity to sing at Constitution Hall.
  The little girl who once scrubbed Philadelphia stoops went

on to become one of the world's most beloved opera singers.

- Under the auspices of the NAACP Legal Defense Fund, Thurgood Marshall, later a Supreme Court Justice, along with Constance Motley Baker, now a federal judge, and others won the landmark Supreme Court decision *Brown v. Board of Education of Topeka*, which decreed an end to school desegregation.
- Rosa Parks's refusal to get off a Montgomery, Alabama, bus helped spark the civil rights movement. After her arrest, the city's Blacks protested by boycotting Montgomery's buses for many months. The Supreme Court intervened and the bus company was forced to desegregate.
- A twenty-seven-day hunger strike by TransAfrica's Randall Robinson challenged the Clinton administration's policy on Haitian refugees. The hunger strikes of internationally acclaimed dancer Katherine Dunham brought similar attention to the Haitians' plight.
- Minister Louis Farrakhan called for a Day of Atonement, which was organized by Dr. Ben Chavis. African-American men from all walks of life answered the call by attending The Million Man March. Viewed by millions of our brothers and sisters in this country and around the world, it was a wondrous day that will go down in history.

There are so many ways that we can help our people. At the Million Man March, for example, Leonard G. Dunston, who is vice president of Preudhomme, Dunston and Associates, and the president of the National Association of Black Social Workers, made a plea for African-American families to come forth and adopt the twenty-five thousand children in need of homes. Since that time, he has reported that over eight thousand have begun the adoption process. What is the importance of this deed? "I think it's important for all of us to remember that Black on Black love is, in fact, adopting Black children. Despite the enormity of problems that plague us as Black people, we should always remember this African proverb: 'Working together, the ants ate the elephant!'" Dunston, who was also the former commissioner of the New York State Division for Youth, stresses.

Think about it! What deed can you perform to help?

Give Back Your Time

Part of Terrie Williams's success is that she gives back to so many. Wanting to share her talents, she opens her agency to nonpaid interns who want to learn the publicity business, and her generosity is well known. "I know how it feels when you just need an answer to a question and can't get that answer," she says. "It's not about being a martyr or anything like that. I'd rather make it easier for someone to get a question answered. So if someone tells me that they want to get into the public relations or entertainment business, there's a place for them here. I always try to give that opportunity."

Even when her schedule doesn't permit it, Williams still manages to accommodate most requests for information. "We were having a screening of this Medgar Evers project for HBO. About five young people had called and wanted to have informational interviews but time didn't permit this. I told them to come and join us at the event. They watched the screening. We gave them materials. And we told them what we were doing as we were doing it. They were also able to ask questions of the other team members."

What else makes Williams give back? "I heard an analogy that I thought was very interesting. People get a little knowledge and they don't want to help somebody else light their candle because they feel that their light will be diminished. Literally, when you help someone else light a candle, all it does is make the world brighter. Yours doesn't go out," says the woman who allows lawyers with aspirations of getting into the entertainment industry to learn the business during their evening hours.

Susan Taylor, Bobbi Humphrey, Ruby Dee and her husband Ossie Davis, Joe Dudley, Sheryl Lee Ralph, Terrie Williams, and others have worked tirelessly to help African-American causes. Through their time and efforts, help has reached many people.

What do you have to give? What difference can you make? Can you be a big brother or sister to an African-American youngster in need? Can you spend some time giving back and help welfare mothers get off public assistance? Can you take a leave of absence and spend a semester helping out a black college? What can you do? Think about it!

Whether through donations, deeds, or time, do give back! Your community depends on it.

‹ 14 ›

Go for It!

*Let your light so shine before men, that they
may see your good works, and glorify your Father
which is in Heaven.*

—Matthew 5:16

When I was a little girl sitting on my grandmother's porch in
Selma, North Carolina, I used to hear the old folks say things
like "Life is short!" and "Time flies!" Being small, I never gave
one thought to the seriousness of these statements. After all, I
was maybe ten or eleven and my whole life stretched out in
front of me. Now, a few decades later, I know what they were
talking about. Like it or not, we have only one life, and that precious gift must be appreciated. If you were given talents or skills
or attributes, you must use them or lose them. And there's no
better time to begin than now.

There's no more time for excuses or fear. There's no more
time to cling to behaviors of the past! It's now or never!

In this infinite wisdom, I began doing something that has
haunted me all of my life. Back when I was a little girl, I was a
bit of a "ham" who loved singing and dancing on the stage. Being an only child who could pry anything out of my parents, I
quickly convinced them to help me shore up my talents and
take me to every class imaginable. Although my working mother
had spent her entire week teaching school and probably de-
served a rest on the weekends, I regularly had her take me to
all kinds of lessons on Saturdays. There were singing, tap, bal-
let, toe, jazz, and late-afternoon skating lessons at Rockefeller

Center. I wanted to be a star. There was no keeping me from Hollywood.

In my teens, I begged my parents to take me to every audition for a play on Long Island and enroll me in the American Academy of Dramatic Arts. In junior high school, I was the lead in every musical. By sixteen, I had starred in a film called *Pigeon*, which aired on PBS. Then something went terribly wrong: I left home for college.

While totally delighted to be away from home and meeting new people, I soon realized that my university's drama department was more theoretical than performance-oriented. While we were required to do all the backstage work of lighting, makeup, props, and even a little directing, we were never given a chance onstage. Dismayed, I soon fell more in love with the civil rights movement that was mushrooming around me than pursuing the dream of acting—although my friends will tell you that I never did stop performing.

After college, I accepted a position as assistant dean of women at a small, upscale liberal arts college in Ohio and began a career in an area that wasn't my first, second, or third choice. Although I had always loved helping others, I should have been on the New York stage or in a Hollywood film.

As time went by, I became more and more entrenched in college work. Switching jobs every two years, I tried to fit myself into an occupation that wasn't meant to be for me. Luckily, I came upon a wonderful vocation that helped steer me in another more satisfying direction. Because former *Essence* editors Marcia Gillespie and Audreen Ballard gave me a chance to write a column for that magazine, I felt that one part of me could pursue something creative. When I had the additional opportunity to write *The Black Woman's Career Guide* and do the subsequent lecturing at colleges, universities, and professional groups that allowed me to "act" or "perform," I was so happy! Even at a book signing event, a Broadway producer told me to write a play and act in it because I had what it takes, I never thought of returning to my first love of theater.

While writing this book, I was fortunate enough to interview Carl Gordon from the television show *Roc*. Halfway through our conversation, he told me he went into acting at age thirty-five. I said, "Wait a minute! Forget the book! Take me to your acting teacher!" When he said that he would, I couldn't forget the inner joy that welled up inside of me. For many months later, it simply wouldn't go away. I kept asking myself, Could I act at this late stage?

On a very bright day in May, I picked up the phone and called Gene Frankel, Carl Gordon's acting teacher and one of the most renowned in the business. His assistant told me to come down and personally interview with Gene. Excited beyond belief, I went to see the man who could change my life and give me another chance at pursuing my dream. We met and he immediately put me in his advanced professional acting class. Hooray! If I could have, I would have done cartwheels down Broadway!

As of this writing, I have been through one full cycle of his class. It's been tough, memorizing monologues in addition to writing this book, but so worth it. I plan to go through many more classes with Gene and become a first-class actress. So when you go into the movie theater and sit back in your seat, don't be surprised to see the credits roll with "Beatryce Nivens starring as _____." It's my lifelong dream and I'm going for it. After all, if not now, when?

What dreams have you hidden under the guise of doing something else in life? Are you really a singer, painter, social worker, preacher, teacher, lawyer, entrepreneur? Has life passed you by without your pursuing what you were put here to do? How many more years will you waste being tied to security and a paycheck? Do you have the guts to go for it?

This book was written to help you free yourself of past restrictions and live out your dreams. After reading the profiles of so many successful African-Americans who took the risk to become all that they could be, it's my hope that you'll follow suit. With this type of motivation, I wish you nothing but sweet success dreams.

Now let's recap what it takes for you to get going:

Uplift Yourself: Boost Your Self-esteem

If poverty, lack of educational opportunities, age, or other factors get in your way, will you surmount them and move on to success? Will you carry the torch of our forefathers and foremothers who had far more challenging times and disappointments than we'll ever experience? Will you have the ability to overcome modest beginnings like Joe Dudley? Or have the courage to achieve despite your advancing age like Bessie Nickens? Or carry the burden of the race on your shoulders like Ruby Bridges? When they call your number, will you rise and say: "Yes! I've done my all!"?

Think Big, Dream Large

Can you think big and act big? Or are you stymied by things getting in your way? If you've hoped for a better tomorrow, what's stopping you from achieving it? Can you climb out of the limitations of your environment and make it to Broadway like August Wilson did with his Pulitzer Prize–winning plays? Can you dream of a career on Broadway and become America's number-one dream girl like Sheryl Lee Ralph? Can you find a passion in something as Bobbi Humphrey did in the flute and blow your way to success? And will you have the vision and dignity of Ruby Dee to believe in your talents and soar?

Wade in the Water: Set Your Goals

Will you summon up the stamina to make your dreams happen by planning for the future? Can you take your hopes and desires to the next level? Will you conquer fear and do what you must to succeed? Will you make goals for a better day and stick to them? Can you take your talents and make them into megasuccess like Nikki Giovanni? Can you follow your dreams and still manage to have the dignity and reserve of Angela Bassett? Will you embrace success at all costs?

Peace Be Still: Affirm Your Success

On a daily basis will you affirm your success by tapping into your subconscious mind? Will you believe that all things are possible with God and the Universe? Can you trust that which is unseen but forever powerful? Will you let go and let God like Senait Ashenafi? Can you turn your life around like Carl Gordon at age thirty-five? Can you cherish life even though you may not come close to losing it like Richard Lawson, and be thankful for every day? Can you count your blessings like Pam Warner?

The Power of Prosperity Thinking

Although you may be caught in a wind of opposition, will you manage the storm to succeed? Can you really feel that all of your blessings make you wealthy? Even in despair, can you see the rainbow around the corner and value all that has been given to you? Can you change your life like Susan Taylor did hers, think positively, and build a champion career as well as a life for yourself? Will you, like Pamela Warner, find prosperity through a special blessing? Can you master your thinking and move to the highest heights?

Standing on the Banks of Jordan: Release the Fear

Does fear keep you bottled up and unable to move beyond the apprehension? Are you prevented from achieving your goals because you're afraid? Has panic made you apathetic and immovable? Like Art Evans, can you step out of fear and create a career? Will you move past any possible fear and make your own way as Jeffrey Anderson-Gunter did? Or will you remain crippled for life, trying to imagine your success but afraid to achieve it?

Blast out of Your Comfort Zone: Taking the Risk

Will you risk everything to become successful? Can you move out of your comfort zone and conquer all? Or will you let your everyday existence continue to stifle you and keep you away from accomplishing your goals? Can you take a risk like Jasmine Guy and leave your familiar surroundings in search of your destiny? Or will you muster up the courage like Marie Brown to abandon the security of a beloved job to start on your own? Can you dare to take the risk of doing something extraordinary as Lawrence Otis Graham did at a young age? Despite a shy personality, will you, like Terrie Williams, do something bold and make your dreams come true?

Honor Your Temple: Take Care of Yourself

Because you can do nothing when you're sick and not feeling well, will you begin taking better care of yourself? Will you watch what you eat, exercise, and reduce stress? While success is desirable, you won't be able to enjoy it without your health. Take care of number one!

Manage Your Stress

Stress can work you into an unhealthy state. As your body struggles to fight over and over again to rise to the occasion, your health can suffer. So decide now to begin taking care of number one—you.

Manage Your Time

Although time flies and it's later than you think, have you mastered the ability to handle time? Do you put first things first or just go with the flow? Have you decided that you'll let time be your friend instead of your enemy? Managing your time well is one of your best assets in your journey to success.

Put Your Principles into Action: Work Your Way to Prosperity

If you don't work at what you love, what's the use? Will you find something to love as Vondie Curtis Hall did? Will you, like Marcia Gillespie, use all of your talents and strong points in your new pursuit? Or will you assume leadership as Franklin Thomas did? Can you chart your own path, following the example of Carolyn Baldwin?

As Marcia Gillespie says, we work too hard and spend too many hours working to slave away at something dull or boring. And if you simply hate your job as so many Americans do, it's worse. So do yourself a favor! Find something that you love and can care about. When you do, you'll really know the meaning of success.

Empower Yourself: Success for the Entrepreneur

If you've always wanted to become an entrepreneur, will you have the stamina, energy, and risk-taking abilities to make it happen? Can you forge straight ahead with your dreams and goals? Will you never, ever give up on your business idea until you achieve success? Will you walk in the paths of Audrey Smaltz, Pierre Sutton, Carole H. Riley, Robert Johnson, and H. Jerome Russell? Can you make it happen?

Give Back

One of the best secrets of life is to give back some of what you make. Most successful people have learned this lesson. They don't hold on to every penny, never offering a dime to anyone else. Instead, they openly give, not for the tax breaks, but because it's the right thing to do! And when they do, they're richly blessed.

Take the lead from actor Ted Lange, who so generously gave some of his earnings from *The Love Boat* to start the Ira Aldridge Acting Competition to help others.

* * *

No one said that it was going to be easy. There have been many times that I felt like giving up on writing this book and returning to a normal life. However, it was important for me to complete it. It was a mission that I felt very committed to achieving. When I did finish it, I looked back at the hard work and said, "Never again!" Then I remembered that I said those same words for the five books before this one.

So remember that success is hard work—very hard work. It doesn't come easy! You have to pursue it every day and never give in. Sometimes a hurricane of problems will land on your lap as you're moving up that mountain. But you can never give up! So work hard and know that success is waiting just around the corner for you!

It's later than you think. If you've ever wanted to be successful, now's the time. You've been given all the tools. What are you waiting for? What's your excuse? Go for it!

Appendix: Business Resources and Professional Associations

Business Resources

American Economic Development Corporation
71 Vanderbilt Avenue, Third Floor
New York, NY 10169
(212) 692-9100
(800) 222-AWED

Offers business counseling, telephone counseling, a hot line, courses, and short-term training in business for women.

Institute for Entrepreneurial Education
23 Gramercy Park South
New York, NY 10003
(212) 982-5200

Provides excellent free Workshop in Business Opportunities for minorities to help "develop real and lasting economic power through business ownership."

Minority Business Enterprise Legal Defense and Education
  Fund
300 I Street
Suite 200
Washington, DC 20004
(202) 347-8259

Helps minority businesses with information and legal
expertise.

National Minority Business Council (NMBC)
235 E. 42nd Street
New York, NY 10017
(212) 573-2385

Specializes in international trade by offering seminars and a
mentorship program for minority businesses.

National Minority Supplier Development Council
15 W. 39th Street
New York, NY 10018
(212) 944-2430

Helps match minority businesses with corporate procurement
programs.

Oversees Private Investment Corporation
1100 New York Avenue, NW
Washington, DC 20527-0001
OPIC Infoline (202) 336-8799

Business-Related Professional Associations

American Association of Black Women Entrepreneurs Corp.
815 Thayer Avenue #1628
Silver Spring, MD 20910
(301) 565-0258

Association of Minority Enterprises of New York
Office of the President
250 Fulton Avenue #505
Hempstead, NY 11550
(516) 489-0120

International Franchise Association
1350 New York Avenue, NW
Suite 900
Washington, DC 20005-4709
(202) 628-8000

Interracial Council for Business Opportunity
51 Madison Avenue #2212
New York, NY 10010
(212) 779-4360

National Association of Black Women Entrepreneurs
P.O. Box 1375
Detroit, MI 48231
(303) 341-7400

National Association of Minority Contractors
13333 F Street, NW
Washington, DC 20004
(202) 543-0040

National Association of Women Business Owners
600 S. Federal Street
Suite 400
Chicago, IL 60605
(800) 222-3838

National Business League
1511 K Street, NW #432
Washington, DC 20005
(202) 737-4430

National Student Business League
7226 E. Forest Road
Kentland, MD 20785
(202) 895-3926

International

U.S.–South Africa Business Council
1525 K Street, NW #1090
Washington, DC 20006
(202) 887-0278

International Minority Business Corporation
Park 80 West, Plaza 1
Fourth Floor
Saddle Brook, NJ 07663
(201) 843-4499

African-American Professional Associations/Organizations

African-American Museums Association
P.O. Box 548
Wilberforce, OH 45384
(513) 376-4611

African-American Travel & Tourism Association, Inc.
P.O. Box 870712
New Orleans, LA 70187-0712
(504) 241-8464

Alliance of Black Entertainment Technicians
1869 Buckingham Road
Los Angeles, CA 90019
(213) 933-0746

Alpha Kappa Alpha Sorority
5656 S. Stony Island Avenue
Chicago, IL 60637
(312) 684-1282

Alpha Phi Alpha Fraternity, Inc.
2314 Saint Paul Street
Baltimore, MD 21218
(410) 554-0040

Alpha Pi Chi Sorority
P.O. Box 1337
Florence, AL 35630
(205) 764-4899

American Association for Affirmative Action
200 N. Michigan Avenue #200
Chicago, IL 60601
(312) 541-1272

American Association of Blacks in Energy
927 15th Street, NW #200
Washington, DC 20005
(202) 371-9530

American Council on Education, Office of Minorities in Higher
    Education
One Dupont Circle, #886, NW
Washington, DC 20036
(202) 939-9935

American Health & Beauty Aids Institute
401 N. Michigan Avenue, 23rd Floor
Chicago, IL 60611-4267
(312) 644-6610

American League of Financial Institutions
900 19th St., NW #400
Washington, DC 20006
(202) 857-3176

Association for Multicultural Counseling and Development
5999 Stevenson Avenue
Alexandria, VA 22302
(703) 823-9800

Association of Black Admissions and Financial Aid Officers of
the Ivy League and Sister Schools, Inc.
P.O. Box 1402
Cambridge, MA 02138
(401) 863-2378

Association of Black Foundation Executives
1828 L Street, NW, Suite 300
Washington, DC 20036
(202) 466-6512

Association of Black Psychologists
P.O. Box 55999
Washington, DC 20040-5999
(202) 722-0808

Association of Black Women in Higher Education
Delores V. Smalls
c/o Nassau Community College
Nassau Hall, Room 19
One Education Drive
Garden City, NY 11530-6793

Bethune-DuBois Fund
600 New Hampshire Avenue, NW #1125
Washington, DC 20037
(202) 629-2900

Black Agency Executives
37 E. 28th Street, #800
New York, NY 10016
(212) 545-0845

Black Career Women
P.O. Box 19332
Cincinnati, OH 45219
(513) 531-1932

Black Caucus of the American Library Association
c/o Sylvia Hamlin, Forsyth County Library
660 West Fifth Street
Winston-Salem, NC 27106
(910) 727-2556

Black Filmmakers Foundation
Tribeca Film Center
New York, NY 10013
(212) 941-3944

Black Psychiatrists of America
2730 Adeline Street
Oakland, CA 94607
(510) 465-1800

Black Retail Action Group
P.O. Box 1192
Rockefeller Center Station
New York, NY 10185
(212) 308-6017

Black Rock Coalition, Inc.
P.O. Box 1054
Cooper Station
New York, NY 10276
(212) 713-5097

Black Women in Church and Society
c/o Inter Denominational Theological Center
671 Beckwith Street, SW
Atlanta, GA 30314
(404) 527-7740

Black Women in Publishing, Inc.
c/o Phelps-Stokes Fund Affiliate
10 E. 87th Street
New York, NY 10128
(212) 427-8100

Black Women's Agenda, Inc.
3501 14th Street, NW
Washington, DC 20010
(202) 387-4166

Black Women's Forum
3870 Crenshaw Blvd. #210
Los Angeles, CA 90008
(213) 292-3009

Black Women's Network, Inc. (Los Angeles)
P.O. Box 56106
Los Angeles, CA 90056
(213) 292-6547

Black Women's Network, Inc. (Milwaukee)
8712 W. Spokane Street
Milwaukee, WI 53224
(414) 353-8925

Blacks in Government
1820 11th Street, NW
Washington, DC 20001
(202) 667-3280

Chi Eta Phi Sorority, Inc.
3029 13th Street, NW
Washington, DC 20009
(202) 723-3384

Coalition of Black Trade Unionists
P.O. Box 66268
Washington, DC 20035-6268
(202) 429-1203

Concerned Educators of Black Students
473 Marathon Avenue
Dayton, OH 45406
(513) 275-9133

Conference of Minority Public Administrators
COMPA ASPA
1120 G Street, NW
Washington, DC 20005
(202) 393-7878

Conference of Minority Transportation Officials
1330 Connecticut Avenue, NW
Washington, DC 20036
(202) 775-1118

Congressional Black Caucus
House Annex 11
Ford Building
Room 344
Washington, DC 20515
(202) 226-7790

Delta Sigma Theta Sorority, Inc.
1707 New Hampshire Avenue, NW
Washington, DC 20009
(202) 986-2400

Edges Group, Inc.
c/o Bell Atlantic
2000 Corporate Drive
Orangeburg, NY 10962
(914) 644-6132

Eta Phi Beta Sorority, Inc.
16815 James Couzens
Detroit, MI 48235
(313) 862-0600

Executive Leadership Council
444 North Capitol Street, #715
Washington, DC 20001
(202) 783-6339

Federation of Masons of the World and Federation of Eastern
    Stars
1017 E. 11th Street
Austin, TX 78702
(512) 477-5380

International Association of Black Professional Fire Fighters
8700 Central Avenue, #306
Landover, MD 20785
(301) 808-0804

International Black Writers
P.O. Box 1030
Chicago, IL 60690
(312) 924-3818

Iota Phi Lambda Sorority, Inc.
P.O. Box 11509
Montgomery, AL 36111-0609
(205) 284-0203

Iota Phi Theta Fraternity, Inc.
P.O. Box 7628
Baltimore, MD 21207-0628
(301) 792-2192

Kappa Alpha Psi Fraternity, Inc.
2322-24 North Broad Street
Philadelphia, PA 19132
(215) 228-7184

Lambda Kappa Mu Sorority, Inc.
1521 Crittenden Street, NW
Washington, DC 20011
(202) 829-2368

Leadership Conference on Civil Rights
1629 K Street, NW #1010
Washington, DC 20006
(202) 466-3311

Links, Inc.
1200 Massachusetts Avenue, NW
Washington, DC 20005
(202) 842-8686

Modern Free and Accepted Masons of the World, Inc.
P.O. Box 1072
Columbus, OH 31902
(706) 322-3326

Most Wonderful National Grand Lodge
Free and Accepted Ancient York Masons
Prince Hall Origin
National Compact, USA Inc.
P.O. Box 2789
Orangeburg, SC 29116-2789
(803) 536-4019

National Action Council for Minorities in Engineering
3 W. 35th Street
New York, NY 10001
(212) 279-2626

National African-American Catholic Youth Ministry Network
P.O. Box 608
Louisville, KY 40202-0608
(606) 253-3305 or (312) 521-4033

National Alliance of Black Salesmen and Saleswomen
P.O. Box 2814
Manhattanville Station
Harlem, NY 10027
(718) 409-4925

National Alliance of Black School Educators
2816 Georgia Ave., NW #4
Washington, DC 20001
(202) 483-1549

National Alliance of Postal and Federal Employees
1628 11th Street, NW
Washington, DC 20001
(202) 483-1549

National Association for Equal Opportunity in Higher
  Education
Lovejoy School Building
400 12th Street, NE #207
Washington, DC 20002
(202) 543-9111

National Association for the Advancement of Colored People
4805 Mt. Hope Drive
Baltimore, MD 21215
(410) 358-8900

NAACP Legal Defense & Education Fund, Inc.
99 Hudson Street #1600
New York, NY 10013
(212) 219-1900

National Association of African-American Catholic Deacons
2338 E. 99th Street
Chicago, IL 60617
(312) 375-6311

National Association of Bench and Bar Spouses, Inc.
5000 S. East End Avenue
Chicago, IL 60615
(312) 493-1688

National Association of Black Accountants, Inc.
7249-A Hanover Parkway
Greenbelt, MD 20770
(301) 474-3114

National Association of Black Book Publishers
P.O. Box 22080
Baltimore, MD 21203
(410) 358-0980

National Association of Black Catholic Administrators
P.O. Box 29260
Washington, DC 20017
(301) 853-4579

National Association of Black Consulting Engineers
2705 Bladensburg Road, NE
Washington, DC 20018
(202) 333-9100

National Association of Black County Officials
440 First Street, NW #500
Washington, DC 20001
(202) 333-9100 or (202) 347-6953

National Association of Black Hospitality Professionals, Inc.
P.O. Box 5443
Plainfield, NJ 07060
(908) 354-5117

National Association of Black Journalists
P.O. Box 4222
Reston, VA 22091
(703) 648-1270

National Association of Black Owned Broadcasters
1730 M Street, NW #412
Washington, DC 20036
(202) 463-8970

National Association of Black Reading and Language
   Educators
2440 16th Street, NW #220
Washington, DC 20009
(202) 232-3623

National Association of Black Social Workers, Inc.
8436 W. McNichols Avenue
Detroit, MI 48221
(313) 862-6700

National Association of Black Telecommunications
   Professionals, Inc.
1025 Connecticut Avenue NW
Suite 308
Washington, DC 20036
(303) 896-8661

National Association of Black Women Attorneys, Inc.
3711 Macomb Street, NW, 2nd Floor
Washington, DC 20016
(202) 966-9691

National Association of Blacks in Criminal Justice
P.O. Box 19788
Durham, NC 27707
(919) 683-1801

National Association of Colored Women's Clubs, Inc.
5805 16th Street, NW
Washington, DC 20011
(202) 726-2044

National Association of Health Services Executives
10320 Little Patuxent Parkway
Suite 1106
Columbia, MD 21044

National Association of Investment Companies
111 14th Street, NW #700
Washington, DC 20005
(202) 289-4336

National Association of Market Developers, Inc.
P.O. Box 4446
Rockefeller Center Station
New York, NY 10089

National Association of Media Women
213–16 126th Avenue
Laurelton, NY 11413
(718) 712-4544

National Association of Milliners, Dressmakers and Tailors, Inc.
157 W. 126th Street
New York, NY 10027
(212) 666-1320

National Association of Minority Contractors
1333 F Street, NW #500
Washington, DC 20004
(202) 347-8259

National Association of Minority Media Executives
1401 Concord Point Lane
Reston, VA 22091-1307
(703) 709-5245

National Association of Minority Political Women, USA, Inc.
6120 Oregon Avenue, NW
Washington, DC 20015
(202) 686-1216

National Association of Negro Business and Professional
  Women's Clubs, Inc.
1806 New Hampshire Avenue, NW
Washington, DC 20009
(202) 483-4206

National Association of Neighborhoods
1651 Fuller Street, NW
Washington, DC 20009
(202) 332-7766

National Association of University Women
1501 11th Street, NW
Washington, DC 20001
(202) 232-4844

National Association of Urban Bankers, Inc.
1010 Wayne Avenue #1210
Silver Spring, MD 20910-5600
(301) 589-2141

National Bankers Association
1820 T Street, NW
Washington, DC 20009
(202) 588-5432

National Baptist Convention of America
1327 Pierre Avenue
Shreveport, LA 71103
(318) 221-3701

National Baptist Convention USA, Inc.
National Baptist World Center
1700 Baptist World Center Drive
Nashville, TN 37202
(615) 228-6092

National Bar Association
377 Park Avenue South
New York, NY 10016
(212) 689-8308

National Bar Association
1225 11th Street, NW
Washington, DC 20001
(202) 842-3900

National Beauty Culturist League, Inc.
25 Logan Circle, NW
Washington, DC 20005
(202) 332-2695

National Black Catholic Congress
320 Cathedral Street
Baltimore, MD 21202
(301) 547-5330

National Black Caucus of Local Elected Officials
c/o National League of Cities
1301 Pennsylvania Avenue, NW #600
Washington, DC 20004
(202) 626-3000

National Black Caucus of State Legislators
444 North Capitol Street, NW
Washington, DC 20001
(202) 634-5457

National Black Child Development Institute
1023 15th Street, NW
Washington, DC 20005
(202) 387-1281

National Black College Alumni Hall of Fame Foundation
127 Peachtree Street, #706
Atlanta, GA 30303
(404) 658-6617

National Black Family Summit
College of Social Work
University of South Carolina
Columbia, SC 29208
(803) 777-4609

National Black MBA Association, Inc.
180 N. Michigan Avenue #1515
Chicago, IL 60601
(312) 236-2622

National Black Media Coalition
38 New York Avenue, NE
Washington, DC 20002
(202) 387-8155

National Black Nurses Association, Inc.
P.O. Box 1823
Washington, DC 20013-1823
(202) 393-6870

National Black Police Association, Inc.
3251 Mt. Pleasant Street, NW
Washington, DC 20010
(202) 986-2070

National Black Programming Consortium
929 Harrison Avenue #101
Columbus, OH 43215
(614) 299-5355

National Black Public Relations Society of America
6565 Sunset Boulevard #301
Los Angeles, CA 90028
(213) 466-8221

National Black Republican Council
440 First Street, NW #409
Washington, DC 20001
(202) 662-1335

National Black United Fund, Inc.
50 Park Place #1538
Newark, NJ 07102
(201) 643-5122

National Black Women's Consciousness-Raising Association
1906 North Charles Street
Baltimore, MD 21218
(410) 727-8900

National Brotherhood of Skiers
2575 Donegal Drive
South San Francisco, CA 94080
(916) 487-4837

National Catholic Conference for Interracial Justice
3033 Fourth Street, NE
Washington, DC 20017-1102
(202) 529-6480

National Caucus and Center on Black Aged, Inc.
1424 K Street, NW #500
Washington, DC 20005
(202) 637-8400

National Citizens Commission for African-American Education
c/o Phelps Stokes Fund
10 E. 87th Street
New York, NY 10128
(212) 427-8100

National Coalition of Black Meeting Planners
8630 Fenton Street #328
Silver Spring, MD 20910
(301) 587-9100

National Coalition of 100 Black Women
38 W. 32 Street #1610
New York, NY 10001
(212) 947-2196

National Conference of Black Mayors, Inc.
1422 Peachtree Street, NW
Suite 800
Atlanta, GA 30309
(404) 892-0127

National Conference of Black Political Scientists
Dept. of History and Political Science
Albany State College
Albany, GA 31705
(912) 430-4870

National Council of Negro Women, Inc.
1667 K Street, NW #700
Washington, DC 20006
(202) 659-0006

National Dental Association
5506 Connecticut Avenue, NW #24–25
Washington, DC 20015
(202) 244-7555

National Economic Association
Office of Vice Provost
Pennsylvania State University
University Park, PA 16802
(814) 865-4700

National Forum for Black Public Administrators
777 North Capitol Street, NE #807
Washington, DC 20002
(202) 408-9300

National Funeral Directors and Morticians Association, Inc.
3390 Peachtree Road, NE #1000
Atlanta, GA 30326
(404) 364-6556

National Insurance Association
P.O. Box 53230
Chicago, IL 60653-0230
(312) 924-3308

National Medical Association
1012 10th Street, NW
Washington, DC 20001
(202) 347-1895

National Naval Officers Association
40 Lake Edge Drive
Euclid,OH 44123
(800) 772-NNOA

National Newspaper Publishers Association
3200 13th Street, NW
Washington, DC 20010-2410
(202) 588-8764

National Optometric Association
2830 South Indiana Avenue
Chicago, IL 60616
(312) 791-0186

National Organization for Professional Advancement of Black
  Chemists and Chemical Engineers
c/o Department of Chemistry
Howard University
525 College Street, NW
Washington, DC 20059
(202) 667-1699

National Organization of Black Law Enforcement Executives
4609 Pine Crest Office Park Drive, #F
Alexandria, VA 22312
(703) 658-1529

National Organization of Minority Architects
Kelso & Easter Inc.
101 W. Broad Street, #101B
Richmond, VA 23220
(804) 788-0338

National Pan-Hellenic Council
IMU #30
Bloomington, IN 47405
(812) 855-8820

National Pharmaceutical Association
12510 White Drive
Silver Spring, MD 20904
(301) 622-7747

National Political Congress of Black Women, Inc.
600 New Hampshire Avenue, NW #1125
Washington, DC 20037
(202) 338-0800

National Society of Black Engineers
1454 Duke Street
Alexandria, VA 22314
(703) 549-2207

National Society of Real Estate Appraisers, Inc.
1265 E. 105th Street
Cleveland, OH 44108
(216) 795-3445

National Students' Support Council for Africa, Inc.
5040 E. Shea Boulevard
Suite 260
Phoenix, AZ 85254-4610
(602) 443-1800

National Technical Association, Inc.
P.O. Box 7045
Washington, DC 20032
(202) 829-8100

National United Affiliated Beverage Association
6216 Woodland Avenue
Philadelphia, PA 19142
(215) 748-5670

National United Church Ushers Association of America, Inc.
1431 Sheppard Street, NW
Washington, DC 20011
(202) 722-1192

National United Merchants Beverage Association, Inc.
609 Ann Street
Homestead, PA 15120
(412) 521-0723

National Urban Affairs Council
P.O. Box 51
Plainfield, NJ 07061
(908) 668-0091

National Urban Coalition
1875 Connecticut Avenue, NW #400
Washington, DC 20008
(202) 986-1460

National Urban League, Inc.
500 E. 62nd Street
New York, NY 10021
(212) 310-9000

New Professional Theatre
443 W. 50th Street
New York, NY 10019
(212) 484-9811

Nigerian-American Alliance
c/o James E. Obi
2 Penn Plaza, #1700
New York, NY 10121
(212) 560-5500

Oblate Sisters of Providence
701 Gun Road
Baltimore, MD 21227
(410) 242-8500

Omega Psi Phi Fraternity
2714 Georgia Avenue, NW
Washington, DC 20001
(202) 667-7158

100 Black Men of America, Inc.
127 Peachtree Street, NE
Suite 704
The Candler Building
Atlanta, GA 30303
(303) 525-7111

Operation PUSH
930 E. 50th Street
Chicago, IL 60615
(312) 373-3366

Opportunities Industrialization Centers of America, Inc.
1415 N. Broad Street, #111
Philadelphia, PA 19122
(215) 236-4500

Organization of Black Airline Pilots, Inc.
P.O. Box 5793
Englewood, NJ 07631
(201) 568-8145

Phelps Stokes Fund
10 E. 87th Street
New York, NY 10128
(212) 427-8100

Phi Beta Sigma Fraternity, Inc.
145 Kennedy Street, NW
Washington, DC 20011-5294
(202) 726-5434

Phi Delta Kappa, Inc.
8233 South M. L. King Drive
Chicago, IL 60619
(312) 783-7379

Positive Afrikan's Image Council
P.O. Box 272086
Columbus, OH 43227
(614) 871-0366, ext. 448

Progressive National Baptist Convention, Inc.
501 50th Street, NE
Washington, DC 20019
(202) 396-0558

Secretariat for African-American Catholics
3211 Fourth Street, NE
Washington, DC 20017-1194
(202) 541-3177

Sigma Gamma Rho Sorority, Inc.
8800 S. Stony Island Avenue
Chicago, IL 60617
(312) 873-9000

Sigma Pi Phi Fraternity ("The Boule")
920 Broadway, Suite 703
New York, NY 10010
(212) 477-5550

Southern Christian Leadership Conference
334 Auburn Avenue, NE
Atlanta, GA 30312
(404) 522-1420

Southern Regional Council
134 Peachtree Street, NW #1900
Atlanta, GA 30303
(404) 522-8764

Student National Medical Association, Inc.
1012 10th Street, NW
Washington, DC 20001
(202) 371-1616

369th Veterans Association, Inc.
369th Regiment Armory
One 369th Plaza
New York, NY 10037
(212) 281-3308

Thurgood Marshall Scholarship Fund
One Dupont Circle #710
Washington, DC 20036
(202) 778-0818

TransAfrica, Inc.
1744 R Street, NW
Washington, DC 20009
(202) 797-2301

Tuskegee Airmen, Inc.
9507 10th Avenue
Inglewood, CA 90305
(213) 678-9763

United American Progress Association
701 E. 79th Street
Chicago, IL 60619
(312) 955-8112

United Black Church Appeal
860 Forrest Avenue
Bronx, NY 10456
(212) 992-5315

United Black Fund, Inc.
1101 14th Street, NW
Suite 600
Washington, DC 20005
(202) 783-9300

United Church of Christ, Commission for Racial Justice
700 Prospect Avenue
Cleveland, OH 44115
(216) 736-2168

United Negro College Fund, Inc.
8260 Willow Oaks Corp. Drive
P.O. Box 10444
Fairfax, VA 22031
(703) 205-3400

UNCF's National Alumni Council
8260 Willow Oaks Corp. Drive
P.O. Box 10444
Fairfax, VA 22031
(703) 205-3400

U.S. African-American Chamber of Commerce
117 Broadway
Jack London Waterfront
Oakland, CA 94697-3715
(510) 444-5741

Zeta Delta Phi Sorority, Inc.
P.O. Box 157
Bronx, NY 10469

Zeta Phi Beta Sorority, Inc.
1734 New Hampshire Avenue, NW
Washington, DC 20009
(202) 387-3103

Suggested Reading

Andersen, U.S. *Three Magic Words: The Key to Power, Peace and Plenty.* Melvin Powers, Wilshire Book Company, 1954.

Anthony, Dr. Robert. *How to Make the Impossible Possible.* Berkeley, 1996.

Bolles, Richard Nelson. *The 1998 What Color Is Your Parachute?* Ten Speed Press, 1997.

Boston, Kelvin. *Smart Money Moves for African-Americans.* G. P. Putnam's Sons, 1996.

Boston Women's Health Book Collection. *The New Our Bodies, Ourselves.* Simon and Schuster, 1992.

Bradshaw, John. *Family Secrets.* Bantam, 1995.

———. *Creating Love.* Bantam, 1992.

———. *Home Coming.* Bantam, 1990.

———. *Healing the Shame That Binds You.* Health Communications, 1988.

Branden, Nathaniel. *The Six Pillars of Self-Esteem.* Bantam, 1994.

Brice, Carleen. *Walk Tall: Affirmations for People of Color.* Beacon, 1997.

Bristol, Claude M. *The Magic of Believing.* Fireside, 1991.

Broussard, Cheryl. *The Black Woman's Guide to Financial Independence.* Penguin, 1996.

Cameron, Julia, with Mark Bryan. *The Artist's Way: A Spiritual Path to Higher Creativity.* G.P. Putnam's Sons, 1992.

Chapman, Audrey. *Getting Good Loving*. Ballantine, 1996.

Church of Today. *Master Mind Goal Achiever's Journal*. Master Mind Publishing Company, P.O. Box 1830, Warren, MI 48090-1830.

Chopra, Deepak, M.D. *Restful Sleep*. Crown, 1994.

———. *Ageless Body, Timeless Mind*. Random House, 1993.

———. *Perfect Health*. Random House, 1991.

———. *Unconditional Life*. Bantam, 1991.

———. *Creating Health*. Houghton Mifflin, 1987.

Chu, Chin-Ning. *Thick Face, Black Heart: The Path to Thriving, Winning and Succeeding*. Warner, 1992.

Coles, Robert. *Story of Ruby Bridges*. Scholastic, 1995.

Comer, James. M.D., and Alvin Poussaint, M.D. *Raising Black Children*. Random House, 1996.

Cook, Suzan D. *Sister to Sister: Devotion for and from African American Women*. Judson, 1995.

Copage, Eric V. *Black Pearls: Book of Love*. William Morrow, 1996.

———. *Black Pearls for Parents*. William Morrow, 1995.

———. *Black Pearls: Daily Meditations, Affirmations and Inspirations for African-Americans*. William Morrow, 1993.

Covey, Stephen. *First Things First*. Fireside, 1994.

———. *The 7 Habits of Highly Effective People: Powerful Lessons in Personal Change*. Fireside, 1989.

Delany, Sarah and A. Elizabeth, with Amy Hill Hearth. *Having Our Say: The Delany Sisters' First 100 Years*. Kodansha, 1993.

Dickens, Floyd, Jr., and Jacqueline. *The Black Manager*. AMACOM, 1991.

Dinwiddie-Boyd, Elza. *Proud Heritage: Eleven Thousand One Names for Your African-American Baby*. Avon, 1994.

Dixon, Barbara M. *Good Health for African-Americans*. Random House, 1995.

Dudley, Joe L. Sr. *Walking By Faith: I Am! I Can! & I Will!*, 1997.

Foundation for Inner Peace. *Course in Miracles*. Viking, 1996.

Edelman, Marian Wright. *Guide My Feet*. Beacon, 1995.

———. *Measure of Our Success*. Beacon, 1994.

Edwards, Audrey and Dr. Craig Polite. *Children of the Dream: The Psychology of Black Success*. Anchor Books, 1993.

Frazier, George. *Success Runs in Our Race*. Avon, 1994.

Gawain, Shakti. *Creative Visualization*. New World Library, 1995.

Getty, J. Paul. *How to Be Rich*. Jove Books, 1965.

Giovanni, Nikki. *Love Poems*. Morrow, 1997.

———. *Racism 101*. Morrow, 1995.

———. *Selected Poems*. Morrow, 1996.

Graham, Lawrence Otis. *The Best Companies for Minorities*. Plume, 1993.

———. *Member of the Club: Reflections on a Racially Polarized World*. HarperCollins, 1996.

———. *Proversity: Getting Past Face Value and Finding the Soul of People*. Wiley, 1997.

Grant, Gwendolyn. *Best Kind of Loving*. HarperCollins, 1995.

Hay, Louise. *Life/Reflections—On Your Journey*. Hay House, 1995.

———. *Meditations to Heal Your Life*. Hay House, 1994.

———. *Colors and Numbers*. Hay House, 1994.

———. *The Power Is Within You*. Hay House, 1991.

———. *You Can Heal Your Life*. Hay House, 1984.

Helmstetter, Shad, Ph.D., *What to Say When You Talk to Your Self*. Pocket Books, 1982.

Hill, Napoleon. *Keys to Success*. Dutton, 1994.

———. *Think and Grow Rich Action Pack*. Plume, 1990.

———. *Think and Grow Rich*. Fawcett, 1960.

Jeffers, Dr. Susan. *Feel the Fear and Do It Anyway*. Ballantine, 1987.

Johnson, John J. *Succeeding Against the Odds*. Warner, 1989.

Kimbro, Dennis. *Daily Motivations for African-American Success*. Ballantine, 1993.

Kimbro, Dennis, and Napoleon Hill. *Think and Grow Rich: A Black Choice*. Fawcett, 1991.

King, Larry. *How to Talk to Anyone, Anytime, Anywhere*. Crown, 1994.

Lewis, Reginald, and Blair Walker. *Why Should White Guys Have All the Fun?* John Wiley, 1995.

Mandino, Og. *Secrets for Success & Happiness*. Fawcett Columbine, 1995.

———. *The Return of the Ragpicker*. Bantam, 1993.

———. *The Greatest Salesman in the World*. Bantam, 1988.

———. *Mission Success*. Bantam, 1987.

———. *The Choice*. Bantam, 1984.

———. *University of Success*. Bantam, 1982.

———. *The Greatest Success in the World*. Bantam, 1982.

———. *Treasury of Success Unlimited*. Pocket Books, 1976.

———. *The Greatest Miracle in the World*. Bantam, 1975.

———. *The Greatest Secret in the World*. Bantam, 1972.

———. *Treasury of Success Unlimited*. Pocket Books, 1982.

McCall, Nathan. *Makes You Want to Holler*. Vintage, 1994.

McMillan, Terry. *Waiting to Exhale*. Pocket Books, 1994.

Morgan, Marlo. *Mutant Message Down Under*. HarperCollins, 1994.

Mosley, Walter. *Always Outnumbered, Always Outgunned*. Norton, 1997.

———. *Gone Fishin'*. Black Classics, 1997.

———. *Little Yellow Dog*. Norton, 1996.

———. *R. L. Dream*. Norton, 1995.

Muhammad, Elijah. *How to Eat to Live*. United Brothers & Sisters Communications Systems, 1992.

Murphy, Joseph, D.D., Ph.D. *Miracle Power for Infinite Riches*. Parker, 1972.

———. *Secrets of the I Ching*. Parker, 1970.

———. *The Cosmic Power Within You*. Parker, 1968.

———. *The Infinite Power to Be Rich*. Parker, 1966.

———. *The Amazing Laws of Cosmic Mind Power*. Prentice-Hall, 1965.

———. *The Power of the Subconscious Mind*. Prentice-Hall, 1963.

———. *How to Attract Money*. Parker, 1955.

Nickens, Bessie. *Walking the Log: Memories of a Southern Childhood*. Rizzoli, 1994.

Peale, Norman Vincent. *The Power of Positive Thinking*. Fawcett, 1956.

Ponder, Catherine. *The Prospering Power of Love*. Unity Books, 1966.

———. *The Dynamic Laws of Prosperity*. Prentice-Hall, 1962.

Ragins, Marianne. *Winning Scholarships for College*. Holt, 1994.

Redfield, James. *The Celestine Prophecy*. Warner, 1993.

Robbins, Anthony. *Notes from a Friend*. Fireside, 1995.

———. *Unlimited Power*. Ballatine, 1986.

———, and Joseph McClendon III. *Ebony Power Thoughts*. Fireside, 1997.

Roman S., and D. Parker. *Creating Money: Keys to Abundance*. HJ Kramer, 1988.

Shenson, Howard L. *Contract and Fee Setting Guide for Consultants and Professionals*. Wiley, 1990.

Sher, Barbara, with Annie Gottlieb. *Wishcraft*. Random House, 1979.

Sher, Barbara, with Barbara Smith. *I Could Do Anything If I Only Knew What It Was*. Dell, 1994.

Shinn, Florence Scovel. *Wisdom of Florence Shinn*. Fireside, 1989.

———. *Your Word Is Your Wand*. Gerald J. Rickard, 1941.

———. *Secret Door to Success*. DeVorss & Company, 1940.

———. *The Game of Life and How to Play It*. Fireside, 1986.

Simmons, Wilson. *Inside Corporate America, A Guide for African-Americans*. Perigee, 1996.

Sinetar, Marsha. *The Build the Life You Want, Create the Work You Love*. St. Martin's Press, 1995.

Taylor, Susan. *Confirmation:* Doubleday, 1997.

———. *In the Spirit*. HarperPerennial, 1993.

Vanzant, Iyanla. *Lessons in Living*. Doubleday, 1995.

———. *The Valley of the Value*. Simon and Schuster, 1995.

———. *A Black Woman's Healing Progress*. Writers and Readers, 1995.

———. *Acts of Faith*. Fireside, 1993.

———. *Power Within*. Writers and Readers, 1992.

Williams, Terrie. *The Personal Touch: What Blacks Need to Succeed in Today's Business World*. Warner, 1995.

Williamson, Marianne. *A Woman's Worth*. Ballantine, 1993.

———. *Illuminata: A Return to Prayer*. Random House, 1992.

———. *A Return to Love*. HarperCollins, 1992.

Wilson, August. *Fences*. Plume, 1986.

———. *Joe Turner's Come and Gone*. Plume, 1988.

———. *The Piano Lesson*. Plume, 1990.

X, Malcolm. *Autobiography of Malcolm X*. Ballantine, 1992.

Index